LA MARINE

The French Colonial Soldier in Canada

1745-1761

Andrew Gallup
and
Donald F. Shaffer

Illustrations by
Joseph E. Lee

HERITAGE BOOKS
2008

HERITAGE BOOKS
AN IMPRINT OF HERITAGE BOOKS, INC.

Books, CDs, and more—Worldwide

For our listing of thousands of titles see our website
at
www.HeritageBooks.com

Published 2008 by
HERITAGE BOOKS, INC.
Publishing Division
100 Railroad Ave. #104
Westminster, Maryland 21157

Copyright © 1992 Andrew Gallup

Other Heritage Books by Andrew Gallup:

The Celoron Expedition to the Ohio Country, 1749:
The Reports of Pierre-Joseph Celoron and Father Bonnecamps

Memoir of a French and Indian War Soldier
"Jolicoeur" Charles Bonin

A Sketch of the Virginia Soldier in the Revolution

All rights reserved. No part of this book may be reproduced or transmitted in any form or by any means, electronic or mechanical, including photocopying, recording or by any information storage and retrieval system without written permission from the author, except for the inclusion of brief quotations in a review.

International Standard Book Numbers
Paperbound: 978-1-55613-711-2
Clothbound: 978-0-7884-7494-1

TABLE OF CONTENTS

List of Illustrations	v
Preface	vii
Acknowledgments	ix
Introduction	1
History	9
Material Culture	53
Uniforms – Firearms and Accessories	
Edged Weapons – Other Equipment	
A Marine's Life	135
Food – Health – Relaxation	
Money – Religion	
Tambour et Fifre	161
Canonniers-Bombardiers	165
Watercraft	173
French Fortifications in Canada	183
Final Thoughts	193
Appendices	
I. Organization of a Marine Company in Canada	199
II. Marine Pay	201
III. Prices and Values	202
IV. List of Marine Officers	205
V. Imported Food at Louisbourg	223
VI. French Artillery Caliber	226
VII. French Small Arms Caliber	227
VIII. Native Americans Allies of the French	228
IX. French Duty Calls for the Drum	233
X. A List of French Forts	235
Terms	239
Bibliography	249
Index	271

LIST OF ILLUSTRATIONS

	page
MARINE c.1700	12
MARINE c.1745	22
MARINE c.1758	30
MARINE c.1758	57
JUSTAUCORPS c.1755	59
BOUTONS	59
VESTE c.1745	62
VESTE c.1755	62
CULOTTE	63
CHEMISE	65
CRAVATE	65
SOULIERS	67
GUETRES	69
GORGET	71
WIGS	72
MARINE IN WINTER DRESS	75
MARINE IN WINTER DRESS	77
MOCCASINS	81
TUQUE	82
BONNET	82
MITTENS	82
FUSIL DE GRENADIER 1734	86
BOUCANIER 1734	86
FUSIL DE CHASSE	86
MARINE 1758	92
BAYONET 1734	95
FLINTS	95
CARTRIDGES	95
WAISTBOX	97
SHOULDER BOX	98
DOUBLE VALVE POWDER FLASKS	100
SINGLE VALVE POWDER FLASKS	101
MUSKET TOOLS	101
SCREWDRIVER	103
HAMMER STALL AND PICK	103
WORMS	103
SPRING VISE	103
PISTOL 1734	109
L'EPEE	111
TOMAHAWK	113
HALBERD	115
SPONTOON	115

BELT	117
KNAPSACK-HAVERSACK, PETIT SAC	119
STRIKERS	119
AWLS	120
RAZORS	122
EYEGLASSES	123
COMB	123
KNIVES	125
ICE CREEPERS	128
ICE SKATES	128
SNOWSHOES	130
TRAINE	131
TENTS	134
PIPES	148
TOBACCO BAG AND TOBACCO	150
COINS	153
PLAYING CARDS AND CARD MONEY	155
JESUIT RINGS	157
RELIGIOUS MEDALLIONS	157
DISCHARGE DOCUMENT	159
DRUMMER AND LACE	162
ARTILLERYMAN	167
CANNON ON GARRISON CARRIAGE	169
MORTAR AND MORTAR BOMB	169
WALL GUN	171
BREECH LOADING SWIVEL GUN	171
BATEAU	179
BASTIONS	186
CROSS OF SAINT LOUIS	204

PREFACE

The reader will not find footnotes or endnotes in this study. The decision not to use notes is based on the idea that, if it is important enough to be included, put it in the text. If something needs clarification or amplification please use the bibliography to locate a source that will perhaps fill the need.

The reader will find an abundance of references to the sources quoted, consulted, or otherwise relied upon. Full citations will be found in the bibliography. These references go beyond legal and ethical requirements. This will provide a trail to the source of the information which may be the starting point for further exploration.

Within quotations the authors have used brackets [ ] to designate material that they have added, usually to identify a person, date, or geographical location.

<u>Travels in New France by J.C.B.</u> is a source that is heavily used in this study. The identification of J.C.B. as *Jolicoeur* Charles Bonin was not part of the 1941 edition. We found this identification noted (handwritten) on the title page of the copy we used. We have used Bonin's name in the text and in the bibliography.

For the purpose of this work, New France refers to the area of North America under French control. This includes the colonies of Louisiana, Canada, Isle Royale, and Acadia. The boundaries of these colonies using modern references would place the present maritime provinces of Canada in Acadia and Isle Royale is Cape Breton Island. Louiciana extended from the Gulf of Mexico to the tributaries of the Ohio River in Indiana and Illinois. Canada encompassed the provinces of Quebec and Ontario, the Old Northwest of the United States (with the exception of southern Illinois and southern Indiana), and the area of western Canada from the Grand Portage to Lake Winnipeg. This "map" is not exact.

The illustrations are speculative. Some are a result of interpretation of period documents. Others are from archaeological specimens from French colonial sites which had marines in residence. The drawing are *one* representation of what might have been in a time before mass production, interchangeable parts, plastics that defy all natural forces, and hamburgers that all taste the same.

INTRODUCTION

The goal of this study was, at first, to revise the ten-year-old "handbook" of the recreated *Compagnie Franches de la Marine du Detroit*, a re-enactment group portraying the French colonial soldiers that garrisoned the settlement of Detroit in the 1750's. The handbook project was designed to incorporate additional facts concerning the equipment used by the marines and cultural aspects of the society of Detroit and New France. When the material collected for the revision was assembled and organized, it was apparent that there was an opportunity to expand the project beyond the handbook and create a product that would be useful to a larger audience than the members of the *compagnie*.

Experience in living history programs that is approaching two decades and a lifetime of interest in history led the authors to believe that fellow re-enactors, armchair historians, visitors to history programs, and professional historians would have an interest in a little-known aspect of the colonial history of North America. Therefore, the revised goal for this work included the substance of the original project, the tools used by the marine, but expanded other objectives, such as the history of the service of the marines and the daily life of the individual. Although this provided a "balance" between the material culture and other cultural aspects, it created new problems.

The limits of the study were difficult to establish. Unlike other European soldiers in colonial service, the marine was absorbed into the colonial society and became part of the culture of the Canada. Consequently, a full treatment of the subject would require a general study of New France, including the activity of marines, especially officers, in the fur trade and other economic aspects of the colonies, relations with Native Americans, and the military activity of marine forces beginning in the late seventeenth century and ranging throughout North America. It was decided to limit this work to the rank-and-file marine and his activity as a soldier, 1745-1761. Further, it was decided to focus on the activity in the colony of Canada with reference to the other French colonies of Acadia, Isle Royale, and Louisiana when appropriate.

The interpretation of the material used in this study has given the authors a view of the marine as a soldier which differs from other historians. The reason for this difference probably lies in the focus on the marine, a subject that has received little, or no, previous study. Most of the previous interpretation of this period has been general and has followed the English/American campaigns. It may be that history is written by the winner, but for whatever reason, the French-Canadian colonial soldier is all but forgotten by most, and if mentioned, descriptions are less than flattering. Usually, the French-Canadian aspects of the struggle for North America are limited to General Montcalm and the corruption of the colonial government.

It will become apparent when reading the text that the authors have a positive view of the French-Canadian colonial soldier. Using the standards of the period he was the equal of his adversaries and may have been superior. Viewpoints to the contrary are probably a result of the lack of detailed inquiry into the service of these soldiers.

This study does not claim to be a detailed inquiry. It will, hopefully, provide new questions in the interpretation of the colonial North American past and thereby benefit historians regardless of their individual method of inquiry.

This study is for and from living history re-enactors. Living history is a method of history interpretation found in programs throughout the world. Although these programs are popular with the public, they have received criticism from history professionals as being

INTRODUCTION

overly dramatic and biased. As with most questions, there are good arguments on both sides. In defense of living history, many similar faults can be found in books, films and other methods of interpretation. It is subject to limitations, as are the other methods. Professionals and volunteers engaged in living history are working hard to present quality programs. The potential and limitations of living history are presented in Jay Anderson's Time Machines, The World of Living History. Anderson concludes,

> Finally, living history rejects a linear view of the past. It argues that, before you study the forest, you must become totally familiar with the trees. Living historians point out that the history establishment has often failed to study, interpret, and experiment with the everyday reality of ordinary people in the past. Museums like Plimoth [Plimoth Plantation, Massachusetts], experimental farms like Butser Hill [experimental archaeology research project in Great Britain], and dedicated buffs like the men and women of the Brigade of the American Revolution are attempting to remedy that neglect.
> The result is an emphasis on new primary sources, especially material culture, and a willingness to try out novel techniques of research and interpretation. Lejre's [experimental archaeology research center in Denmark] use of imitative experiments and the colonial Pennsylvania Plantation's attempt to interpret historiography itself are excellent examples. Living historians dart rapidly about that Bruegelesque painting of man's past, comfortably moving from one historical period to another. Their goal is not to discern a grand pattern of relationships, but to steep themselves in the

historical context of a particular place and time and come to understand, appreciate, and feel the life of the people who once lived there and then. When asked why they are attempting to communicate with their counterparts in the past, the living historian's quiet answer is: It's about time (Anderson 1984:192).

The information generated by living history programs is of great value and beyond the critique of individual programs. Professional and volunteer historians have brought forth massive amounts of historical data through research for their programs. This information would, quite probably, never have been available if traditional "book" history and scholarly conferences had been the only market.

Living history practitioners are not limited by disciplinary boundaries. They innocently dive into primary sources, secondary works, archaeological reports, museum collections, period literature and music; any and all sources are important. This is a missionary effort.

As Anderson suggests, much of the information gathered by re-enactors concerns the material culture of the past. A large part of most programs are the "things" that people made and used in their daily lives. Yet, it is debatable if tangible artifacts are the only items that fall within the world of the living historian's material culture. Anthropologist James Deetz has a wide view of what constitutes material culture.

> Material culture is usually considered to be roughly synonymous with artifacts, the vast universe of the objects used by mankind to cope with the physical world, to facilitate social intercourse, and to benefit our state of mind. A somewhat broader definition of material culture is useful in how profoundly our world is a

INTRODUCTION

product of our thoughts, as that sector of our physical environment that we modify through culturally determined behavior, this definition includes all artifacts, from the simplest, such as a common pin, to the most complex, such as an interplanetary space vehicle. But the physical environment includes more than what most definitions of material culture recognize. We can also consider cuts of meat as material culture, since there are many ways to dress an animal; plowed fields; even the horse that pulls the plow, since scientific breeding of livestock involves the conscious modification of an animal's form according to culturally derived ideals. Our body itself is a part of our physical environment, so that such things as parades, dancing, and all aspects of kinesics - human motion - fit within our definition. Nor is the definition limited only to matter in the solid state. Fountains are liquid examples, as are lily ponds, and material that is partly gas includes hot air balloons and neon signs. I have suggested in Invitation to Archaeology, that even language is part of material culture, prime example of it in its gaseous state. Words, after all, are air masses shaped by speech apparatus according to culturally acquired rules (Deetz 1977:24-25).

Deetz's definition includes areas of study beyond the interest of most, but not all, individuals doing living history. By performing the tasks of daily life using reproductions of artifacts they are, voluntarily or involuntarily, investigating the areas Deetz would include. The historians doing living history can use this active material culture to propose ideas concerning life in the past, and these ideas send them back to the research phase.

The ideas that arise from doing history may never occur to an armchair historian. Living history is more than a method of history interpretation, it is a method of inquiry.

Living history is in its infancy and an avocation to most practitioners. Not unlike other disciplines in their early years, living history is in need of structure. The archaeologists of the nineteenth century would be considered "pot hunters" today. That structure will come in time.

A part of the development of living history is the distribution of information. This work falls into that category. The colonial period of North American history, by comparison to others, has been ignored. The nineteenth-century historian, Francis Parkman, still retains a place of prominence on local library shelves. If one wishes to delve into the history of the French in this period, pickings are scarce.

This work is not meant to make great inroads into French colonial history. It will not present new facts. Its limited purpose is to bring together information from various primary and secondary sources concerning the life of French colonial troops in Canada during the final French and Indian War. This study will focus on the material culture of the common soldier, including description, illustration, and documentation. Related subjects, officers' equipment, artillery companies, and boats, for example, will be briefly covered. The reader is encouraged to use the bibliography to pursue further information or for clarification concerning particular subjects.

Information concerning other cultural aspects of the life of the Independent Companies of the Marine will be included. Unlike other military forces, these men were assigned to garrison isolated posts for long periods and French policy encouraged them to become permanent settlers. Consequently, they became a part of the development of individual communities and Canada.

INTRODUCTION

One of the dangers of history interpretation is that by repetition, speculation becomes truth. Every attempt will be made to clearly identify speculation by the authors of this study or authors of material included in this study.

This work may replace earlier efforts. This is not meant to comment on the quality of these works. They were pioneering efforts and the authors are to be commended. This study will soon become dated; the "doers" of history will see to that. The authors of this work encourage them to continue to bring forth more information.

What follows is for the "doers". It is for the use of re-enactors, interpreters, researchers, experimenters, for all those who get their hands dirty digging into history.

HISTORY

The success of the French colonization and exploitation of North America was in doubt for more than one hundred years. Various attempts to settle and profit from the new land had met limited success. The first attempt, near Quebec in 1541, was abandoned the following year. The next attempt, Port Royal in 1605, became the first permanent settlement and the colonial capitol of Acadia (Nova Scotia, New Brunswick, Prince Edward Island, and part of Maine). Fisheries, agriculture, and trade promised a good future.

Acadia's founder, Pierre du Gast (Gua, or du Gaust), sieur de Monts, was a Huguenot. This may have been the reason that, despite considerable wealth and influence, he did not receive the monopoly he had been seeking from the Crown (Costain 1954:50). This setback did not deter him. He looked toward the St. Lawrence Valley on the advice of one of his assistants, Samuel de Champlain.

In the fifty years following the settlement of Port Royal, Champlain, the Church, and various trade groups, such as the Company of One Hundred Associates, formed by Cardinal Richelieu, played in New France. Their competition for furs, the primary export, came not from other Europeans, but from the Iroquois Confederacy that served as a middleman between the western Indians and the English and Dutch. The trade rivalry fueled a perpetual war. The Iroquois had achieved major successes by 1661. They attacked French settlements and maintained a blockade of the Ottawa River, the principal trade route to the furs of the west, threatening the life of the colony.

By 1663, Louis XIV had seen enough. He reorganized the political structure of the colony.

The system of government that was inaugurated between 1663 and 1666 was derived from that of provincial France

but made more simple and effective by
the absence of feudal vestiges and
institutions that cluttered the French
political scene and occasionally jammed
the administrative machinery. All
power rested with the King, who ruled
with divine right, and was delegated to
a series of royally appointed officials
through a clear cut chain of command.
The most senior of these was the minister of the marine, who resided at court
(Zoltvany 1969:9-10).

    The Minister of the Marine delegated the
supervision of the colony to the Governor and
Intendant. The former was senior and the head
of the military; the latter looked over the
judicial and financial aspects. These individuals were part of the Sovereign Council
which included the Bishop, the Attorney
General, and various counselors. Although the
general population was excluded from participa-
tion in this "official" government, there were
consultive and deliberative assemblies. The
King's instructions were that the authorities
should govern by maintaining a bond with the
colonists by gaining their confidence, not by
force. (Zoltvany 1969:11, 12).
    The first governor under the new system,
Jean Baptiste Colbert, accomplished much in the
first five years. He instituted the governmen-
tal structure and brought the economic problems
under control. However, the immediate problem
of the Iroquois and the ever-present threat
from the British were, perhaps, his toughest
problems.
    Colbert could call on militia companies
composed of the settlers. In addition, the
King sent four companies of the Carignan
Salieres regiment to New France. They arrived
prior to the French commander, Alexandre de
Prouville, Marquis de Tracy. Tracy landed at
Quebec, June 30, 1665, with the troops he had
in the West Indies. These men were from the
regiments of Poitou, Orleans, Chambelle, and
Lignieres (Costain 1954:253).

HISTORY

Three campaigns were conducted and, in 1667, the Iroquois made peace with the French. The government offered inducements to the Carignan Salieres to remain in Canada. Four hundred settled on the Richelieu River, one of the routes for Iroquois war parties moving north (Eccles 1974:62-64, 67). The policy of providing incentives to soldiers to settle in Canada remained in effect until France surrendered the colony.

Problems with the Iroquois began again in the 1680's. The Ministry of the Marine sent forces for the defense of the colony. These soldiers, *Les Compagnies Franches de la Marine*, the Independent Companies of the Marine, were raised and maintained by the Ministry of the Marine for service in the colonies, guards for Ministry property in France, and for duty on ships. They were independent of the regular army.

Troops of this type were first organized as the Independent Companies of the Marine by Richelieu in 1622. At that time, they were temporary forces and discharged in 1627. Companies were raised again in 1671. In 1690, they were reorganized by Louis Phelipeaux, Comte de Pontchartrain, as a permanent organization (Petard 1976:20).

It must be noted that these forces have various titles in primary and secondary sources. Les Compagnies Franches de la Marine and Troupes de la Marine are the most common. Also, they are referred to as Canadian Regulars, companies of La Marine Regiment, colony troops, colonial troops, Compagnies Detachees de la Marine, Compagnies Francaises, or simply, marines (Petard 1976:20. Eccles 1974:101. Hamilton 1962:131. Hamilton 1967:1. McLennan 1973:47). As these companies were the only professional military forces in Canada after the Iroquois Wars of the 1660's (the Swiss Karrar Regiment, under contract to the Ministry of Marine, served at Louisbourg), any reference in the literature to "regulars" between the mid 1680's and June 1755, can be assumed to mean marines. After June 1755,

MARINE c. 1700

regular army regiments began to arrive in Canada.

Les Compagnies Franches de la Marine served throughout New France. Full companies and small detachments garrisoned posts from the Canadian maritimes to the Great Lakes. There were twenty-eight companies in Canada at the beginning of the eighteenth century (Eccles 1974:132). The marines entered Louisiana with the first settlers and served from the Gulf of Mexico to Illinois.

The marines adapted to the foreign environment they faced in Canada. For seventy-five years they successfully served a dual role as policeman and soldier. Many became settlers after, or even during, their service. Of the 63 settlers at Detroit in 1708, 29 were married soldiers of the 100-man garrison (Eccles 1974:136). While most of the rank and file were recruited in France, young Canadians of the upper class became officers in the companies. A list of officers in 1722 states that more than half were Canadian by birth (Douville and Casanova 1968:74). Unlike the regular army troops sent to the North American colonies by both sides in the final French and Indian War, it was the government's intention that the marine become part of the civilian society they served. (Many men of the army also stayed after Canada surrendered.)

The organization of the companies of the Ministry of the Marine by Pontchartrain in 1690 called for twenty-four independent companies each commanded by a naval lieutenant and two ensigns (the lieutenant became the company captain, the senior ensign, a lieutenant, and the junior ensign, a marine ensign). The company was to have 100 men; a captain of arms, 4 sergeants, 8 corporals, 2 drummers, 1 fifer, and 84 privates (Petard 1976:20). Apparently, this organization was subject to modification. In New France the company seems to have been, at times, half of the regulation size. Although it retained the three officers, there were only 2 sergeants, 4 corporals, 1 drummer, 1 fifer, and between 35 and 80 men per company

(Hamilton 1967:1-2). A second ensign and two cadets (the senior cadet was cadet a'aiguillette) were added to each company after 1742 (McLennan 1983:47). The cadets were young men training to be officers. They were treated as senior soldiers and received the same pay, rations, uniforms, and equipment as did the soldier. Their promotion was based on ability and the availability of openings in companies. It was not unusual for a cadet to wait ten years before he became an ensign. One cadet, a member of the Verendrye family, was a junior cadet for nineteen years, 1728-1747 (La Verendrye 1968:509). Influence was probably used to obtain preference. By 1753, cadet positions were reserved for the sons of serving officers (Eccles 1987:115).

Overall military command in the colonies rested with the governor. There are references to the companies in Canada being under the command of a "major" in each of the three districts: Quebec, Montreal, and Three Rivers (Hamilton 1962:131). Another source refers to the major at Louisbourg (McLennan 1983:47). This was a "brevet" rank made necessary in a garrison with more than one company. Although not part of the company organization (Appendix 1), garrisons may have had sergeant majors and barrack sergeants (McLennan 1983:47. Kalm 1987:601).

The marine company was independent of the complex organizational structure common to most armies. In the 1750's, Governor Vaudreuil attempted to introduce a battalion structure but this was vetoed by Paris (Hamilton 1962:132). Montcalm did form a marine battalion in 1757, for the expedition against Fort William Henry (Bougainville 1968:152). Levis, who commanded the French forces in Canada after the death of Montcalm, organized two marine battalions in 1760.

There can be little doubt that the chain of command provided little day to day oversight of the individual company, especially those stationed on the frontier. The great distances and harsh environment of Canada isolated indi-

HISTORY

vidual units. A marine captain had far more freedom of action than his counterpart in the regular army. This was balanced by much less support than would have been available if part of an army.

The commander had to rely on his junior officers, NCO's (Non-Commissioned Officers), and the men of his company. Sergeants were given substantial responsibility. Chaussegros de Lery, a Canadian-born marine officer, cites two occasions in 1754, where sergeants commanded substantial parties, one totaling 100 men. (De Lery 1940:27, 40).

The quality of the individual soldier in a marine company was probably much the same as his counterpart in other military forces. As with any military or naval force, the Ministry of the Marine wanted to recruit quality. Economics, need, and human nature would, of course, modify that plan.

An ordinance in 1689 set the minimum age of a recruit at eighteen. In 1723, the age was reduced to sixteen and it seems even fifteen-year-old boys were recruited. Physical condition or other requirements of the recruit were probably left up to the company (Petard 1976:21).

The background of the recruit is open to question. The first companies to serve in New France were said to be "hastily recruited in the grogshops of Rochefort" (Eccles 1974:115). Another historian was even more critical.

> While in theory the soldiers of this regiment were supposed to be competent professionals, actually they were far from it, recruited as they often were from the slums of Europe. Governor de la Jonquiere wrote home to the Minister of Marine in 1750 that the recently arrived recruits for La Marine were "cripples from birth, men 60-70 years old... married men with women and children, foreigners... mostly Spanish who could neither speak nor understand French, rogues and scoundrels who

should be in the gallies." A slightly later report stated that it was useless to try to teach La Marine the new drill since the majority of the soldiers could not understand French. The officers were better men, many drawn from the sons of the Canadian noblesse, while others came from regiments disbanded in France after the Peace of 1748. The training of the soldiers of La Marine was better than that of the militia, but the poor quality of the men, their lack of battalion organization and the small experience of many of their Canadian officers made it impossible for them to be really effective troops. They probably were really more policemen or gendarmes than combat soldiers. The Marquis de Vaudreuil, who succeeded to the governorship in 1755, was Canadian born and of course proud of the soldiers of La Marine. He boasted that they knew how to make bloody war on the British, while Montcalm's French regulars, he said, fought in too gentle and conventional a manner. The soldiers of La Marine numbered less than a thousand in all (Hamilton 1962:132).

The criticisms above are not fair. The study of any European army of the seventeenth and eighteenth century will find "scum, rogues, scoundrels, and slum dwellers". This was the grist of the mill. The words of Governor de la Jonquiere might derive partially from class bias and a growing separation of French and Canadian identities. Also, it is not clear whether this is an observation over time or one year's replacements which represented 150 men (Kalm 1987:540).

As to the men being Spaniards, this would not be surprising. European armies made soldiers, voluntarily or forcibly, from foreigners, especially in times of need. The British army had German regiments. The French army had

HISTORY

Scots. The Prussians weren't choosy. Mercenary regiments, most notably Swiss, fought for many nations. As mentioned before, the Swiss Karrar regiment served at Louisbourg and companies of this regiment served in Louisiana.

What proportion of the marines were not French is unclear. The lists of soldiers in Louisiana presents names that appear to be French (De Ville 1986:15-32). The available information suggests the marine companies in Canada were French, although foreign troops were used to fill companies in 1757 (Bougainville 1968:144).

The quality of service as soldiers, or gendarmes, could be debated. It is questionable if the marines should be compared to twentieth-century standards or even regular army standards of the eighteenth century. The fact that they had no battalion organization is consistent with their role as guards or police. The history of warfare in North America in the colonial period is that of the small unit, mobile, engagement, *la petite guerre*. This seems ideally suited to the company size unit. The quality of a particular company would probably be unique to that unit, dictated by the care in recruiting, quality of officers, and experience in Canada. References to any particular company, good or bad, should not necessarily reflect the ability of the Troupe de la Marine as a whole. The Canadian-born Governor of Canada, Pierre-Francois de Rigaud, marquis de Vaudreuil-Cavagnal, seemed to understand how to use the marines in 1755.

> His strategy was to employ the troups de terre [regular army] sent from France to secure the approaches to the central colony, and then to use the colonial regulars, the Troupes de la Marine, the Canadian militia, and the Indian allies to ravage the Anglo American frontier, and oblige the English colonials to use their vastly greater numbers to defend their frontier settlements. Initially, this

strategy enjoyed success.... Half a century earlier the Canadians had experienced the same sort of attacks in the Iroquois war and initially they had suffered heavy casualties, but they had mastered the art of guerrilla warfare and then beat back the Iroquois by using their own tactics of surprise, ambush, and swift assault where least expected. In that cruel war the Canadian military tradition was born (Eccles 1974:173).

In the unconventional warfare of the final French and Indian war the French were highly successful. A large part of this warfare was conducted by the marines, often with militia and Indians, commanded by Canadian-born, marine officers. The characterization that marines were not effective combat soldiers demands further documentation, as does the comment, quoted earlier, concerning the inexperience of Canadian officers. The senior officers, and many of the junior officers, had more than ten years of experience, including combat in King George's War. The marine captains were, with few exceptions, over forty years old. As they had joined the marines as teenagers, they had twenty to thirty years of experience. This is not to suggest that these units or individuals were appreciably better than the French regulars or their English opponents. The evidence suggests they were much the same as other European or colonial soldiers and performed as well as any other force.

Part of the problem might stem from applying modern ethical standards to eighteenth-century warfare. Forest warfare was brutal when compared to conventional European military tactics. Montcalm sent Joseph Marin, a Canadian-born marine officer, with a party to attack Fort Edward in advance of his campaign against Fort William Henry. The General wrote to Governor Vaudreuil with apparent disgust that, "... he [Marin] was unwilling to amuse himself with prisoners; he brought in only one and 32 scalps." (Steele 1969:106). What Montcalm could not realize was that the Canadian experience in warfare included a century of small fights where death in battle was preferable to capture and the "slow fire". The French-born marine surely learned this lesson from his Canadian officer.

The assignment for the marine companies was to protect the interests of the King. This seems to have left a considerable amount of time for personal interests. Those officers (and to a lesser extent the rank and file) who found themselves in a frontier outpost took advantage of financial opportunities when they were presented.

By 1720 the price of beaver had begun to rise and competition from the English caused the Canadian authorities to move aggressively westward. Major sites, Michilimackinac, Niagara, Detroit, were strengthened. In order to minimize costs, many of the lesser posts were leased to the commandant. He was required to maintain the garrison including a priest, surgeon, and blacksmith. Regardless of the expense, many officers made their fortune in just a few years (Eccles 1974:146).

This opportunity was a source of rivalry between marine and regular army officers in the late 1750's. The regulars were finding it difficult to maintain themselves in Canada.

> They [Montcalm and others] ask for an increase in pay for the regular troops in Canada, the same as those in Europe have been allowed, and observe, that the pay of those troops is not to be compared with Colonial troops, as the latter have sources from their families, from trade, from contracts, the intrigue of the country and trading posts (O'Callaghan 1969, X:859).

The economics and the government corruption of Canada in the late 1740's and 1750's is beyond the scope of this study. Bougainville, however, saw the business of the colony as the

cause of problems related to the fighting of
the war.
M. Mercier leaves for Montreal. He
doubtless has [private] Business there.
Such is the way of the colony. The
Indians come to make coup and go home.
The militia men do the same; also the
officers of La Marine. For the next
fortnight they will all come to ask to
leave under the pretext of poor health,
of business, of trade, of commerce, of
bills of exchange. They will have completed three weeks or a month of campaign. In truth this is very long
(Bougainville 1968:250).

Bougainville's criticism is valid. It
would be difficult to campaign with disruptions
in the command structure. The marine officer
could, however, counter argue that the commerce
of Canada was also critical and as a leading
citizen of the colony they, like the militiaman
who was both soldier and farmer, had to do double duty.

A marine officer in the West who was accu-
mulating a fortune would counter similar complaints by arguing that his service in the
"outback" deserved reward and what reward there
was was diminished by the costs not reimbursed
by the government. Joseph Marin, commanding at
Green Bay shared in profits of 150,000 livres
per year, however, he made sure that his
expenses were known. "It has cost me at least
10,000 livres to restrain that large war party
as well as several others and to make them
agree to remain at peace" (Eccles 1974:148).
He was also responsible for maintaining the
fort and the services of a priest and blacksmith. We can only speculate on the accuracy
of the accounting methods applied in any part
of the system.

As was the case with woods warfare, the
marine adapted to the economic opportunity present at a frontier post, learning the necessary
skills from his Canadian officer. In a court
case concerning marines charged with desertion,

the accused claimed they were only out to do a little trading and hunting and they had received permission (Wright 1990:11). Other marines, when stationed in, or near, settlements, worked for nearby farmers or in a trade or craft. This activity is consistent with the desire of the government that these soldiers become settler upon leaving the service. Also, these activities helped decrease the material support need from the government.

The War of the Austrian Succession (King George's War), 1744-1748, marks a pivotal point in the service of the marine companies in Canada. Although they had conducted campaigns in the past (the Fox war campaigns of 1730, 1731, and 1734), they were now called on to conduct expeditions and establish new forts on a regular basis. Raiding parties of marines, Canadians, and Indians attacked New York and New England, including Saratoga and settlements near Albany and Boston (Eccles 1974:151).

The role of campaigning soldier was now added to garrison duty. This new responsibility was due to the need of the government and the availability of the marines. Yet, the success of the French military activity during the final one and one-half decades of marine service in Canada speaks well of the men assigned this task.

The major action of King George's War was the siege of Louisbourg in 1745. An American provincial force, assisted by the Royal Navy, maintained an artillery bombardment for seven weeks which caused heavy damage to the fortress and town. Marines were a substantial part of the Louisbourg garrison which fought honorably but unsuccessfully. Their service was in question as they had mutinied the year before (Eccles 1974:151). A relief force from Canada to Louisbourg led by a marine officer, Pierre Marin, was also unsuccessful (Wrong 1970:679).

The change of role for the marines was due to more than the war. There was a change in the geography of the broader colonial conflict. The focus of King George's War had been in the East, the Champlain Valley and Louisbourg. Now

MARINE
c. 1745

attention turned West. France saw the English attempting to divide New France by making an establishment in the Ohio country. The French claimed but, due to poor economic conditions, did not exploit the lands along the Ohio river. The English aggressively took advantage of the inattention of the French.

English traders, most notably George Groghan, were well-established in the region by the 1740's profiting from new markets caused by a shift in the Indian population in the Ohio country during the first half of the eighteenth century. The was a potential danger. The Shawnee, Miami, Delaware, and Wyandot, to name just a few, were competing for resources. The problem was enhanced by the fact that the Iroquois, a long time enemy of the French, claimed the lands by right of conquest.

From Pennsylvania, to present day Indiana, to the south shore of Lake Erie, English traders bartered goods for furs at an exchange rate the French could not match. Three hundred English traders were in the area of Fort des Miamis (Fort Wayne, Indiana) in 1749, according to the fort commandant, the Comte de Raymond (Eccles 1974:157).

King George's War had not ended when the new, and final, conflict began. In 1747, Groghan reported that the Iroquois killed five French traders near Detroit (Downes 1968:47). In a similar incident, very likely the same incident, called the Conspiracy of Nicholas, a Wyandot leader named Orontony, or Nicholas, was accused of killing five French traders near Sandusky while they were traveling back to Detroit from winter trading on the Cuyahoga River (Tanner 1987:44). Three *voyaguers* were killed while traveling between Detroit and Michilimackinac, and two canoes were attacked near Lake Michigan (Eccles 1974:153). These were just a few of the incidents related to the aggressiveness of the English traders in the Ohio country.

The French began their countercampaign in 1749 by sending a major expedition, that included 20 marines and 180 militia, through western Pennsylvania and down the Ohio River. The party was led by an experienced, Canadian-born, marine officer, Pierre Joseph Celoron de Blainville. Celoron was born in Montreal in 1693, he became a Chevalier de St. Louis in 1741, and served as commandant of Detroit, Michilimackinac, and Niagara (Wallace 1963:126). Celoron met with the Ohio Indians and buried lead plates inscribed with the French claim to the territory.

The English responded. Between 1748 and 1752, Pennsylvania paid as much for Indian relations as they had in the previous 30 years (Downes 1968:51). They did, however, refuse a request by the Indians to construct a fort on the Ohio River. The fort would have given the English dominance in the region.

The French had not been sitting on their hands. The English-dominated trading center at Pickawillaney (Piqua, Ohio) had been unsuccessfully attacked in 1751, by an expedition under the command of a marine officer, the Sieur de Bellestre. The next year Charles Langlade, with a party of Indians and a few marines, repeated the attempt and succeeded, killing the chief, Old Britain, and burning the village. In the north, the French sent Pierre Paul Marin to establish a chain of forts from Presque Isle (Erie, Pennsylvania) south toward the forks of the Ohio river. Fort Presque Isle and Fort Le Bouef were built in 1753, and Fort Machault at Venango in 1754.

The French saw their Ohio forts as a guarantee of the line of communication between Canada and Louisiana and a method to retain the loyalty of the Indians. They also protected the Ohio river which was the gateway to Louisiana and even Mexico, and according to Governor La Galissoniere, there were broader implications.

> ...In fine, nothing must be spared to strengthen these colonies, since they may, and are to be considered the bulwark of America, against the attacks of the English; since they alone can make up for

the want of Naval forces, and the outlay
they will occasion will save more considerable expense whereof the effects are much
less certain, especially if we allow ourselves to be reduced to the necessity of
having to transport reinforcements thither
from France, in order to preserve these
colonies in time of war; and since they
cannot be abandoned to their actual
strength alone, without being delivered
over in some sort to the English, who, by
the wealth they would draw thence, to the
exclusion of other nations, would most certainly acquire the superiority in Europe
(Zoltvany 1969:165).

Perhaps the government in London shared
the grand strategy view of La Galissoniere.
However, English colonial organizations, such
as the Ohio Company, and individual traders
were less worried about superiority in Europe
than they were the loss of a major economic
resource, the Indian trade in the Northwest.
Pressure was building, and although activity
had been reasonably non-violent to this point,
at least compared to what would happen in the
next seven years, the rewards were too great
and the rivalries contained too many memories.

Pennsylvania's failure to resist French
activity allowed Virginia to get into the act.
George Washington was sent to the French posts
in western Pennsylvania with the demand,
politely worded, to get out. The French
replied, as politely, no. In 1754, Virginia
sent an expedition to the forks of the Ohio to
establish a fort. The French moved south
before construction was very far along and sent
the Virginians home. They destroyed what the
Virginians had started and began to build Fort
Duquesne (Pittsburgh, Pennsylvania).

Marines were involved in the construction
of, and were part of the garrisons at, the new
posts in western Pennsylvania. The 800-man
expedition which left Montreal in early
February of 1754 to go to the the head of the
Ohio contained marines and militia. One hun-

dred men were left at Niagara and 200 at Fort Presque Isle. After the removal of the Virginians at the forks of the Ohio, 300 men were to remain at Duquesne and 100 were to go to Venango and the same number would go to Le Bouef (Eccles 1974:163, 167).

This assignment did not prove easy for the marines or the Canadians with whom they served. The days of occasional guard duty, hunting, fishing, and maintaining a garden which they had enjoyed at the posts in the North were over. They faced hard work, short rations, and unpredictable Indian relations.

> The largest number maintained at one time appears to have been less than 1400, and many of these were workmen employed on the construction of the fortifications or voyaguers transporting supplies. The only way this many could be maintained was by reducing the bread ration from two to one and a half livres per day. This did not improve morale, and the desertion rate gave cause for concern.
> Considering the back breaking work the men had to perform, up at three in the morning, hard at it to ten at night, on a diet of bread, stew, and salt pork, the officers frequently running short of wine, and with a heavy drain from sickness, it is amazing that the men gave such a good account of themselves (Eccles 1974:167).

Lack of food and hard work were not the only problems.

> Fort Duquesne was almost completed when Commander Contrecoeur sent some savages with Frenchmen to reconnoiter. The detachment returned at the end of several days, and reported that the English had settled in Virginia, some forty leagues away, and were building storehouses, probably with the inten-

HISTORY

tion of attacking Fort Duquesne. Upon this news, the commander determined to send an officer with an escort to carry a summons to the first English officer that he could find, but with care to be on guard against surprise attack from either the English or the savages,... (Bonin 1941:57-58).

The detachment, led by the Sieur de Jumonville, contained thirty-four men and an interpreter. A marine ensign, Droullon, and two cadets, Boucherville and Du Sable, were with the party (De Lery 1940:28). Presumably, some of the rank and file were marines. Jumonville was an experienced officer. He was born in 1718, in New France at Vercheres. In 1739, he served in an expedition against Indians in Louisiana, and later he was stationed in Acadia.

Jumonville's party did not find the English, the English found them. On the morning of May 28, 1754, a force of Virginians and Indians, led by George Washington, ambushed Jumonville, killing the officer and nine others. The remainder were made prisoner except for a man, Mousseaux, who escaped to tell the story to the commander of Fort Duquesne (Bonin 1941:58-59. DeLery 1940:19).

If Claude Pierre Pecaudy, Sieur de Contrecoeur had any doubts about his response to the attack on Jumonville, two events strengthened his resolve. Shortly after learning about the attack, he received a message from Quebec informing him that the English government had sent a plan for an attack on Canada to all their colonial governors. Then on June 26, Captain Louis Coulon de Villiers, Jumonville's brother, arrived at Fort Duquesne with 130 Indians, Nepissings, Algonkins, Abenakis, and Hurons (De Lery 1940:17). He asked for command of the expedition that was being sent in retaliation to the attack on the Jumonville party. This expedition of 100 men, which included marines, was now reinforced with the Indians that had come with Villiers (Bonin

1941:60). (Note: Bonin states that Villiers came from Fort de Chartres. He may have been confused concerning two marine officers. Francois de Villiers, brother of Louis, and serving in Illinois, did come to Fort Duquesne and was active in the raiding taking place from that post, capturing Fort Granville in 1756. Louis passed Lery on Lake Erie on his way to Duquesne. (De Lery 1940:17)

On the third of July the French met the English colonial forces, commanded by Washington, at a spot referred to at that time as Great Meadows. Washington was aware of the French party and had constructed a small stockade with exterior trenches (Fort Necessity). Washington believed that all of the men at Fort Duquesne were coming and estimated he was facing 900 of the enemy, enough to successfully assault his position. After some brisk firing from both sides, a rain, coupled with the English position being on low ground, filled the trenches with water. That evening the two sides met and Washington agreed to take his men east (Harrington 1957:64, 65). The French commander and another participant stated that two Frenchmen and one Indian were killed (Harrington 1957:64. Bonin 1941:63). As period documents regularly separate French and Canadians, the dead were probably marines.

The next year British regulars and colonial troops moved on Fort Duquesne under the command of General Edward Braddock. Joseph Gaspard Chaussegros de Lery, had come from Detroit and apparently convinced Contrecoeur that the fort could not withstand a siege. The commandant faced the decision to retreat or attack the oncoming English (Stanley 1968:98, 99). At 8 a.m., July 9, 1755, Contrecoeur sent a party of 72 marines (also 13 marine officers and 23 cadets), 146 militia, and 637 Indians under the command of Daniel Hyacinthe de Lienard de Beaujeu (born in Montreal, 1711) against the English force (Steele 1969:84. Stanley 1968:99. Wallace 1963:40. Kopperman 1977:267-269). The officers and cadets with Beaujeu were:

HISTORY

Captains: Dumas, Lingneris.
Lieutenants: Courtmanch [Contemanche?], La Bourque [Le Borques?], Mommidy, Carqueville.
Ensigns: Lonqueville, La Peyrade, Bailleul, Corbreare [Corbiere?], Bleury, Chevalier [Jean Baptiste?] de Celeron.
Cadets: Pecudy, Courtmanch, Beulac, St. Cherre, Hartell, Cabanac, De Muy, Rocheblas [Rocheblave], Saqueped [Sacepecs?], Soanna, St. Simon, La Bourque, Linctot (elder), Linctot (younger), Daillebout [D'aillebout?], La Framboise, Normanville, Roctorade [Rockloyade], Calaron, Blanville, St. Ours, Morandiere [Montimidy?]. (Kopperman 1977:267-268).

    Accounts of the battle state that the action began at 12:30 p.m. when the French first encountered the English advanced guard. The English soldiers formed for battle and brought their artillery into the action. The French commander, Beaujeu, according to Captain Jean Dumas, attacked before his troops were in order and they fired their first volley while out of range (Kopperman 1977:251-252). This criticism illustrates the difference in thinking between the European-trained Dumas and the Canadian-born Beaujeu. On the fields of Europe the game followed the rules; in the forests of North America a quick, determined attack often decided the issue.

    The third volley from the British killed Beaujeu and command went to Captain Dumas. Dumas had noted that the French militia had run and he ordered, in despair, the remaining troops, probably all marines, to advance. He sent Le Bourque and Rocheblave to lead the Indians against the British flanks. The French attack captured the British artillery. With the silencing of these guns, the Indians became bolder. The British, were pressed on three sides, and with the fear of being encircled, broke. There was no organized pursuit by the French. The battle lasted between two and four hours. (Kopperman 1977:251-252. Bonin 1941:82-83). The French losses were extremely light. In addition to Beaujeu, two officers, Lieutenant Carqueville and Ensign La Peyrade,

MARINE
c. 1758

three Canadians, two marines, and fifteen
Indians were killed (Stanley 1968:100).
Lieutenant La Bourque, Ensign Bailleul, and
Cadets Hartel and Normanville were wounded
(Kopperman 1977:267-269).

The British loss was in excess of 700,
killed and wounded. Included in these casualties were Braddock and more than 50 other officers (Hamilton 1959:54-58). This is a high
ratio of officers and men killed for an
eighteenth-century battle and would not have
been found on the "formal" battlefield. This
introduction to war in the North American forest was a costly lesson for the British regulars.

This battle established Dumas's reputation
as a military officer. He was born in France
and had been a Captain in the Agenais Regiment.
He arrived in Canada as a marine captain in
1750. In 1760, he returned to France and continued his military career attaining the rank
of field marshal (1780) (Wallace 1963:204).

The victory was not only important to the
state of affairs in the Ohio country, it helped
make up for the defeat at Lake George that same
year of a French force, including army regulars, under Dieskau, by British colonials under
William Johnson. The French blamed lack of
discipline on the part of the Indians as the
reason for the disaster. Yet, they apparently
made the same mistake as Braddock's men: they
attempted to use formal European tactics
against experienced woods fighters. There were
a few marine soldiers with Dieskau. Marine
officers served with the militia and Indians.
Jacques LeGarduer de St. Pierre, who had entertained Washington in Pennsylvania, died leading
the Indians. Celoron de Blainville commanded
the marines and militia. Also present were
Raymond, Vassan, and Repentigny. There may
have been as many as nine marine officers and
seven soldiers killed or wounded (O'Callaghan
1969, X:319, 321, 331, 356, 361, 383).

Marines played a part in every major
engagement of the war and countless nasty little fights undocumented and forgotten. The

defeat of Braddock opened Pennsylvania, Maryland, and Virginia to attack. Fort Duquesne became a base to launch raids to the east of the Appalachians. Dumas, who now commanded in the Ohio, saw this as the best way to prevent another attack by the British which could result in the loss of Fort Duquesne. Montcalm, although he had not seen the fort, supported de Lery's evaluation saying it was, "...not worth a straw" (O'Callaghan 1969, X:416). Marine cadets and junior officers led Indians on raids to Fort Cumberland and beyond. Lieutenant Alexandre Dagneau Douville was killed on a raid on a small fort in Hampshire County, Virginia (O'Callaghan 1969, X:423 note). Ensign Niverville de Montizambert attacked Fort Shirley and Bigham's Fort in June 1756. In August of that year, Francois de Villiers with 23 soldiers and 32 Indians captured Fort Granville (Lewiston, Pennsylvania). That same month Philippe de Rocheblave, a cadet who had been at Braddock's defeat, captured a small fort beyond Fort Cumberland (Stanley 1968:148. Robinson 1965:234).

Now that the French were masters of the Ohio, Governor Vaudreuil turned his attention to another English threat, Oswego. Oswego was established on the south shore of Lake Ontario to divert Indian furs from the French. Aside from the economic threat, this post sat between Fort Frontenac and Fort Niagara, posing a strategic threat as well. It was an embarrassment to French prestige.

In preparation for an expedition against Oswego in the campaign of 1756, Lieutenant de Lery led 362 men, including 27 marines, in a raid to disrupt supplies and communications to the fort. The supply line was the most exposed at the Onieda carry, the portage from the Mohawk River to the Oswego River. The English had built forts at each end of the portage, Fort Bull on the Oswego end, and Fort Williams on the Mohawk.

The French chose to attack Fort Bull, as it was the weaker of the two fortifications, little more than stockaded storehouses. They

HISTORY

reasoned, correctly, that it contained the supplies that were critical to Fort Oswego. Failing to surprise the garrison, Lery was forced to assault the fort. Lery's men stormed the gate under fire from the English. Rushing into the compound, they received a volley of musketry and grenades. Surprisingly, French losses were very light; however, nearly all the English defenders were killed. The fort, and supplies not carried off, were destroyed. (Hagerty 1971:vii. O'Callaghan 1969, X:404, 405).

The campaign to destroy Oswego continued with a force of 1200 men, under Louis Coulon de Villiers, harassing and all but isolating the post. On July 10, he led part of his command against a British convoy traveling south for additional supplies.

> With four hundred men he attacked a convoy of three to four hundred bateaux, each with two men, and three companies of soldiers. The English companies here are of one hundred men. Some have been reduced to sixty two. (They were) returning from Oswego, where they had carried food and munitions, and had gone up again after more provisions. Villiers put them to flight and knocked off a great number, and would have knocked off a lot more were it not for the poor quality of the tomahawks furnished by the King's Store, took twenty four scalps and killed or wounded in their flight, according to his estimate, about three hundred men. We lost in this affair a colony officer, six Canadians and colony soldiers and one Indian (Bougainville 1968:6).

In August, Montcalm, who had replaced Dieskau, led approximately 3000 men with artillery against Oswego. The French found the English defenders in three fortifications, Fort Ontario, Fort George, and the old Fort Oswego.

The advanced guard of Montcalm's force, made up
of 400 marines and the Indians, covered the
landing of the army (Bougainville 1968:24, 25).
Using conventional siege tactics, French artillery soon began bombarding Fort Ontario from
close range. The English position was hopeless
and the garrisons of Fort Ontario and Fort
George retreated to Fort Oswego. Montcalm sent
a force to cut off any retreat from this post
and turned his guns on the last stronghold.
The French cannon breeched one of the walls and
the English, expecting an assault, surrendered
(Roberts 1980:372).

The reduction of Oswego removed the most
serious threat to the French lines of communication and supply to the west. This allowed the
French to turn their attention to yet another
problem, the Champlain Valley. Johnson's victory over Dieskau had established British control at the south end of Lake George (Lake St.
Sacrement). The French established a camp at
Ticonderoga and began building Fort Carillon
early in 1756. Carillon, like Duquesne, became
a base for raiding parties Mixed parties of
marines, militia and Indians, ranged south
toward Albany and into New England, "taking
prisoners almost within sight of Boston ..."
(Bougainville 1968:35).

The 16th [May]. Messrs de La
Fontaine and Sacapes, volunteer cadets,
returned from the detachment commanded
by M. Le Borgne, with eight Indians,
and 16 French, to inform us that, having found no one at Sarosto (Saratoga)
to attack, they had burned two large
guard houses, and had killed 30 horses
on the spot, without counting a large
number of wounded.

The 21st [May]. At noon, M. de La
Colombiere set out at the head of a
party of 415 men to go and burn the
boats of the Enemy which are beneath
the cannon of the fort of Ledius [Fort
Miller, between Saratoga and Fort
Edward]. This detachment consists of

Messrs de St. Martin, Lieutenant, de
Villejoint, de Lanoix, senior ensigns,
de Boucherville, junior ensign; of
Messrs de Montarville, of both
Sacepecs, of both Grosbois, La
Fontaine, Hiche, De la Colonnerie, all
cadets, of 52 Indians, two gunners and
349 soldiers of the Marine, and
Canadian Militia. That this party will
succeed is not doubtful, if the main
army of the enemy has not yet arrived
(De Lery n.d.:129, 131)

Colony troops were part of the garrison at Fort Carillon (Ticonderoga) from its construction in 1756, until it was abandoned in 1758. The journal of Joseph Gaspard Chaussegros de Lery details activity of the marines during May and June 1756, in and around Fort Carillon. He states, "we have also, this year, an increase of 1200 men to bring to full complement our troops in this country, each company of 70 men" (De Lery n.d.:129). This suggests that replacements may have been used to fill out existing marine companies, as well as to form new companies. The replacements came from foreign recruits and from small detachments (12-24 men) of regular troops. The regulars were from the regiments of Bigoree, Bresse, Brissac, Flandres, Saint Chaumond, Vatan, Chasseurs, de Fisher, and Volontaires de Flandres (Chartrand 1984:23).

It is interesting that, although regulars were available, marines were used to scout and attack the British advanced troops on Lake George (De Lery n.d.:131). That marines were chosen for this duty seems to argue against the contention that they were second-rate soldiers (or worse). Also, Governor Vaudreuil kept detachments of marines, militia, and Indians in the field throughout the winter (O'Callaghan 1969, X:457). This duty would not have been familiar to the regular soldier.

The garrison of Fort Carillon in the winter, 1756-1757, was composed of 150 French regulars and 100 marines. In January, they were called on to go to the relief of a supply party that had been attacked going to Fort St. Frederic for forage and brandy. The mixed party of 100 regulars and marines, including five cadets, was joined by a band of Ottawa Indians under the command of Ensign Charles Langlade. They ambushed the English, a detachment of Rogers' Rangers, and followed the initial gunfire with a bayonet charge. The ranger rearguard formed a defensive line which held the French until dark when the rangers withdrew (Bougainville 1968:81. O'Callaghan 1969, X:569-570).

Rogers' account states that his party consisted of 74 men. He admits to having fourteen killed, six wounded and six missing. He estimates that the French had 250 men and they lost, killed and fatally wounded, 116 (Rogers 1966:39, 44, 45). His estimates are high if compared to the French account. The French report of casualties state that there were nine soldiers, one Canadian, and one Indian killed. Twenty-seven of the French force were wounded, three later died. They freed four of the seven men captured by the Rangers earlier. The Rangers killed the other three (Bougainville 1968:81).

Early in 1757, a winter expedition was formed to attack Fort William Henry. This expedition, planned by the colonial government, and the summer campaign of Montcalm that same year, illustrate the differences in strategic thinking of the French and the Canadians. The winter attack, attempting to capture the fort by surprise, was part of harassment on a wide front to force the British to act defensively, guarding their frontier. Montcalm's plan was that of a conventional soldier. He understood the annual campaign, formal battlefield, and the siege, not the Canadian's *la petite guerre*.

The winter expedition consisted of 300 regulars, 896 marines and militia, formed into 16 companies, and 300 Indians. Each company had 17 marines, 33 militiamen, and was led by two marine and one militia officer. There was a cadet in each company and two sergeants

HISTORY

(Bougainville 1968:85-86).

The command of the force was given to de Rigaud, the brother of the Governor General. The military ability of Rigaud is unclear. His second in command was an experienced marine officer, de Longueil, King's Lieutenant at Quebec. The brigade major was Sieur Dumas. He was assisted by Mercier, the colonial artillery commander. Also, the French detachment was commanded by Poulharies, the grenadier company commander of the Royal Roussillon Regiment (Bougainville 1968:86). According to Montcalm, the assignment of Dumas and the other subordinate officers by the Governor was related to the ability of the commander (O'Callaghan 1969, X:551). The head of the party may have been questionable, but it did have a backbone.

They may have planned to attack the fort. Ladders were taken along. The ladders were in three sections of five feet, eight inches, that fit together to make one ladder of thirteen and a half feet. The ladders, it was later said, were a ruse. There is no mention of artillery with this force. Special combustibles were to be used to burn the fort, but they got wet and did not work (Bougainville 1968:94-97).

The success of the raid, according to the government, was measured by the burning of: Four cruisers (ships), ten to fourteen guns; a number of (50 oar) long boats; 350 bateaux; boatbuilding materials; campaign carriages; a stockade with foodstuffs and military equipment; a saw mill, hospital; other buildings; and a large quantity of firewood (O'Callaghan 1969, X:542-545).

The French found room to criticize.

> The success they had in this expedition is proof that the marquis de Montcalm was entirely right in wishing for a detachment of only six to eight hundred men at most. They would have accomplished the same objectives with more glory, have cost less in money and food, and we would have been able to

get started as soon as the ice went out
(Bougainville 1968:97).

Montcalm's plan for William Henry, in
contrast to Rigaud's raid, was conventional and
methodical. While parties of French and
Indians, under the command of marine officers,
including Joseph Marin and Charles Langlade,
raided south of Lake George, Montcalm gathered
his forces. By July 29, 1757, he had assembled
in and around Fort Carillon an army of 8019
men.

A large part of the marine contingent was
organized as a battalion of 525 men formed from
the "detached companies of the Marine" which
had been filled by recent arrivals from France
(O'Callaghan 1969, X:599, 636). Officers of
the battalion were "those who would be least
fit to go with the Indians and exercise the
business of harassing" (Bougainville 1968:132).
It is quite probable the men for the battalion
were chosen using the same qualifications. The
marine battalion was part of La Reine brigade,
comprised of the Languedoc and La Reine regiments (Bougainville 1968:152-153). The establishment of the marine battalion and its
assignment to an Army brigade would, in effect,
take a large number of marines away from
Rigaud, commander of the colonial forces.

Marines, including all the cadets and 66
officers, served with the six militia brigades
(Stanley 1960:75). The marines assigned to the
militia were the "old marines", the experienced
woods fighters. The distribution of marines
within the militia brigades is open to speculation. A possibility is that they were appor-
tioned between companies, similar to the system
used for the winter expedition against William
Henry. There were 1000 marines with Montcalm
for this campaign (Bougainville 1968:120).
Some marines were with raiding parties to the
south. It is a reasonable assumption that each
militia brigade (411-473 men) may have had as
many as 70 marines in its ranks.

The formation of the marine battalion had
not been without problems.

HISTORY

The Marquis de Montcalm this afternoon went to the camp at the Falls [near Carillon] and the one at the Portage, where he gave orders for the formation of the battalion of La Marine troops, a large and difficult operation and one which those charged with are having much trouble accomplishing (Bougainville 1968:134-135).

This job was given to Dumas who was also charged with organizing the militia. The order to organize the marines was given about July 20 (Bougainville 1968:131-132). If the marines were able to function as a battalion by August 1, the day the French left Carillon, it was a military miracle.

The army was divided into two detachments. Chevalier de Levis commanded a 2488 man detachment that would march overland. This force included half the militia, which may have been another attempt to dilute Rigaud's influence. A picket of 100 marines from the battalion went with Levis, as did a 300-man unit known as Villiers' Volunteers. Villiers men led the advance (Stanley 1968:159). The remainder of the force, including the marine battalion, went by water with Montcalm. The army left at two in the afternoon on August 1, with the La Reine brigade first to embark. The lead bateau was under the command of an officer named Jacquot who may have been a marine (Bougainville 1968:156).

The capture of Fort William Henry, August 9, was the result of a formal artillery siege. The most notable infantry action was an assault by Villiers Volunteers on the English trenches. Bougainville saw the fight as useless (Bougainville 1964:167). A Jesuit missionary describes the action,

> Monsieur de Villiers, brother of Monsieur de Jumonville, an Officer whose name is a eulogy, improved these advantages [French siege works] by coming at the head of a body of Canadians,

to attack the outer intrenchments. The
action was sharp, disputed for a long
time, and deadly for the enemy
(Thwaites 1959:167).

The marine battalion, with the La Reine
brigade, served very close to Montcalm during
the campaign. It is difficult to know if this
was an honor or if the general wanted to keep
watch on them. There was little trust between
the French and Canadians.
The French army's contempt for the colonial government and some of the colonial military officers was not hidden. Montcalm wrote
to Levis, August 17, 1756,

... remember that Mercier is a
weakling and an ignoramous, St. Luc a
garrulous braggart, Montigny admirable,
but a looter, Villiers and Lery good,
Langly excellent, Marin brave but stu-
pid; the rest are not worth mentioning,
not even Rigaud my senior lieutenant
general (Fregault 1969:61).

The date of Montcalm's letter should be
noted. He was making his judgment having been
in Canada for a short time. Most of the criticism by French officers was directed at the
government, especially Bigot the Intendant and
his group which included Mercier, Pean, and
others. Often the marines, officers and rank
and file, were praised. Bougainville's journal
often mentions the quality of individuals. As
mentioned earlier, marines comprised the
advance party for the campaign against Oswego
and were at the head of the advance toward
William Henry. This included raiding parties
of marines and Indians under Langlade,
Montegron, and Joseph Marin who were causing
problems beyond Fort Edward (Stanley 1968:159).
As in 1757, 1758 began with a fight
between Rogers' Rangers and a French detachment
from Carillon. Rogers had left Fort Edward on
March 10, with 180 men to scout in the vicinity
of Carillon. On March 13, he received word of

HISTORY

the approach of 96 of the enemy, mostly
Indians, and he deployed his men in an ambush.
The initial volley from the Rangers killed, in
Rogers' estimation, more than 40 men. The
Indians broke and were pursued by the Rangers.
They ran into the main body of 600 (again,
Rogers) French and Indians (Rogers 1966:79, 84-85).

The French force of 250 (French report)
consisted of regulars, marines, militia, and
Indians under Montegron (Bougainville 1968:198-199). The battle raged between small groups in
rough terrain. After an hour and a half,
Rogers, having lost more than 100 men,
"...thought it most prudent to retreat...."
His total loss was more than 120. He claimed
to have killed 150 and wounded the same number
(Rogers 1966:87,88-89).

The French casualty report states that two
cadets, a Canadian, eighteen Iroquois, and an
Abanaki, were wounded. Three Iroquois and a
Nipissing were killed. The Indians took seven
prisoners and 144 scalps (Bougainville
1968:198-199).

In July, the English moved on Carillon in
force. General James Abercromby led a force of
6300 regulars and 5900 provincials north
(Hamilton 1962:216). The 3500-man garrison at
Carillon contained only 150 marines. They were
placed, with 250 militia, on the far right of
the French line outside the newly built fortification, half a mile from Carillon.
Abercromby, in one of the great military blun-
ders, sent his battalions to assault the French
position without artillery support. He lost
men and his nerve and retreated. Although not
directly attacked by the British, the marines
and militia did fire on troops that came within
range from behind an abatis of tree branches.
Twice they were ordered to sortie against the
enemy (Bougainville 1968:231-233). Apparently,
these orders were ignored.

The marines had twenty-eight casualties at
Carillon. Montcalm reported to Governor
Vaudreuil on the conduct of the marines and
militia.

The Colonial Troops and the Canadians have caused us to regret that there were not in greater number. Chevalier de Levy, under whose eyes they fought speaks highly of them (O'Callaghan 1969, X:749).

Montcalm's report to his superiors was quite different and less than favorable. Although he also recognized the valor of Captain Raymond, he reported,

> I must say in truth that the colonial troops and the Canadians behaved very indifferently. M. de Trecesson, the Commandant, has been obliged to fire on some of them who were abandoning their post... (O'Callaghan 1969, X:754).

Vaudreuil found out about the "other" report and sent his own account to Paris.

> The troops of the Marine, the Canadians and Indians, who were stationed at the weakest point, were fortunately not attacked. But they rushed boldly from the intrenchment and made a flank attack on the column which appeared most determined to clear the intrenchment. They displayed so much valor that even during the action they took most of the prisoners (O'Callaghan 1969, X:795).

It appears that Bougainville, who also recorded the event, upon reflection, did not wish to leave an impression that the service of the marines was less than honorable. In a summary of the action, which was written to counter attempts by certain Canadians (Mercier and de Lotbiniere) to take undeserved credit, and to all but accuse them of being cowards, Bougainville makes the following remarks.

HISTORY

At the first sortie which the Chevalier de Levis ordered the Canadians and colony troops (to make), Sieur Raymond, who commanded them, called for men of good will to follow him. A small number stepped forward with Sieur Nigon, an officer come from France in 1757 and placed in La Marine regiment. These volunteers advanced; the enemy fired on them once, all disappeared. Sieur de Raymond returned alone, and Sieur de Nigon, wounded by a shot in the thigh, scarcely found anyone who would bring him back.

It was the same on the second sortie; Sieur Denys la Ronde, lieutenant, was the only one who followed M. Raymond. Note: Many soldiers of La Marine (among them is a great number of very good ones.) wished to share with the regulars the risks and the glory and fought in our defenses. It was there, and beside the Chevalier de Levis that Sieur Langy Montegron was wounded (Bougainville 1968:238).

The poor relations between the governor and the General Montcalm continued even in the light of the great victory at Carillon. Montcalm points out to the governor certain shortcomings in military protocol.

Sir, after my three years service under your orders, to prescribe to me useless or minute details, which I should blush to prescribe to the lowest captain; that proceed from your secretary having but one mould wherein to fashion instructions and letters for all officers, from me to the colonial ensign (O'Callaghan 1969, X:779).

Vaudreuil had his own complaints concerning the general.

If the troops of the Marine have
not exploded so openly, we are indebted
for their restraint to their subordina-
tion, but their pain, though secret, is
not less acute, seeing that M. de
Montcalm, far from doing justice to
their services, attributes these to the
troops of the Line. This proceeding
disgusts both officer and soldier
(O'Callaghan 1969, X:780).

Although Bougainville is very loyal to
Montcalm, his journal seems to find some middle
ground between the governor and the general as
his description of the events at Carillon,
quoted above, suggests. He becomes more and
more critical of high-ranking Canadians as time
goes on. He does not, however, degrade the
ability of the marines or militia. In a letter
to Governor Vaudreuil he states a plan for
fall, winter, and spring expeditions and reor-
ganizing the military forces. Part of his
scheme is:

I would bring up all companies of
regulars and colony troops to sixty
men, incorporating in them elite
Canadians who would serve the whole
campaign with pay furnished by the King
or even the parishes; this mixture
would give each troop good shots, good
canoemen, and good workmen of all kinds
whose mutual emulation would make
excellent warriors (Bougainville
1968:272).

Bougainville's plan shows an ability to
adapt to the situation as it was in Canada. It
was, perhaps, fortunate for the British that
Bougainville was between a governor who was too
tangled in politics to act and a commanding
general who could not adapt to the environment.
Bougainville and Levis (second in command of
the French regulars) were, however, in accord.
Levis had suggested as early as 1756, that
Canadians and marines be used on the flanks and

as skirmishers. As commander of French forces after the death of Montcalm, he incorporated militia into the regular battalions to be used as light troops. His reorganization worked better than expected at Ste. Foy as Canadian militia plugged a hole in the French line caused by a mistake of a regular battalion (Nicolai 1989:70-72).

The success at Carillon, which preserved French control of the Lake Champlain invasion route for another year, was tempered by the loss of Fort Duquesne. A British army, led by General Forbes, moved methodically toward the fort on the Ohio in the autumn. In August, Fort Frontenac, with a garrison of 110 men commanded by 60 year old, Captain Pierre Jacques Payan de Noyan, had been captured and destroyed by the English provincial troops under Lieutenant Colonel Bradstreet. Although the French re-established a post at the site, the damage was done. Frontenac contained supplies for the Ohio posts and the boats to move them. Fort Duquesne was in peril but saw some hope when the English advance was dealt a series of setbacks.

Captain Charles Philippe, Sieur de Aubry, a marine officer from Louisiana, led a party of 500 against Major Grant who, with 800 men, had been sent by General Forbes to attack the Indian camp near the fort. (It is possible that Captain Francois Marie le Marchand de Ligneris, who had succeeded Dumas as commander in the Ohio country in 1756, actually commanded the French.) The battle, fought on September 14, resembled Braddock's defeat in that the French fought from cover and the English in the open. The English were routed (Bonin 1941:101-102. Bougainville 1968:295). Grant commented, "Fear had got the better of every other passion, and I hope I shall never again see such a pannick among troops" (Stanley 1968:189).

On October 12, Aubry engaged a detachment near the English base at Loyalhanna. Although outnumbered, he blockaded the British camp for two days. A month later, on November 12, a party of 30 Canadians and 140 Indians, under de Corbiere, raided the English army. Forbes sent Mercer and Washington with 500 men each to deal with the raiders. They succeeded in engaging each other in the dark (Stanley 1968:189).

These French successes had no lasting effect. Unlike Braddock's army, Forbes continued the advance on Duquesne with a force of nearly 7000 men. Further resistance by the French was useless when their Indian allies made peace with the English. In November, Ligneris, the commandant of Fort Duquesne, ordered the fort destroyed and he fell back on Fort Machault. (Eccles 1974:178-179. O'Callaghan 1969, X:952).

The loss of Fort Duquesne opened the back door into Canada. The front door, Louisbourg, had also fallen in 1758. This opened the St. Lawrence river to the English. These setbacks enabled the English to threaten Canada from three directions. In 1759, they seized the opportunity.

In the west Fort Niagara was besieged. In the east an English fleet carrying Wolfe's army threatened Quebec. Amherst, the English commander in chief in North America, moved from the south on Lake Champlain. The French forces were too few to successfully resist on all fronts. Bougainville estimated, in 1758, that the English could bring 20,000 regulars and an equal number of militia against a total French force in North America (without Indians) of approximately 11,700 men, including 3500 marines. His estimate of the forces available in the Champlain Valley area was about 7000, including 300 Indians. The marine force was 1112 (Bougainville 1964:251, 255).

The English arrived at Fort Niagara on July 6. The French garrison consisted of 10 officers and 486 men, including 183 marines, marine artillery, and 133 militia. An additional two officers and 70 men, marines and militia, arrived on July 10 (Dunnigan 1986:33). Some of the marines were German and they were mutinous (Stanley 1968:219. O'Callaghan 1969, X:989).

HISTORY

The marines were stationed throughout the fortifications. Thirty men were in the outerworks to the left (lake side) of the ravelin and thirty more were posted to the river side (the right). Forty marines were on the beach under the high bank and thirty were at the west end of the covered way (Dunnigan 1986:37).

On July 9, Captain Walter Rutherford of the Royal American Regiment, came to the Fort with the English demand to surrender. When he returned to his lines with the French refusal he reported that the garrison was mostly Canadians (Dunnigan 1986:36). Since not quite a third of the garrison was Canadian, it would be interesting to know if the captain's remarks were based on the marines being indistinguishable from the militia or if the English considered the marines Canadian rather than French.

The French attempted to lift the siege of Niagara by attacking the English base camp at Oswego and sending a relief force from the west. On July 5, a mixed force of 1200 Canadians and Indians, under St. Luc de la Corne, attacked about the same number of English troops at Oswego. The English commander, Frederick Haldimand, had been warned the day before and had built barricades using the bags and barrels of supplies. The French attack failed (Roberts 1980:351-352).

In the west, a relief force of 800 marines and militia and 500 Indians was organized. The French force, made up of the men from Forts Machault (Venango) and Presque Isle and reinforcements from Illinois and Detroit, was under the command of Lignery (Ligneris) and Aubry (Dunnigan 1986:76. Knox 1980:210. Stanley 1968:216). Joseph Marin and Philippe Rocheblave joined this force fresh from an expedition to "insult Fort Pitt" (Robinson 1965:235).

The English learned of the relief expedition and sent a force to meet it. They fortified a site to the west of Niagara at La Belle Famille. The topography of the battlefield forced the French to attack in a column 12 men wide. This tactic, unusual for marines, allowed the English to concentrate their fire. The results were devastating. The French were routed with the loss of 344 men, 250 killed. Lignery and Aubry were wounded. Lignery died on August 29 (Dunnigan 1986:77-80. O'Callaghan 1968, X:992). Marin and Repentigny were among those captured (Robinson 1969:235. Knox 1980:210).

The defeat at La Belle Famille made the defeat of Niagara only a matter of time. The fort surrendered on July 24. The garrison had lost, killed and wounded, 43 marines, 26 militia, and 40 regulars (Dunnigan 1986:105).

Marines were part of a 400-man garrison at Fort Carillon when Amherst arrived on June 18. As in the previous year, the French defended the outerworks. The English, however, would not repeat their mistake. They erected artillery positions to bombard the fortifications. The French withdrew on June 26, exploding mines to destroy the fort (Bonin 1941:110).

The third part of the campaign was Quebec. Marines played an important role in the siege and the final battle on the Plains of Abraham. When the British arrived, marines were part of the force stationed at Point Levis on the south side of the St. Lawrence River. They retreated to the city when, after skirmishing with the British light infantry, Brigadier General Monckton brought the grenadiers and Highlanders forward in overwhelming numbers (Knox 1980:134-137).

Wolfe constructed batteries at Point Levis to bombard Quebec. An attempt to attack this position was led by Dumas. He, with a mixed force of 1500 militia and Indians, found the British defenses more imposing than they had expected. Dumas sent for a reinforcement of 300 marines. Dividing his command in two sections, Dumas marched on the British position. For some reason the lead section did not launch the attack and when they returned they were fired on by the second section. Not knowing who their attackers were they returned the fire. Seventy men were killed or wounded (Knox 1980:146-147).

Governor Vaudreuil's account states that it was a marine detachment that was on guard at Ance au Foulon, later called Wolfe's Cove, the night of the British landing. Bonin supports this in as much as he states that a marine officer named Vergor was in command of the post (Bonin 1941:114). Louis Du Pont de Chambon Vergor was born in France. He came to Canada as a marine officer in 1751. It is quite possible that he was part of Bigot's group. He was given command of Fort Beausejour in 1754, which he surrendered with less than a token defense the following year. There was a court martial in 1757, concerning this incident and Vergor was acquitted. He returned to France following the war (Wallace 1963:770).

Vaudreuil also states that marines were part of the French forces that harassed the British flanks on the Plains of Abraham (Zoltvany 1969:182, 183). It is thought that most of the British casualties were inflicted by the fighting on the flanks before and after the main engagement (Eccles 1974:182). When the French regulars broke and ran, the 78th Regiment (Highlanders) threw down their muskets and pursued with swords and dirks. Lieutenant Frazier of that regiment states, "It was at that time and while in the bushes that our regiment suffered most." It appears that the Scots turned to meet the flanking fire of "skulking fellows, with small arms" (Stanley 1968:232). It is estimated that this rearguard action held the British for one half hour (Nicolai 1989:69-70).

The French force under Levis, who marched to retake Quebec in 1760, contained 800 marines in two battalions (Stanley 1968:244). After defeating the British at Ste. Foy, where the British lost 1100 killed, wounded, and missing, the French besieged Quebec from April 27 to May 16 (Knox 1980:248). Levis was forced to fall back on Montreal when the British fleet appeared (Hamilton 1967:21, Bonin 1941:118).

The English closed in on Montreal, taking Fort Levis on August 25 (Bonin 1941:119). Montreal could not be defended with 2200 regulars and 200 marines. The English numbered 17,000 (Jenkins 1966:147).

> It [the English force] was more than was needed against a paltry town, overpowered on all sides, which had only a shirt and ten or twelve bad cannon; we were reduced to less than three thousand men (Bougainville 1968:326).

The loss of Montreal was the loss of Canada. The terms of the capitulation, signed September 8, 1760, allowed any French soldier, regular or marine, to stay in Canada (Zoltvany 1969:187). It seems many took advantage of this opportunity. The marines in the western garrisons went to the Louisiana colony.

It is estimated that 107 marine officers and 1052 other ranks returned to France (Stanley 1960:96). Some officers were reassigned. The enlisted men were discharged.

> It may be noted that all the free companies of the Marine coming from Canada were discharged at Harve by government order. Each individual was given a full discharge with thirty francs to take him home. As some soldiers had several years' pay due them, the government ordered eight months' pay on account given them. It was different with the troops of the line. They were ordered to rejoin their regiments by short marches (Bonin 1941:135).

The service of the men of Les Compagnies Franches de la Marine in Canada was honorable, if not distinguished. They performed the duty that was asked of them. This performance is unjustly criticized by historians using standards such as regular European armies of the period, or even the military of today. Such criticism is faulty. The marines must be judged on the job they were asked to accomplish, to guard the interests of the King in the colony. For 75 years they maintained the peace and successfully resisted attempts by the English and their Iroquois allies to expand their influence. Setbacks such as the capture of Louisbourg in King George's War are better attributed to lack of support than to a lack of skill or valor by the marines.

When called on to actively campaign in the final conflict, a role that they were not intended to play, they gave a good account of themselves. This was never better shown than it was at Quebec where they continued to fight as the regulars broke and ran. As many marines had settled in Canada, and others intended to, it may have been that they were no longer fighting for France; perhaps now, here in Canada, they were fighting for their home.

MATERIAL CULTURE

Introduction

The uniform and equipment of Les Compagnies Franches de la Marine is a source of questions and continuing debate. Opinions concerning their appearance range across the spectrum, from uniform and "spiffy", to something resembling pirates or *coureur de bois*. Documentation provides hints and suggestions, archaeology some possibilities. These pieces coupled with the use of analogies from military history present a picture that suggests each of these conclusions may be correct.

As suggested earlier, the quality of the men of Les Compagnies Franches was probably no better and no worse than other European soldiers. They were subject to the same environmental and cultural forces as were their opponents. These forces, also effecting their uniforms and equipment, included, but were not limited to, the attitude of their commanders, the availability of supplies, the surrounding cultural and natural environment, and personal preferences.

It would seem a reasonable assumption that the handful of men at an isolated post such as Fort Sandoske would present a different appearance than the garrison at Quebec, who might be called on to parade before the governor. Some documents suggest that frontier posts did not receive replacement uniforms.

In the western outposts of Canada such as Michilimackinac and probably Louisiana, uniforms were at first sent to the garrisons, but this proved too expensive. As a result, soldiers who were sent to these posts clothed themselves with trade and Indian goods (Leliepvre and Chartrand 1974:22).

When, and if, uniforms were sent, did the canoes make it to the posts in the west or did the bales of marine supplies sink in Lake Huron or Lake Erie? Perhaps the post commander decided to use the space allocated to marine supplies to bring more trade goods to the fort.

> The commander at Presque Isle, M. de Portneuf, preferring his own profit to the good of the service, has loaded his bateau with brandy and merchandise instead of flour and salt pork,...
> (Bougainville 1968:107).

In Louisbourg, unscrupulous officers, indifferent soldiers, and poor quality equipment were factors governing the soldiers' appearance.

> The problem of distributing and paying for the uniforms caused various abuses, especially in the early days of the Fortress and affecting the Compagnies Franches. "Almost all the captains are playing merchants with their soldiers" to the point where they exploit them, wrote Pierre-Auguste de Soubras in 1714, whereas the soldiers, for their part, often preferred to spend their money on drinking, rather than paying for their uniforms. Thus they were forced, in 1719, to purchase the clothes they needed upon receipt of their wages.
> These difficulties were compounded by the quality of the materials sold to the soldiers. For the entire history of Louisbourg are found documents issued by the colonial or metropolitan authorities which makes clear the wretched quality of the fabric used in manufacture of the uniforms. The cloth was of poor quality, the material too thin and the linen too coarse. A memorandum written in 1751 by Governor Jean-Louis de Raymond is particularly eloquent concerning the supplies for the soldiers of Isle Royale. As well

MATERIAL CULTURE

as being poorly clothed, the soldiers are unhappy with their equipment: "...our soldiers are without belts, cartridge cases or accouterments. We would be greatly embarrassed if the occasion arose where we would have to defend ourselves or repel attackers. I beg of you monseigneur, that you order the shipping of the armaments for six companies, next year". So wrote St. Ovide de Broullan in 1727 (Proulx 1971:1-2).

The memorandum by Raymond, mentioned above, says much the same as Broullan twenty years earlier. He complains of the cloth in the coats as being too thin and loosely woven. The coats themselves are poorly made. The color is impractical as they quickly get dirty. The shoes have single rather than double soles. The gaiters never fit. The shirt linen is too thin and the hats are of poor quality (Egli 1984:18).

Again in 1758 there is evidence of poor quality in supplies. Bougainville points to the system that is making Canadian contractors rich.

> The deerskins, the tanned shoes, the tobacco are of a bad kind; the deerskins, the tanned shoes, the tobacco come on contract. The coats, breeches, mitasses, are of poor material, too short, too tight; the coats, breeches, mitasses come on contract. The hatchets, shovels, picks are almost always useless; the hatchets, shovels, and picks come on contract.
> Still this is not all. These contractors use the King's workmen and their pay is charged to the King's account. One could continue on this subject at length (Bougainville 1964:257).

It is an exaggeration to say that appearances changed daily. However, the harsh environmental conditions and the poor quality of the uniforms would have changed the appearance of the troops in perhaps as short a period as a few weeks. "Since clothing for the troops was provided last year [1755], we have had to use all sorts of ways, this year, to provide for the needs of said troops..." (Proulx 1971:2).

What does "all sorts of ways" include: Civilian clothes or soldier produced clothing? Blue mazamet, used for regulation small clothes manufactured in France, was sent to the Louisiana colony (Brain 1979:298). What other materials were used: trade cloth, blankets, animal hides? Speculation can be enjoyable, endless, and at times, frustrating. How extensive was a marine's adaptation to the environment of the western post? What did a particular captain allow? What became necessary because of lack of supply?

What follows does not directly answer those questions. The regulation uniform and equipment is presented with possible adaptations. The examples included are documented, as used by marines, contracted to be manufactured and issued to marines, or otherwise available to these soldiers. How items were used, altered, or combined, is left to the imagination of the reader.

UNIFORMS

Marines were to be issued two uniforms in alternate years. The first year they received the "full dress": justaucorps (uniform coat), breeches, two shirts, two cravats, a hat, a pair of stockings, and two pair of shoes. The following year they received "small dress"; waistcoat, breeches, two shirts, two cravats, a hat, a pair of stockings, and two pairs of shoes. This uniform, established in 1718, saw only minor changes through the end of the final French and Indian War (Proulx 1971:5-6). What follows is a discussion of a complete marine

MARINE
c. 1758

uniform. As suggested above, on the North American frontier this may have been rare.

Le Justaucorps (Uniform Coat)

The battalion was the army unit with which the eighteenth-century soldier identified. The uniform of each battalion was unique. Le justaucorps provided the soldier his identity. Differences in the coat from one battalion to another might be found in the color of the cloth, the type of metal used in the buttons, the number and placement of the buttons on the coat body, cuffs, and pockets, and the shape of the pockets and cuffs. For the purpose of uniforms, the marine companies, though independent, can be considered a battalion, as there is no evidence to suggest that there were differences between companies. Although the basic elements of the marine justaucorps can be illustrated, many specifics remain unclear.

The coat was made of a gray-white woolen Lodeve cloth during the early eighteenth century. After 1732, the cloth was manufactured in Marseilles. The shade of gray-white depended on the raw material. The following quote concerns the regular army but there is no reason to believe it would not apply to the marines.

> During the 18th century white was the standard colour for the Line Infantry. This was not as spectacular as might be imagined however, since this was the colour of the coarse undyed wool that was used, dyed cloth, apart from distinctive cuffs and collars, being reserved for the Guards, Cavalry and foreign corps (Thorburn 1976: 7).

The cuffs and lining of the justaucorps were blue wool. The tails of the coat could be turned back as was common of military coats of the period. It had eighteen large buttons in front, four on each cuff, and four on each

JUSTAUCORPS 1755

BOUTONS

pocket (page 22). The four button pattern for cuffs and pockets represents a change from an earlier period. Illustrations c.1718 show five buttons on the pocket and three on the cuff. There was a button at the top of each tail pleat and one on the rear slit. Two smaller buttons closed the pleats. The buttons in front were evenly spaced from neck to hem. This may been changed to follow fashion, c.1750, by using just nine buttons extending only to the waist (page 59). The buttons were brass, except in the early part of the eighteenth century, when they were pewter. (Petard 1976:22. Proulx 1971:11. Protz and Marsala 1989:1).

There is debate as to whether the justaucorps had a collar. Most of the documentation would suggest the coat was collarless. Petard, however, states that there was a blue collar with narrow descending points. His sources are a 1751 document and period paintings by Joseph Vernet (Petard 1976:22). Proulx does not state that the trimmings included a collar but quotes a 1741 document that describes the coat as having a "small white buttoned collar" (Proulx 1971:6). It is very probable the collar in this description is actually the neck stock.

It is also suggested, based on period documents, that the "sea service" marine justaucorps had a collar but the coat of the land-based marine did not (Chartrand 1984:13). Yet, the Conseil de Marine decided in 1716 that the troops serving in the colonies should be dressed like naval troops (Proulx 1971:5). Additionally, there is a drawing of a soldier, identified as a marine c.1755, showing a dark collar and cuffs (Sullivan 1981:33).

In 1757, a coat with a collar was issued to the Naval Regiment which was part of the French Army in Europe (Funcken 1977:61). The regiment is found, in 1758, in the order of battle for the Army of the Lower Rhine (Kennett 1967:Table 1). The drawing mentioned above may be of a soldier in this regiment. The date of the drawing may be incorrect and/or the coat

MATERIAL CULTURE

may have appeared before the "official" issue, which was not uncommon.

A coat, with collar, appears in a description by an English officer at the surrender of Louisbourg in 1758. He identifies the unit as the 43rd, Royal Marines. The coat is grayish white with blue collar and cuffs and wrought pewter buttons. The hat is trimmed with silver lace (Knox 1968:258). As small detachments of French army regiments serving in Europe served in North America, it is possible that this may have been the uniform of the Marine Regiment (numbered, 44th, in Funcken 1977:60). What relationship, if any, this regiment had to the Ministry of the Marine is unclear. This unit may, however, contribute to the conflicting uniform descriptions. As it was organized as a regiment, it seems unlikely that it has any direct relationship to the Independent Companies of the Marine.

The conflict between the descriptions and illustrations may well demonstrate change over time, the difference between troops in France and those in the colonies, variations due to cost-conscious contractors, or modifications by the soldiers. Also, history provides many examples of a time lag in providing frontier soldiers with new equipment. The illustrations and documents are few and interpretation from such a small sample must be suspect.

La Veste (Waistcoat)

The marine waistcoat had sleeves and was made of blue Mauye wool serge in 1719, blue Mazamet drape in 1730, and blue Boisseson serge in 1732. It was lined with yellow linen or blue serge. The sleeves had no cuff and were slashed, closing with two buttons. It had eighteen buttons in front and four on each pocket flap. This may have been reduced to nine in front, c.1750, following the change in the justaucorps (page 62). Unlike the coat which had false pockets, the veste pockets were functional (Pelard 1970:22. Proulx 1971:12).

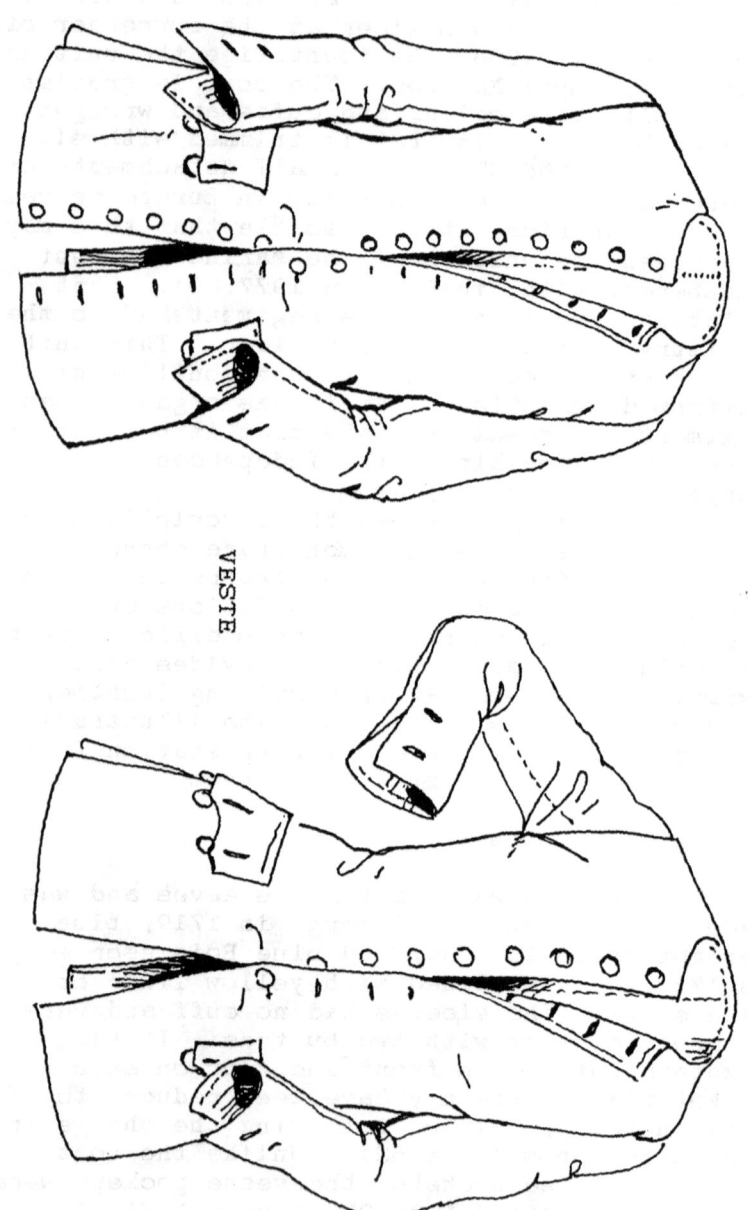

VESTE

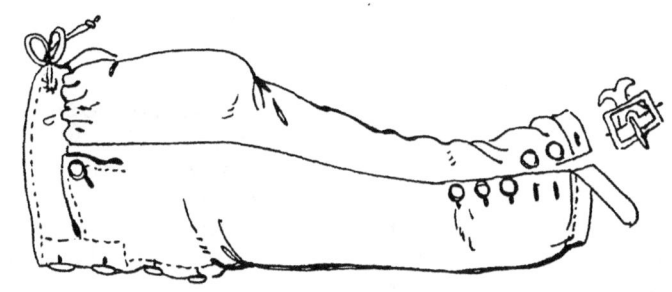
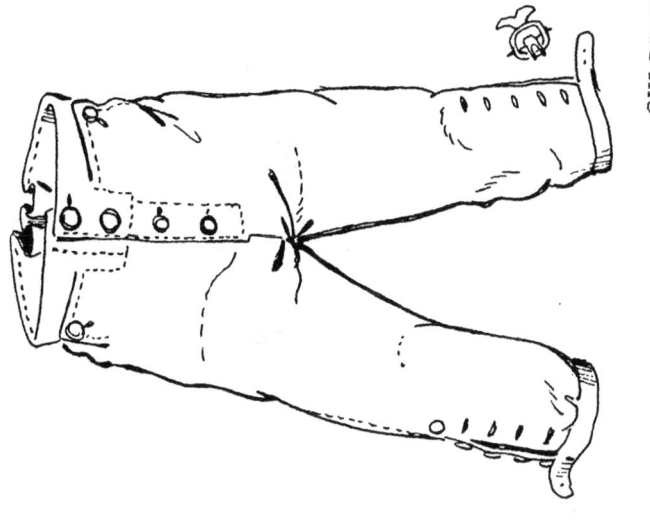

CULOTTE

As the veste also required three dozen buttons it is quite possible that it had buttons at the top of the side vents, as did the coat. These buttons would have provided support for the waist belt (Egli 1984:14).

La Culotte (Breeches)

The breeches were made of blue Boisseson serge and lined with gray linen (the fabric was probably the same as the veste and changed as noted above). It had two pockets which closed with buttons. The breeches had a vertical fly front which closed with four or five buttons. A gusset and drawstring in the back of the waist adjusted the garment to the wearer. The legs had five buttons and a buckle at the knee (Petard 1976:22. Proulx 1971:12. Egli 1984:14-15. Diderot 1959:Plate 441).

La Chemise (Shirt)

The shirt was made of linen. The material was left in its natural color, a light brown. The garment was made full in the body and in the arms. The arms were one piece. There was a heart-shaped gusset or reinforcement at the base of the front opening. There were components described as side pieces and shoulder pieces. They can be interpreted as either reinforcements or gussets (Petard 1976:22. Proulx 1971:10. Egli 1984:15).

La Cravat (Tie, Neck Stock)

The soldier wore a "tie" which was a single piece of white Saint-Jean de Lyon linen wrapped around his neck (on top of the shirt collar). It tied in front with long ends. In the final decade of marine service in North America a neck stock was introduced made of white and later black material, perhaps muslin. The black variety may not have been issued in North America or it may have been limited to shipboard marines. The stock tied, buckled, or buttoned behind the neck (Petard 1976:22.

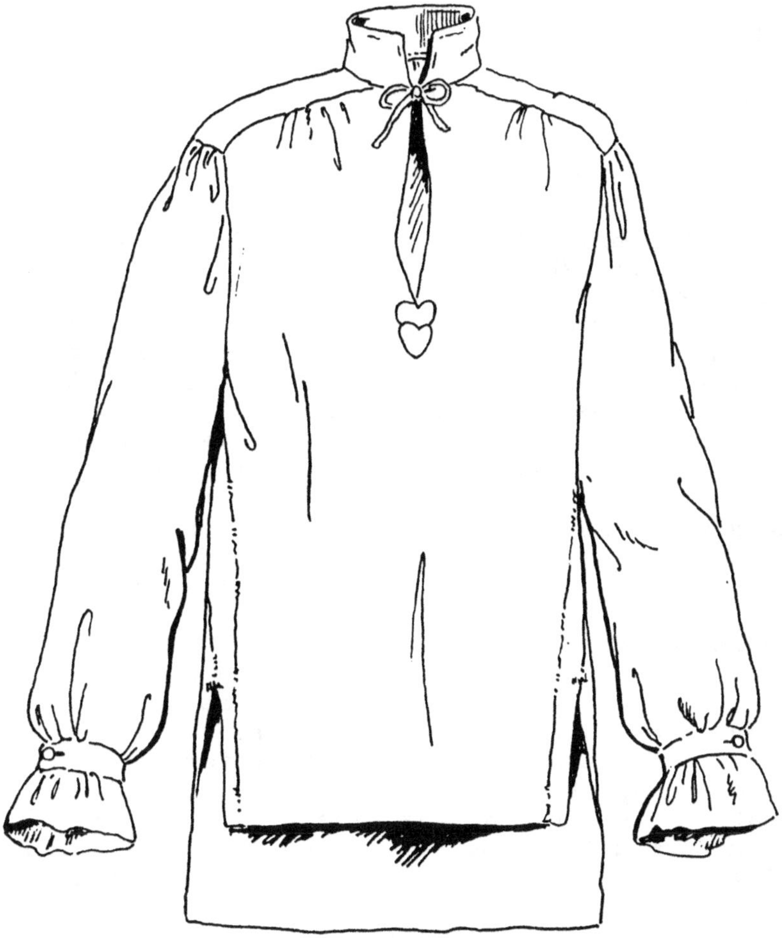

CHEMISE

CRAVATE

Proulx 1971:10. Egli 1984:15. Protz and Marsala 1989:1).

Le Chapeau (Hat)

   The marine wore a Caudebec style hat (adopted in 1732) turned up on three sides (page 22). It was trimmed with false gold lace (one pouce wide) on the edge of the brim. The hat also had cords and a black cockade fastened with a button. In 1746, the King ordered the hats to be made from good quality lamb's wool. It had a lining and leather band (two pouces wide) on the inside. Apparently the quality was not all it was supposed to be and, with hard usage on the frontier, it can be suspected that the hat was a perishable item (Petard 1976:22-23. Proulx 1971:12, 57. Egli 1984:16).

Le Bonnet de Police (Fatigue Cap)

   The fatigue cap, or bonnet, was not an issue item. (A "stuff cap" was requested to be sent to Louisbourg. This might refer to a fatigue cap [Proulx 1971:57]). It is probable that the fatigue cap was made by the soldier from worn uniform parts such as the veste (Egli 1984:16-18). This was a practice in other armies.
   Style and color varied. A typical cap would be a tapered bag with a turned up "cuff" at the head opening. This may have been edged in a contrasting color and an anchor or fleur-de-lis sewn on the front (page 82).

Les Souliers (Shoes)

   The ship Machault sank in 1760 carrying military supplies destined for the soldiers in New France. The cargo included 500 pairs of shoes. These shoes are the typical square-toed buckled shoe of the eighteenth century. The French shoes were made with double and single soles, the double-soled variety for cold climates. Both styles were shipped to Canada. Metal heel plates were used, with examples in

SOULIERS

the Machault cargo and in the archaeological collection of Fort Michilimackinac (Petard 1976:23. Proulx 1971:12. Egli 1984:16. Sullivan 1981:80. Stone 1974:81, 87).

Les Bas (Stockings)

After 1722 the marines used a stocking that was sewn from blue woolen cloth (St. Maixent weave). The stocking was fastened with a garter of some sort below the knee (Petard 1976:26. Proulx 1971:12. Egli 1984:15). Examples of stockings can been found in the Machault cargo and in period illustrations (Sullivan 1981:82. Klinger 1967:27).

Les Guetres (Gaiters)

Gaiters were protective clothing, a canvas legging that extended from the top of the shoe to above the knee. Gaiters may not have been considered a regular part of the marine uniform but might be better classified as additional equipment. A period illustration (1755) shows a marine(?) with gaiters (Sullivan 1986:33). Apparently, marines at Louisbourg were not regularly issued this garment.

> It seems that gaiters did not form a part of the usual apparel of the soldiers at Louisbourg. In fact, one reference dated 1743, in which there is talk of 800 pairs of gaiters to be shipped to Isle Royal, is the only reference we have been able to find prior to 1745. Furthermore, it is to be noted that not a word is said about Canada and Isle Royale in the shipping statement for the colonies covering the clothing of the troops, while gaiters are usually mentioned for the Windward Islands. The wearing of gaiters became a general practice only after the year 1751, ... (Proulx 1971:14).

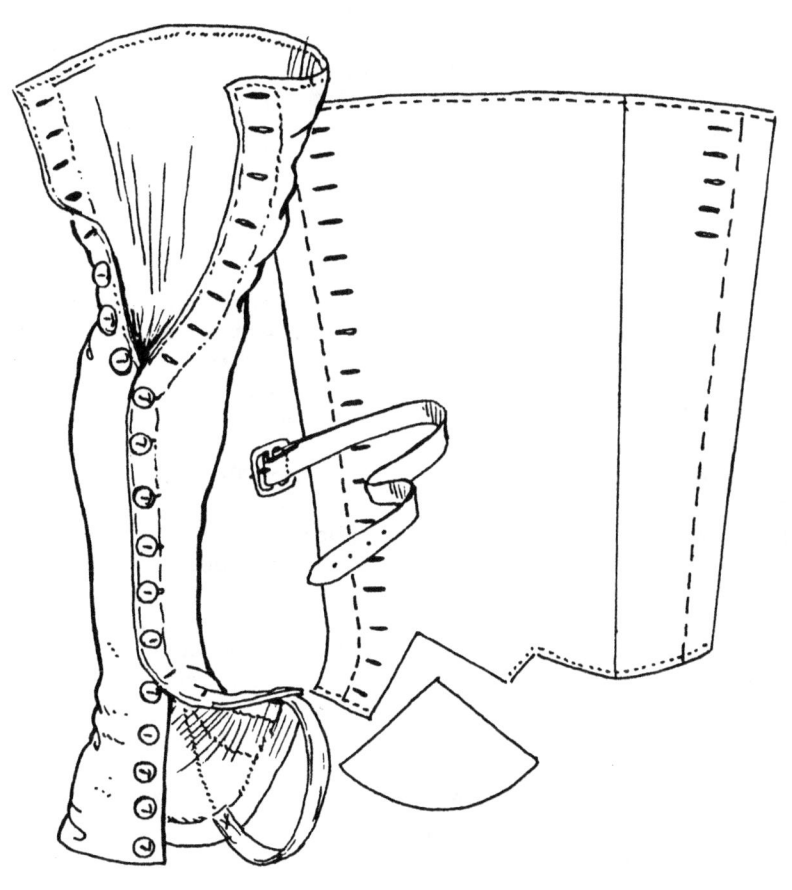

GUETRES

The gaiters were made of heavy canvas. A strap ran under the shoe. They buttoned on the outside of the leg to the bottom of the leg of the soldiers' breeches. At this point the buttons closing the breeches leg buttoned through the gaiters. Additionally, a garter held the gaiter below the knee. The type of button used on gaiters is not known but may have been leather. (Petard 1976:26. Egli 1984:16. Sullivan 1986:78).

Buttons

Justaucorps, veste, and breeches buttons, after the early eighteenth century are believed to be brass, convex in cross section with a flat "flange" rim. They had a wire loop soldered to the rear (page 59). Archaeological work has uncovered 78 examples of this type at Fort Michilimackinac, all within French occupation areas (Stone 1972:49). Similar buttons were found at Louisbourg. This strongly suggests that these are indeed French military buttons. The 78 specimens include two different sizes, 17.0 mm - 19.5 mm and 23.5 mm - 24.5 mm (approximately 3/4 inch and 1 inch). These two distinct size groups support the contention that the buttons used on the small clothes were similar in design, but smaller than, the justaucorps buttons.

These domed brass buttons may mark a particular period. The uniform of 1741 was to have flat copper buttons (Proulx 1971:6). Other descriptions call for copper sheet buttons on wood (Proulx 1971:11). It is quite possible these buttons were actually brass, as that is the metal given in a 1744 inventory in Quebec (Petard 1976:22). Reference to copper buttons may be a problem in translation.

Officers and Non-Commissioned Officers

A 1697 contract of uniforms for the marines states that officers' uniforms included gray-white justaucorps with blue cuffs, blue breeches and stockings, gilded buttons and the

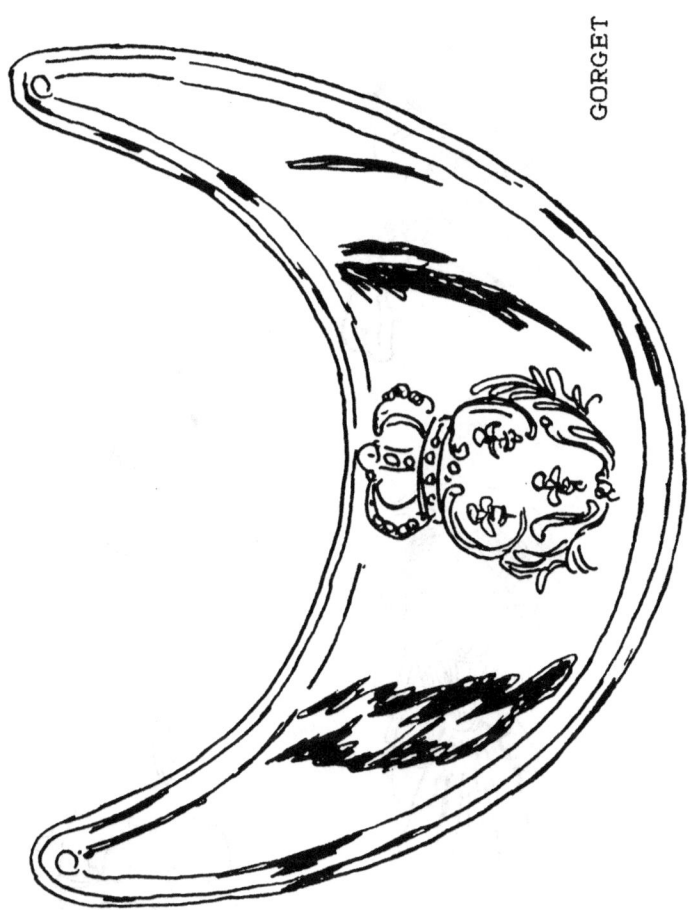

WIGS AND WIG BAG

MATERIAL CULTURE 73

hat edged in gold with a white plume (Proulx 1971:7). This is similar to the soldier's uniform, but the material would have been of superior quality. In the absence of specific information concerning later periods, it may be speculated, cautiously, that this relationship continued. The officer, of course, provided his own uniform and probably had some latitude in design and decoration. Officers would have worn a gorget and carried a sword (Kalm 1987:447). On formal occasions the officers awarded honors such as the Order of St. Louis would wear their decoration (page 204). A sash was not used (Protz and Marsala 1989:2).

Better-quality material is also found in the sergeant's uniform. The justaucorps and veste construction was to be of "fine" cloth. Rank was indicated by trim on the cuffs and pockets, a "fine gold Lyon braid", one inch wide. The same material was used to trim the hat (Proulx 1971:8-9. Protz and Marsala 1989:2).

There may have been men serving as sergeant majors in large garrisons such as Louisbourg, Quebec, Montreal, Detroit, and New Orleans. This rank is indicated by two strips of lace, one above and one below the buttons on the cuff of the uniform coat (Protz and Marsala 1989:2).

CLOTHING IN CANADA

> When the French are traveling about in this country, they are generally dressed like the natives (Kalm 1987:560).

It seems that if the marines were part of Canadian society and exhibited similar cultural traits they would have also adopted the clothing styles of the common people. This would, of course, be tempered by their belonging to a military organization.

Evidence of supply problems and poor quality of uniforms and equipment is presented throughout this study. However, there are contrary viewpoints.

> Marine soldiers were from France and shipped to Canada annually. Only marine officers were Canadian born. It is hard to imagine a native born Frenchman no matter his frontier post casting aside European born customs, mode of dress and behavior. Fur traders could go Indian in terms of dress but not marines....
> Evidence suggests that even western outposts such as those in Michigan, Illinois and Wisconsin that marines there were amply supplied with marine military clothing. The idea that supplies of such items were low or nonexistent is false. There was even evidence suggesting that marines sent to fur trading posts north of present day Minnesota and North Dakota dressed well. There is sufficient evidence (from Mackinac and Montreal) supporting the idea that there were enormous quantities of European cloth on hand. There was not a shortage of cloth especially when its importance in trading is considered (Protz and Marsala 1989:2).

These two views are not necessarily contrary to one another. That the Canadian adopted native dress does not mean that he was wearing only a breechcloth and moccasins. It must be remembered that Kalm, a Swedish naturalist, had only recently arrived in Canada and minor deviations from European dress may have caught his eye. Also, the Indians had adopted certain European clothing such as the shirt. It is quite possible that in the manner of dress they did not present a great contrast.

As to the dress of marines, the examples of lack of uniforms, or environmental adaptations, detailed in period documents are not meant to suggest these men went native. These

WINTER DRESS

Joe Lee
91

sources merely support the supposition that marines, including officers, by necessity and/or choice, obtained clothing from local sources. If they had the resources and opportunity they might have purchased clothing from a tailor in Quebec. If at a frontier post, they may have had to contract with a woman in a nearby Indian village to make clothing or do it themselves.

The marine arriving from France had a complete uniform. However, the uniform of the European soldier rarely survived very long away from the home country. Local environment, difficulty of supply, and, in some cases, neglect, allowed and demanded adaptation. A marine serving in Canada faced all of these forces. He may have adopted civilian dress to save his uniform.

> He [a marine] had previous to going to Sandoske left his uniform coat and some shirts with Norman Coutuier, a Detroit tailor, and his hat with Dr. Chapoton, the Detroit garrison Surgeon (Wright 1990:12).

It is not clear as to whether replacement uniforms were regularly sent to western posts. Large posts, like Detroit, had a tailor who could produce new uniforms. Part of the Detroit garrison, retreating to Illinois at the end of the war, wintered in Illinois, one reason being, " ... their uniforms and shoes were in a very bad state" (Kellogg 1936:66).

As references quoted at the beginning of this chapter suggest, supply of French-produced uniforms was a problem at garrisons such as Louisbourg. If the front of the supply line had problems it is questionable if the "tail end" did better. Certainly, seventy-eight buttons found at Michilimackinac, lost over forty-five years, do not present a strong case for a steady supply of uniforms. This would have been sufficient for one uniform.

Even if uniforms were available, the French-made garments would not have been suit-

WINTER DRESS

able for the Canadian winter. Adaptation would be necessary for comfort and not survival. The equipment list for the men on winter expeditions lacks formal military clothing.

February 17-28 [1757]: On the eighteenth at St. Jean the equipment was issued. It is well to list here of what this equipment consists. This list will show once and for all how these winter expeditions are equipped. (the money value of part of this equipment may be taken instead, if one chooses.)

EQUIPMENT

One overcoat
One blanket
One wool cap
Two cotton shirts
One pair mitasses
One breechclout
(A soldier has breeches and drawers instead of a breechclout.)
Two hanks of thread
Six needles
One awl
One tinderbox
One butcher's knife
One comb
One worm
One tomahawk
Two pair of stockings
Two siamese knives
One pair of mittens
One waistcoat
Two pair of deerskin shoes
One dressed deer skin
Two portage collars
One drag rope
One pair of snowshoes
One bearskin
One tarpaulin per officer, one large one to every four men.
(Bougainville 1968:87)

MATERIAL CULTURE

Capot

The cold Canadian weather certainly called for an outer garment in place of, or in addition to, the justaucorps. The Ministry of Marine made some effort to provide this additional item. Louisbourg records mention Lodeve cloth capes for guards. The color is given as gray-white (Proulx 1971:14). A soldier of the Sandoske garrison mentions a "munitions coat" which had been made into a capot (Wright 1990:12).

Armies of the eighteenth century provided outer garments, watch coats or capes, for guards but this would not solve the problem for a soldier at other times. The capot was a common garment in Canada and it was issued to the members of expeditions which probably included marines (Bourlamarque n.d. Bougainville 1964:87).

The capot is often depicted as a crude garment made from a few rectangular pieces of blanket material. This type of blanket coat would be the product of a marine, Canadian, or Indian who had little knowledge of tailoring methods. This was not the limit of fashion.

A period illustration shows a well-tailored capot with back pleats and cuffs (Acker 1982). A nineteenth-century, factory-made, capot in the Smithsonian Institution is very similar to the illustration, although shorter in length (Hanson 1981:14).

A capot differed from a cloak or coat as it had an attached hood (Petersen 1968:28). As they were tailored, it is very likely that they were produced from wool cloth rather than blankets, although this may have been similar material such as duffle. Also, they probably were produced in a variety of styles (material, length, cuffs, edge binding) and colors (Seguin 1968:44-51). The capot was normally secured at the waist with a finger woven woolen sash.

Mitasses (leggings)

Military leggings were not an "issue" piece of equipment until the late 1740's (see Gaiters). Although marines were garrison troops, the occasional patrol, hunting, or the cold weather would call for leg coverings in addition to stockings and breeches. It seems rather likely that marines, especially on the frontier, would have adopted the leggings worn by the native population.

The mitasses were wool or leather sewn to form a tube that extended from the ankle to the knee or the upper thigh. A long pair would have "ties" that fastened to a waistbelt. A knee-length pair would be fasten with a leg garter below the knee. This garter, also used on the long pair, might be a scrap piece of cloth or a colorful woven braid (Hanson 1983:8).

Moccasins

Shoes were issued to the marine but supply problems and poor quality were ever present. If serving on the frontier he would trade for a pair of moccasins from the local Indians. This footwear varied in design from tribe to tribe so what he wore was regionally distinctive.

If the marine was in garrison in Quebec, Montreal, or near another French settlement he would be able to purchase a pair of moccasins produced by French Canadians. This footwear, whether low cut for summer wear or high topped for winter (souliers de boeuf, bottes sauvages), had a one-piece sole of cowhide formed on a wood last (Hanson 1981:16). The uppers were of lighter leather. Wild animal hides were used as well as domestic.

Tuque (Stocking Cap)

Perhaps nothing is more French Canadian than the tuque, a woolen stocking cap. The marine had access to this headgear. The tuque

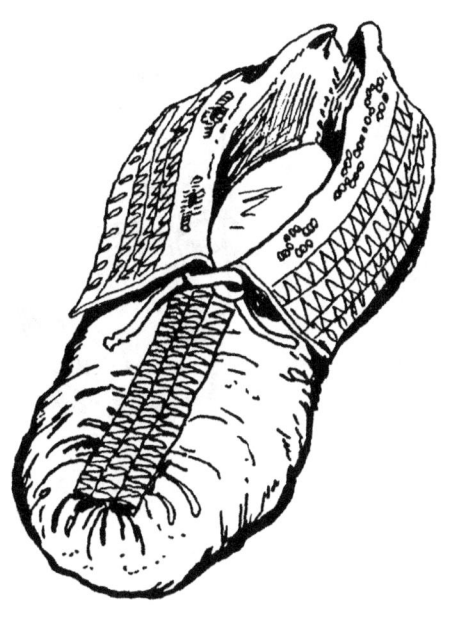

MOCCASINS

TUQUE BONNET

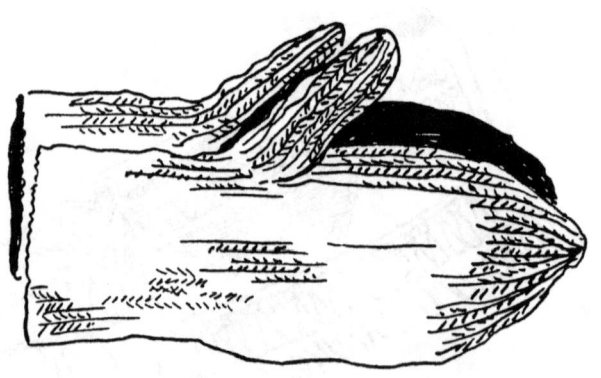

MITTENS

MATERIAL CULTURE

was an issued item in 1757 (Bougainville 1964:87). They were made in various weights, "single caps" or "double caps". They came in various colors, blue and scarlet being most popular. Tuques were knitted as tubes. An example from the Machault cargo is of two-ply yarn knitted in stocking stitch (Hanson 1981:11. Sullivan 1986:82).

Mittens

Mittens would be as necessary as other warm clothing and were issued in the 1757 expedition referred to above. These may have been made of two pieces of wool cloth sewn together. Mittens were also knitted, a specimen was recovered from the Machault cargo (Sullivan 1986:82). The mittens may have been joined by a cord which passed around the wearer's neck.

Summary

The information available concerning the clothing of the marine in Canada is insufficient to allow confident conclusions. It is possible to speculate, with a chance of being correct, that the uniform changed over time and the marine used non-regulation clothing, produced in Canada, that was suited to the environment.

There were changes in uniforms and equipment throughout the period of marine service in North America. Most of these changes were minor until the late 1740's and 1750's. It is at this time haversacks and gaiters appear in the documents. Also at this time, uniform changes, justaucorps with collars and buttons extending to the waist, buttoned cravats/neck stocks, may have been seen in Canada. Most likely, these new uniforms would have arrived on new marines. Replacements were arriving as late as 1756 (De Lery n.d.:129). It is debatable if the men on the frontier ever received a "new model" uniform.

Perhaps those stationed in a regular port, Quebec or Louisbourg, may have had access to resupply. The marines at posts with tailors quite likely had uniforms, but these would have been constructed in the style with which they were familiar.

Regardless of the availability of uniforms, marines adopted outerwear used by the Canadian settler and Native Americans. Capots, mitasses, tuques, and mittens were regular items of winter dress. The poor quality of shoes made the use of moccasins a necessity. This footwear was available from Canadian and native sources.

As the small amount of documentation causes highly speculative remarks concerning marine uniforms in general, any attempt to comment on individual companies would be futile. Service at different posts would give them unique experiences that would, over time, effect their appearance in terms of material culture. The number of men in the garrison, its degree of isolation, the activity of nearby native tribes, and the personality of the marines themselves (to list only a few possibilities), gave the post, and its company, a specific identity.

FIREARMS AND ACCESSORIES

Le Fusil (Musket)

European soldiers, and their colonial counterparts, in the eighteenth century carried a muzzle loading, smoothbore, flintlock musket. Although all of these firearms were substantially the same, there were decorative and minor functional differences. Evidence strongly suggests that the marine was supplied with a musket different than that used by the soldiers of the French army. The bore diameter of the barrel was slightly smaller than the army musket and the marine received a grenadier model which meant it had a leather sling. Unlike the army musket that fixed the barrel to

MATERIAL CULTURE

the stock with bands, the marine musket had a pinned barrel with one barrel band to mount a sling swivel.

The Tulle manufactory (Tulle, France) was the primary supplier of arms to the Ministry of the Marine and the Ministry represented the primary market for the armory's product beginning in the late seventeenth century (Ravenshear 1986:44). Tulle supplied arms for all aspects of Ministry activity: trade, ships, and colonial troops.

A copy of a contract between the Ministry of the Marine and Jean Martial de Fenis, Sieur de la Combe, owner of the arms manufactory at Tulle, provides information concerning marine muskets at one point in time. This agreement, dated 1734, gives specifications for muskets to be built for the marine troops (Ravenshear 1979:10-11). As this arm represents the type used near the mid-point of marine service in North America it is important. Although France did constantly change the design of the military musket in the first half of the eighteenth century, many of the changes were minor. Consequently, it can be assumed (cautiously) that the models used before and after the 1734 musket were similar.

The musket of 1734 (M1734) was described as a "grenadier" musket, meaning it had a sling (a grenadier would sling his musket to free his hands for throwing grenades). The octagon to round 44 3/4 inch barrel was to have a bore of approximately .66 inches. The front sight/ bayonet lug and four tenons were to be braised to the barrel. It was to have iron furniture. A partial barrel excavated at Louisbourg is very similar to that described (Ravenshear 1979:11).

Contact specifications called for a walnut stock with the butt being 15 1/2 inches long, 5 3/4 inches wide, and 2 1/4 inches thick. The tang of the butt plate was to be short or "snub nosed," an obvious difference from the butt plate with a long tang used on the army musket (Ravenshear 1979:12).

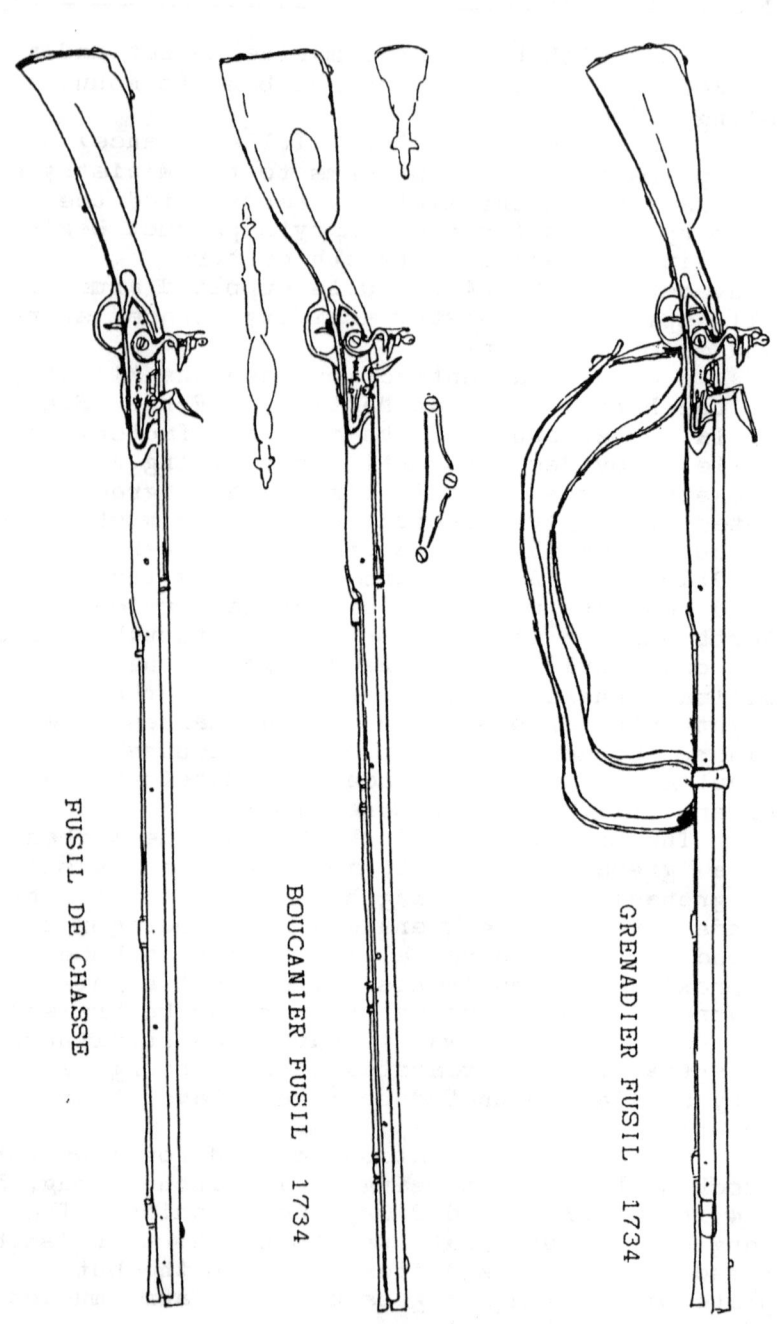

MATERIAL CULTURE

The sling, called for by the use of the term "grenadier", makes sling swivels necessary. Artifacts from Louisbourg show these swivels to be "D" shaped rather than round which was the case on the army musket. The "D" ring is also present on an earlier model in the French Naval Museum. The mounting of the forward swivel would have required a barrel band. Excavated artifacts at Louisbourg include two bands with "D" shaped rings (Ravenshear 1979:12).

The lock plate was flat, as was the plate of the army muskets, M1717 and M1728. However, the 1734 contract calls for "locks of the new design". Evidence suggests that this means the use of the bridle connecting the pan and frizzen used on the M1728 rather than the bridle system used on the M1717 which connected the frizzen to the base of the frizzen spring (Ravenshear 1979:13).

The barrel length would suggest four ramrod pipes were used, however, one was probably replaced by the barrel band. The ramrod was wooden. The side plate was to be "S" shaped. The "collar" at the muzzle was a sheet iron band folded into the barrel channel (Ravenshear 1979:12).

The 1734 contract and the artifacts excavated at Louisbourg strongly suggest that the M1734 musket was an arm used at that fortress. An example thought to be from a French sloop sunk in Lake Champlain has the characteristics of this arm (Ravenshear 1986:46). It seems reasonable to assume this model was supplied to other companies.

Fort Michilimackinac was garrisoned by les Compagnie Franches de la Marine. The site of this fort has received extensive archaeological excavation. The small sample of firearm parts found includes several specimens that may have come from marine weapons. Two lock plates attributed to the French are most interesting. They have anchors engraved in front of the position of the cock. These, and a third plate, attributed to the French, are similar in that the portion of the plate forward of the frizzen is, by comparison to other lockplates, short. This is similar to a M1728 lock excavated at Louisbourg. This lock provided a model for the design of the lock used on reproduction arms for the reconstruction at Louisbourg (Hamilton 1976:21, 24. Ravenshear 1979:15).

Other parts found at Michilimackinac include a butt plate which has a short tang. There are also examples of trigger guards which could be attributed to military weapons. Finally, a sample of balls shows a concentration in the sizes from .54-.61 inches (Hamilton 1976:8, 12, 33). The larger of these may have been used in a barrel with .66 inch bore.

The 1734 model was but one example of marine weapons. There are documents concerning supplies to Louisbourg from Tulle with dates of 1719, 1728, 1746, and 1751 (Proulx 1971:13). This supports Tulle as the primary supplier of firearms for the marines.

The Ministry of the Marine purchased muskets from Saint Etienne (known for army muskets) in the 1740's. These were similar to the army's 1728 model (Chartrand 1984:21). It should be noted that Chartrand states that St. Etienne replaced Tulle as the supplier of marine muskets. Yet, another source states that Tulle was still a supplier for the Ministry of the Marine as late as 1758 (Proulx 1971:13). Also, the Intendant Bigot wrote to to Ricouart, February 22, 1745.

> I am writing to the Abbe de Lacombe [Tulle] to attend to (the supplying) of 450 grenadier fusils...
> (Hamilton and Fry 1975:113).

It is interesting that Bigot appears to be bypassing the Ministry of the Marine and ordering directly from the manufacturer.

How similar was the St. Etienne musket purchased by the Ministry of the Marine to the Tulle M1734? If it was based on the army M1728, there would have been major differences between the M1734 and the St. Etienne musket.

MATERIAL CULTURE 89

The barrel of the M1728 is longer (46 3/4 inches) than that of the M1734 and has a bore of approximately .69 inches (examples run larger). The tang on the butt plate is 5 3/4 inches long instead of the short version found on the 1734 Tulle musket. Also, the barrel is held by three bands rather than pinned to the stock (Neumann 1972:70). The archaeological evidence from Michilimackinac would not support the use of the St. Etienne weapon at that site.

A term, "fusil a'domino", was used to label a soldier's arm with a banded barrel produced after the early 1740's at Tulle (Ravenshear 1986:44). This could be a Tulle version of the musket referred to as being manufactured by St. Etienne. (The term a'domino may refer to the muskets' metal parts being blued or browned as protection from the environment.) The grenadier musket a'domino, iron ring with bayonet appears on the governor's list of equipment needed in Canada, 1758 (O'Callaghan 1969, X:864). Grenadier muskets also appear in the inventory of the stores of Fort de Chartres when it was surrendered to the British in 1765 (Keefe 1992:43).

The reason the Ministry of the Marine purchased muskets from St. Etienne in the 1740's may well have been due to the increased need for arms caused by conflict with England. How similar these muskets were to the army M1728 is questionable. The marine muskets retained the smaller bore. In 1756, grenadier muskets are issued to the marines while regulars in the same expedition received muskets of the ordinary caliber. At the same time, the regulars received fixed ammunition and the marines received powder and ball (Bougainville 1968:20). Also, the order for supplies from France in 1758, that includes grenadier muskets and flints for those muskets, lists balls 20 to 22 per pound (livre) (O'Callaghan 1969:864).

If the firearm used by the marine in 1756 was the 1740's model, it is likely that this new weapon was an improved model based on the M1734, perhaps using a banded barrel and eliminating the pins. A period drawing of a marine(?), c.1755, shows a banded musket (Sullivan 1986:33).

Old military muskets may have been used in the Indian trade in addition to weapons designed specifically for this purpose. These trade guns may have been used by the marines as personal hunting weapons or, if supplies were short, on duty. A letter from Intendant Bigot to the Ministry of the Marine states that the recent shipment of muskets (probably military) was rusty and "barely fit for service" (Ravenshear 1979:16). Although shortages may have resulted in some improvising, it would be uncharacteristic for an officer to allow his soldiers to serve with non-uniform weapons that would not take a bayonet.

The arms of Germans serving as marine replacements at Fort Niagara were less than ideal. Only 140 muskets were fit for service and only some had bayonets. Some men of the garrison were armed with knives tied to sticks (Stanley 1968:219). Shortages might be the reason for a call in 1758, for a variety of arms to be sent to Canada. One item on the list is 6000 fowling pieces (thules de chasses) with their bayonets (Peterson 1956:331). It is possible these were meant for militia use (Ravenshear 1986:44).

That the fusil de chasse manufactured at Tulle was used in North America is without question. It was a major item in the Indian trade with 6000 being sent to Canada between 1729 and 1734 (Coulter 1985:10). The common weapon would not, however, accept a bayonet as called for in the 1758 document. The stock of the fusil de chasse terminated very near the muzzle. Although not a difficult procedure, the stock would need to be cut back a few inches and a bayonet lug attached to the barrel. If the modified weapon did exist, it may have had much the same characteristics as an existing example.

    Total length: 4' 11.6"
    Barrel length: 3' 7.8"

MATERIAL CULTURE

Calibre: 28 balls/lb. of lead. (It may otherwise be described as .62 calibre or 20 gauge.)
Barrel characteristics: Tapered, octagon-to-round. The octagon shape breaks down to 16 flats about 9.5" anteriorly from the breech. These flats run for 2" into a double wedding band. The barrel then is round, tapering gently to the mouth. It is fixed to the stock by four lugs set equidistant. The octagonal breech is 2.5". The sight is 0.6" located 4.4" from the muzzle. A crowned fleur-de-lis proofmark is present on the top flat.
Lock plate: 6.25" stamped in front of the cock with a crowned fleur-de-lis and "TVLLE" [Tulle] below. The lock has the square profile of the period and is fastened by two screws.
Stock: Dark walnut, 4' 11.2" long with no decoration.
Ramrod: Wood, secured by 3 thimbles.
Fittings: Side plate of iron, 3.5"; butt plate of iron, 8.25"; trigger guard of iron, 11.2" (Coulter 1985:10-11).

Ravenshear has noted the use of a fleur-de-lis, crown, and TULLE on these locks and also mentions an example with just TULLE on the lock plate. The .61 inch bore is similar to the example above (Ravenshear 1986:45-46). The TVLLE/TULLE mark provides some help in dating as TVLLE was used prior to 1745 and TULLE after (Bouchard 1980:100-101).

Late in 1757 Rogers' Rangers captured a marine sergeant who said, "500 Rangers were lately raised in Canada, each man having a double barreled fuzee,..." (Rogers 1966:73). An example of this weapon has "Compagnies Franches de la Marine" engraved on the top of the center rib. This is not to suggest that all marines were armed with this weapon. It does point out, however, that a gun thought to be a

MATERIAL CULTURE 93

sporting weapon for gentlemen in the eighteenth century was available to the common soldier.

A 1749 inventory of the Kings Magazine in Quebec lists 414 buccaneers. This musket is usually associated with the West Indies colonies and French ships. Naval contracts with Tulle specify an 18 calibre (.69 inch) bore. The overall length of this weapon was 5 feet 10 inches (Hamilton 1980:51). The length of this gun would make it difficult to manage in the woods. This problem, and the small number in the inventory, would suggest it may have been reserved for fortification defense. The long barrel would have given it a advantage in range and accuracy in comparison to the common musket. If accuracy was not important they could be used with more devastating results.

> Some buccaneer firelocks, of an uncommon length, were found by our men today, buried in an orchard adjoining to the great water mill [on the Island of Orleans, near Quebec]; upon examining them, they were loaded with two balls each, besides a piece of squared iron, four inches long, the edges of which were wickedly filed rough, like the teeth of a saw (Knox 1980:139).

It is very likely that marine officers carried shoulder arms. An equipment list shows a gun worm and flints being issued to officers. It is unclear, however, if the officers were regulars, marines, or militia (Bourlamarque n.d.). Officers of all armies in North America appear to have replaced the traditional spontoon with a fusil. These may have been issued weapons or guns purchased by the individual officers. If a personal weapon, the design and ornamentation was to personal taste and therefore presenting a representative model based on archaeological evidence or surviving examples is difficult. Marine officers recruited from the Canadian population would have been well acquainted with the use of a shoulder weapon and, given their knowledge of warfare, would have resisted exchanging a firearm for a symbol of rank.

La Baionnette (Bayonet)

The bayonet was a standard military weapon, part of the equipment of the regular soldier, including marines. The plug bayonet, that fitted into the bore of the musket, was replaced by the socket bayonet in the first few years of the eighteenth century. The system of fixing the bayonet to the exterior of the musket's barrel was superior as it allowed the musket to be loaded and fired with the bayonet attached.

The bayonet used on the Tulle muskets was unique, as the neck, which connected the blade to the socket, was much longer than other bayonets. The 1734 contract gives specifications for this weapon and an archaeological specimen found at Louisbourg corresponds to these measurements (Ravenshear 1979:14). A similar specimen was found at Fort Beausejour (Bouchard 1980:97). Another example, attributed to c. 1690-1710, measures 19 1/4 inches (Neumann and Kravic 1975:31). This corresponds with examples depicted in a 1703 illustration (Chartrand 1984:15).

Ammunition

The method of carrying and maintaining an ammunition supply by a marine changed over time. In the late seventeenth century the soldier had iron tubes filled with a measured amount of powder in a slung box. The balls were kept separately. This appears to be an adaptation of carrying charges suspended from a shoulder belt which had previously been the fashion. The box provided better protection for the powder.

If the charges in the iron tubes were exhausted in battle the soldier would use a powder flask to refill the tubes or, as one authority suggests, the powder was dumped into

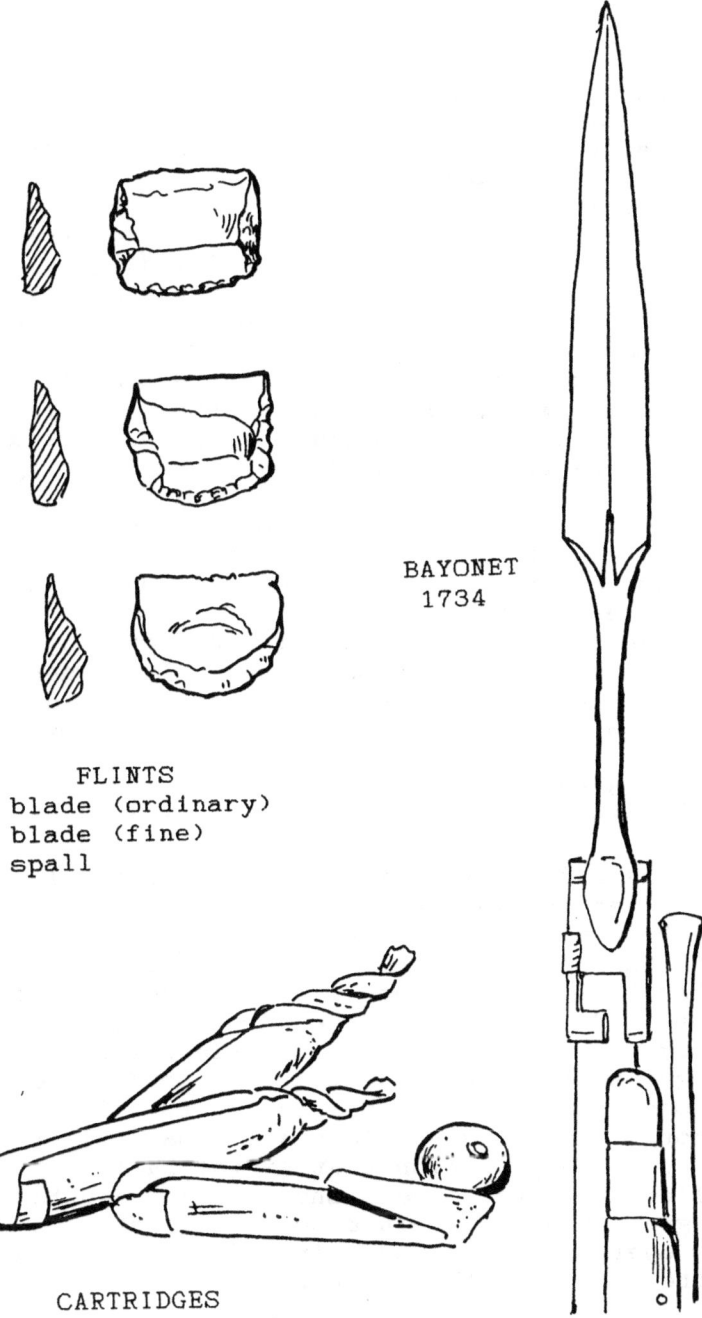

the box and a single tube was used to scoop a measure of powder (Peterson 1956:229). That this dangerous system of loading was changed should come as no surprise.

Perhaps as early as 1700 the Compagnies de la Marine were equipped with a cartridge box worn on a waist belt. In 1702, the King approved the use of paper cartridges, although the technology was available before that date. The paper cartridge or, "fixed ammunition", was designed to make the loading of the musket quick and simple. It can be assumed that fixed ammunition was reserved for a time when speed was important. At other times, such as going on guard, the soldier probably used his flask and a patched ball. As the soldiers were allowed to hunt they were familiar with the superior accuracy of a patched ball over that of a paper cartridge.

The cartridge adopted at the beginning of the eighteenth century contained only powder. In 1738, instructions on how to construct a cartridge which included powder and ball were issued. As with the issuance of all regulations and drills, the written word may well have followed the established practice in the field.

The 1738 instructions called for a ball .65 inches in diameter. This size ball would have been used by the army muskets of 69 caliber. The paper for this size of ball was 6 3/8 inches by 2 9/16 inches. This was rolled into a tube and pasted along the edge as was the bottom over the ball. The cartridge was then charged with a measured amount of powder and the open end sealed by folding or twisting. Although these instructions are apparently for the army, they mention that if the ball size is smaller the paper dimensions must be adjusted (Margrand n.d.:69). This would suggest that this system may have been intended to be used by the troops of the marine.

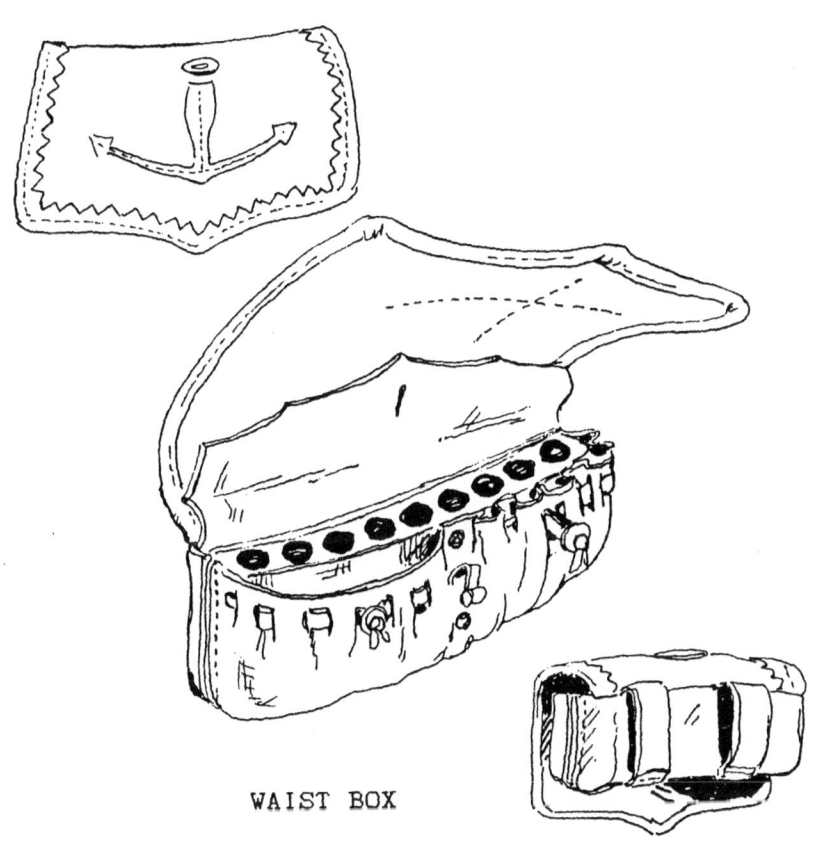

WAIST BOX

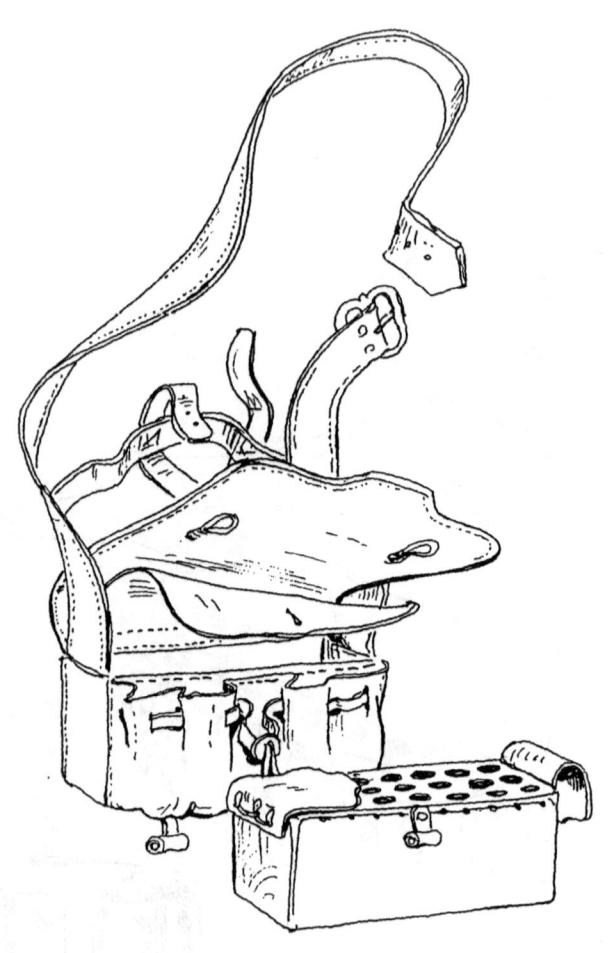

SHOULDER BOX

MATERIAL CULTURE

Le Gargoussier/La Giberne (Cartridge Box)

Until the final French and Indian War the marines were equipped with a cartridge box (le gargoussier) which was carried on the waist belt. They were made of calf skin until 1739 when, in response to reports that the calf skin did not hold up to the Canadian environment, cowhide was used. The new boxes were red leather and had the white anchor emblem until the late 1740's when it was replaced by the King's arms. The new boxes did not totally replace the older model (Proulx 1971:13. Protz and Marsala 1989:2).

The box contained an elm wood block, slightly curved to conform to the waist. It was drilled to hold nine cartridges (Petard 1984:78. Chartrand 1984:24). This minimal amount of ammunition, compared to the thirty-round box carried by the army, would suggest that the role of the marine was not to engage in major battles.

The marines did receive a thirty-round, shoulder slung, box (la giberne) in the 1750's (It is possible that this box may have accommodated grenades and cartridges). This increase, however, did not call for the powder flask to be discarded. It was still carried but now it was attached to the strap of the box rather than being carried on its own belt (Chartrand 1984:24). The issuing of these boxes supports the speculation that the role of the marines had changed: they were now to be capable of campaigning.

Le Fourniment (Powder Flask)

The powder flask was standard equipment for the marine. The flasks used by the marines have two variables, the body and the charger. The body was of leather, wood covered with leather, or horn, and the charger spout was single or double valve.

The leather used for the powder flask, heavier than that used in the calfskin cartridge boxes, proved equally unsuited to the

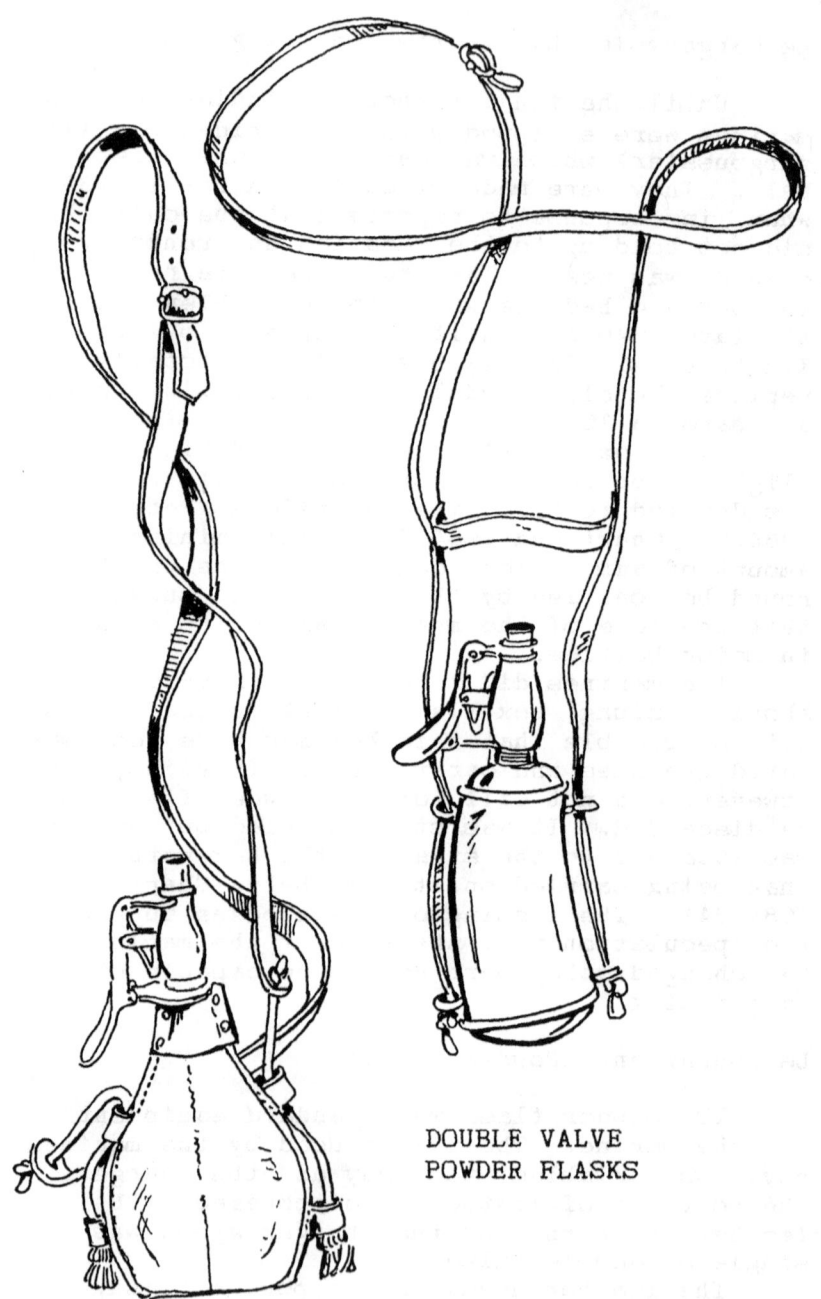

DOUBLE VALVE
POWDER FLASKS

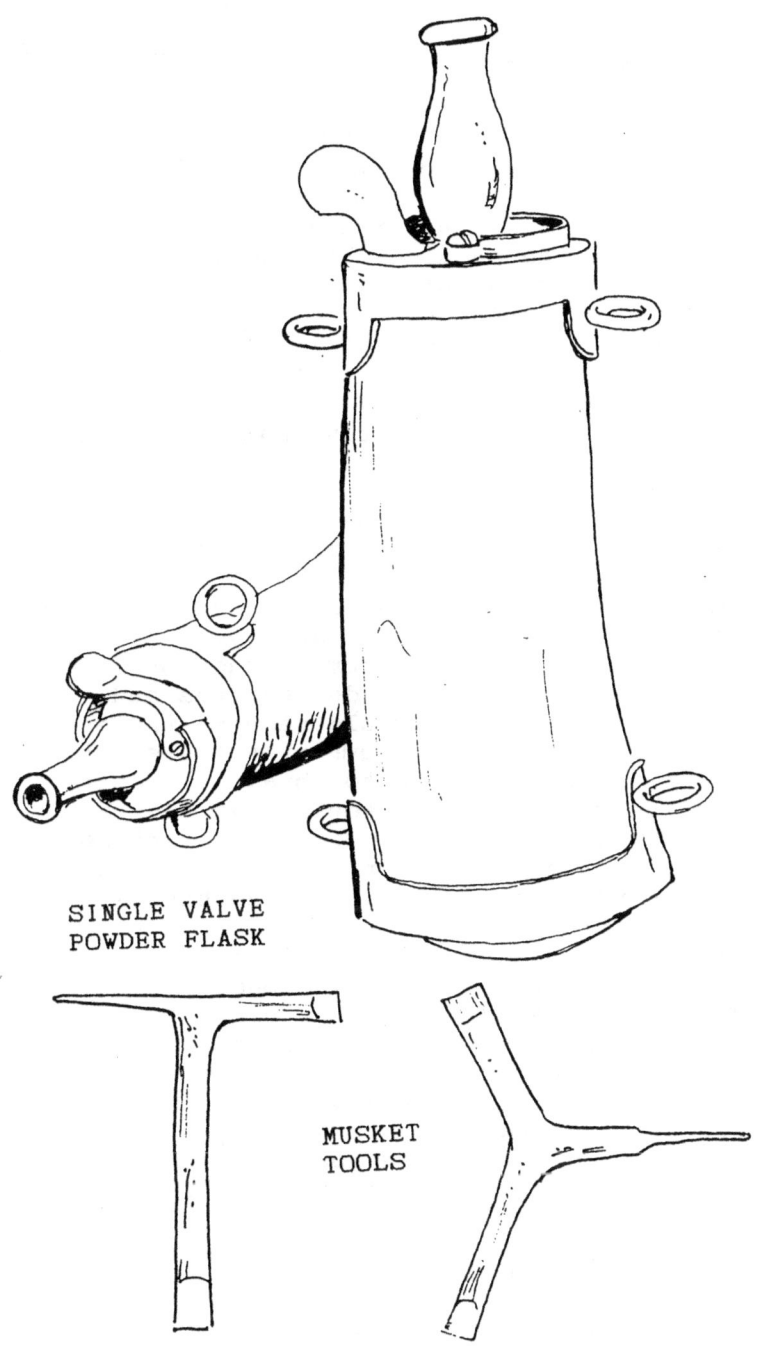

environment of New France. It was replaced with horn at Louisbourg in 1737. This material, though superior in terms of being waterproof, cracked, and powder was lost (Proulx 1971:13). Both varieties were suspended from the shoulder by a strap that attached to loops on the body of the flask. As noted above, when the thirty-round cartridge box was issued to the marines the flask was attached to the box's strap (Chartrand 1984:24).

Period illustrations show leather and horn powder flasks with double valve spouts (Petard 1984:76. Chartrand 1984:19). An example of a horn powder flask in the Museum of the Fur Trade (Chadron, Nebraska) is similar to those in period illustrations except that the spout has a single valve, or gate, rather than a double valve (Hanson 1981:31). Parts very similar to those present on the Museum of the Fur Trade specimen were found at Fort de Chartres and Louisbourg. This system would require the soldier to hold a finger or thumb over the spout while depressing the lever to obtain a measured amount of powder. A flask would have been more convenient than a conventional powder horn as the soldier would not be concerned with a separate powder measure or replacing the horn's plug or stopper.

It seems a reasonable assumption that common powder horns would have also been used by marines if the issued items were prone to damage, although no existing examples of Canadian horns can be attributed to use by marines (Swayze 1978:49-51. Hanson 1981:30). Any primary source references to "powder horns" must be viewed with suspicion as horn was also used as the body of the flask, so the term could refer to either item.

Other Items Relating to the Musket

The musket required a few small tools and other items for its maintenance and use. This includes flints, screwdriver, vent pick, pan brush, worm, and hammer stall. The latter item

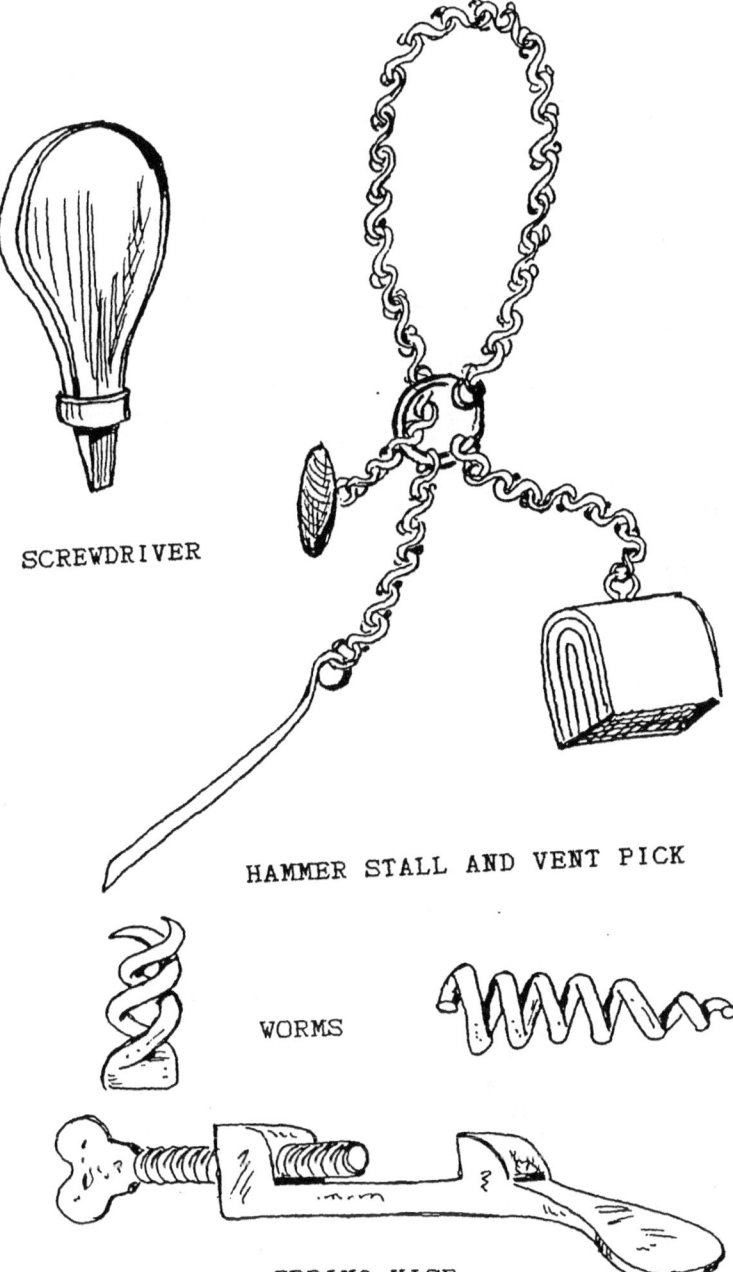

is simply a leather sleeve that fits on the frizzen of the musket lock to prevent an accidental discharge. (Note: Frizzen is a modern term for this part of the lock, the period term would be hammer.) The 1704 marine drill addresses the use of this item.

> There must be careful attention paid that all of the fusiliers have small leather stalls over their hammers, their pan covers open, and their cock springs eased; the stalls, which are attached to the trigger guards by a small metal chain, are to prevent accidents (Houlding 1988:38).

Gun worms were very important. They were wire twisted into a spiral which attached to the ramrod. There were two varieties of worm, one using a single wire and another with two wires. Both varieties were ordered for the Louisiana colony (Brain 1979:296). The marines carried their muskets loaded, although they might not have occasion to fire. If this load remained in the barrel for a long period, especially in damp weather, it became doubtful if the weapon would fire. "The fog in this country [Louisbourg] obliging arms to be unloaded very frequently, one wad hook [worm] per fusilier should be sent..." (Proulx 1971:58). The charge in the barrel had to be removed in order to load a fresh one. The soldier could accomplish this by firing the weapon. If the weapon wouldn't fire or the soldier did not want an enemy to know his position, the ball had to be withdrawn with a gun worm. Worms were regularly issued (Bougainville 1968:23, 87).

It would seem a safe assumption that, even in the absence of direct evidence, the individual marine had access to screwdrivers, vent picks, and brushes. They were a necessity to the operation of the firearm. Also, the shoulder slung cartridge boxes (la giberne) were designed to carry these items. Spring vises were a company item. "...and since the locks

MATERIAL CULTURE 105

have to be taken apart very often for cleaning, two clamps [spring vises] at least would be needed per company" (Proulx 1971:58).

Gunflints

Apparently, the authorities were particular in providing flints to the troops. A request for supplies includes gunflints as two separate items.

> Clear and transparent flints for grenadier muskets.
> Flints for fowling pieces (Peterson 1956:331).

Clear and transparent flints were regarded as superior quality flints. However, as was common in other categories of equipment, what they wanted and what they got were often very different. Bigot and Du Quesnel to Minister of Marine, December 5, 1740.

> We also lack good gunflints: in store there is a quantity of some thousands which are condemned (Hamilton and Fry 1975:113).

Again, Bigot to Ricouart, February 22, 1745.

> I am writing to the Abbe de Lacombe to attend to (the supplying) of 450 grenadier fusils... I charge you similarly to see to it that the gunflints that are requisitioned on this account are of good quality and well selected, because complaint is made that those sent to the Colony in the last several years were found to be of poor quality (Hamilton and Fry 1975:113).

The contract for gunflints issued in 1740 gives the desired length as 34-36mm (Hamilton and Fry 1975:110). Given this dimension and allowing for wear it would seem possible to identify flints that were "probably" used by marines, especially if they are located in or near a known garrison site.

Gunflints used in the mid-eighteenth century were primarily of Dutch or French origin. Although there is a Nordic and English tradition in gunflints, their use, at least in the French area of activity, is minimal if it exists at all. There are no examples of these types at Louisbourg (Hamilton and Fry 1975:107).

French and Dutch gunflints are found at French sites and are quite different from each other (page 95).

> Dutch gunflints were basically spalls struck individually from the surface of the nodule flint. A typical spall gunflint bears a bulb of percussion on the upper conchoidal surface in the area of the heel, with the face sloping down to the edge. ... the heel and sides are shaped by secondary chipping. The bottom face or bed of the Dutch flint often shows the negative impressions of portions of other spalls previously removed.
>
> Both the English and French made their gunflints from a long blade struck from a core with a prepared striking platform, but once the blade had been struck off all similarities ceased. The French broke their blades into more or less uniform lengths which were dressed on the sides and heel, usually in the same manner as the Dutch gunflints, giving the product a sort of gnawed appearance on those three sides. Ideally, the best quality French gunflint, is trapeziform in outline when viewed from the side [known as "fine", if triangular, "ordinary"]: the flat upper face, parallel to the bottom face or bed, furnished a firm gripping surface for the lead or leather cap which cushioned it between the jaws of

the cock (Hamilton and Fry 1975:107-109).

There is a question as to whether any flints were actually of Dutch manufacture. The authors of the statement above include the following;

> Therefore, it is the senior author's opinion at this time that the term "Dutch" should be used with reservation; that it should refer to style of manufacture rather than source, and that until conclusively proven otherwise, its three sub-types should always be kept in mind (Hamilton and Fry 1975:121).

A later work by another researcher is more definite.

> The term "Dutch" is no longer applicable. In the remainder of this paper, French gunflints made from flakes will be spoken of a "gunflints" and those made from spalls will be called "gunspalls" (Brain 1979:210).

The details of this problem are beyond the scope of this study. Evidence, apparently, lies in the identity of the source of gunflint material. Readers interested in further pursuing this issue should refer to the studies cited in the bibliography.

The study of Louisbourg flints by Hamilton and Fry shows a wide range of sizes, quality, and type (French or Dutch). The authors give only a few paragraphs to the dimensions of the locks that may have held the flints, and this is limited to French army weapons (Hamilton and Fry 1975:123). What seems apparent is there was a lack of uniformity in the flints supplied and, as the letters quoted above suggest, the quality, at least at certain times, was poor.

A time factor may enter into the use of French or Dutch flints. The Dutch dominated

the market from about 1650 until 1750. The
French industry gained steadily through the
latter half of this period (Hamilton and Fry
1975:107). This is possibly confirmed by the
study of gunflints at Fort Michilimackinac.
The spall gunflints (Dutch) outnumber the blade
type (French) 6 to 1. However, the blade type
may not have appeared until sometime between
1730 and 1740 (Stone 1974:263). This may well
indicate that the French blade industry was
sufficiently developed in the mid 1730's to
meet normal demands of the Ministry of Marine
to supply even its most remote posts. The fact
that the use of Dutch flints continue through
the entire occupation period might be due to
additional needs of a growing fur trade and the
conflicts of the 1740's and 1750's.

Pistols

The military use of pistols in the eighteenth century is often thought to be the realm
of officers. However, Tulle made large amounts
of pistols for the Ministry of the Marine
(Bouchard 1980:54). These may have been
intended for shipboard use.
It would not be surprising that marines
carried pistols. A second shot in a single
shot world could save a life. The marine,
through trading or other activity, had the
resources to obtain the weapon. One of the
soldiers at Fort Sandoske carried a pistol when
he was going hunting and trading, or perhaps
deserting (Wright 1990:11).
The auction of the effects of an officer
at Louisbourg in 1752 included a pair of
wheellock pistols. In the absence of similar
examples it seems appropriate to consider these
arms to be an exception rather than a rule as
the wheellock was obsolete. As they brought
thirty livres, which was the amount paid for a
worn waistcoat, the condition of these pistols
and the market is questionable (Proulx
1971:69).

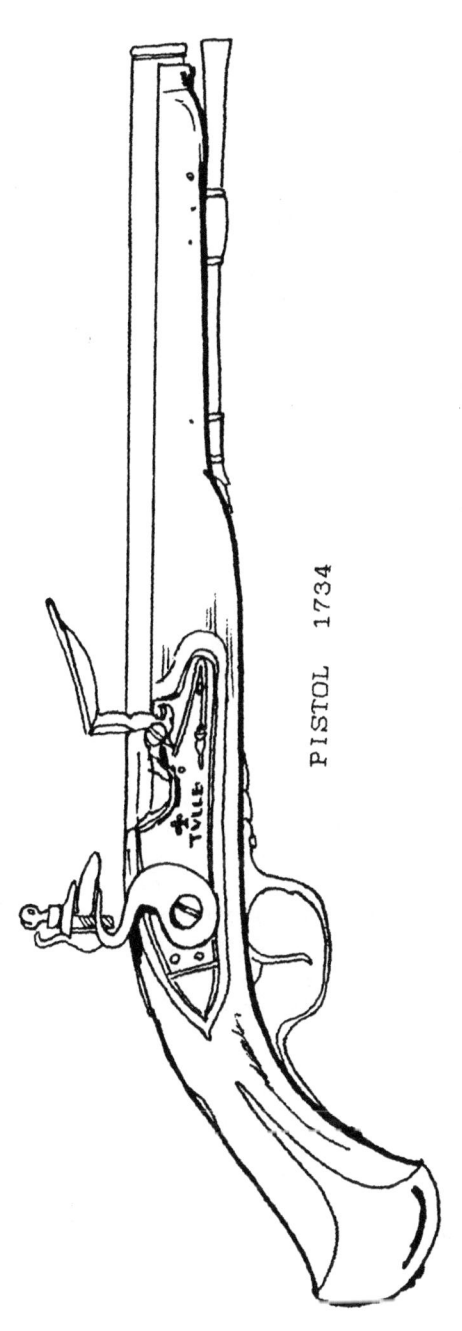

PISTOL 1734

Summary

French military arms changed constantly throughout the eighteenth century. It seems reasonable to assume that the firearms used by the marines also saw change. Archaeological evidence (note: a small sample) supports Ravenshear's model of the M1734 Tulle musket. Documentary evidence suggests a new model was developed in the 1740's based on the army musket M1728. This firearm was produced at St. Etienne and/or Tulle.

What seems consistent is that the marine used a musket with a sling. The gun had a smaller bore size, .66 inches, than the military arm, .69 inches. Also, the marine weapon was functionally plain, having iron furniture with no decorative features.

EDGED WEAPONS

L'epee (Sword)

Eighteenth-century military officers carried a sword as evidence of their social rank. This was a personal weapon. Swords were issued to soldiers in this period, although it is quite possible that the marines were sent to Canada without them. Louisbourg documents (1730, 1734, 1746) request that this item be sent from France and state that they were issued (Proulx 1971:11). That enlisted men's swords existed is clear. If they were regularly used is not clear.

A list of equipment for an expedition in 1757 calls for a tomahawk (Bougainville 1964:87). It might be argued that the sword, like the musket, was carried but not mentioned, but it is doubtful that both sword and tomahawk were part of the soldier's kit. The tomahawk was superior as a hand-to-hand combat weapon in a forest environment; the sword was a nuisance in the woods. The British recognized this and Braddock's troops left their swords behind dur-

1750-1764

1680-1750

L'EPEE

ing the first campaign of the final French and Indian War (Hamilton 1959:77). If the newly arrived British adjusted to the environment quickly it seems likely the marines, with seventy years of experience in North America, would have made similar changes. It is quite possible that the sword was reserved for formal occasions, required by individual commanders, or in elite companies. The artillerymen in Quebec in the early 1750's carried swords. This may have been due to their status as grenadiers (Bonin 1941:15, 16). This followed military fashion of the time. It is also possible that, at least in Quebec and other garrisons, non-commissioned officers and musicians would have also carried swords.

One incident in which enlisted men had swords happened when five marines left Fort Sandoske on a hunting expedition. One of the men returned to the fort and reported that the others intended to desert. He said he had been threatened by the others with their swords (Wright 1990:11).

The style of enlisted man's sword changed through the period. Although the straight, double-edged, blade was retained, the grip was changed from wire-wrapped to cast brass. Blade length varied from twenty-six inches to thirty inches. Scabbards were of wood covered in red leather (Neumann 1973:77. Petard 1985:41).

Tomahawk

The tomahawk carried by the marine, like the knife, may have been obtained from civilian sources, a fur trader, or local blacksmith. Consequently, the marine's tomahawk was of personal preference limited by finances. The colonial government provided this item on occasion. Tomahawks are included in the 1757 equipment list of an expedition against Fort William Henry. The King's tomahawks were of questionable quality. "Villers put them to flight and knocked off a great number, and would have knocked off a lot more were it not for the poor quality of the tomahawks furnished

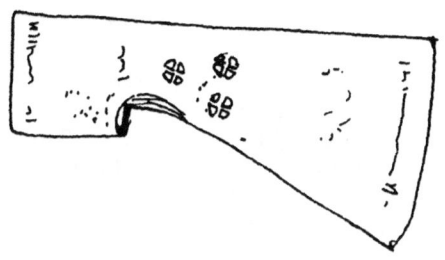

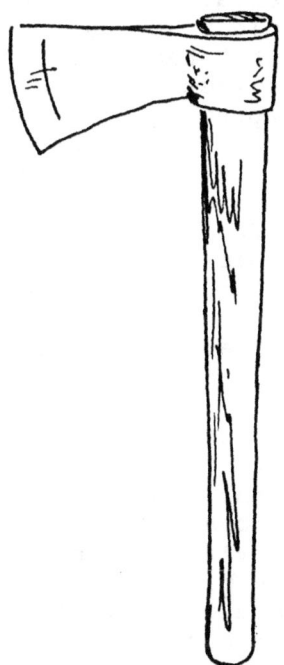

TOMAHAWKS

by the King's Store,..." (Bougainville 1964:6, 82).

Things had not improved by 1758.

> All the hatchets were of plain iron without steel [edges], also all bent like pancakes at the first blow. The colony had missed destruction through the poor quality of the hatchets. Where would we have been without our abatis [Carillon]? (Bougainville 1964:256)

It seems within the realm of reasonable speculation to believe that the tomahawk selection might have been based on requirements other than combat. A marine working on a construction project may have obtained a tomahawk or hand axe that had a hammer poll. Also, this weapon, regardless of design, would have been used for chopping or splitting small pieces of wood on the trail or in garrison. This would argue against the use of decorative or ceremonial types intended for the Indian trade.

Limited funds and hard daily use would suggest a simple tool with consideration given to a good cutting edge. There are ample examples of this type. There is a particular type of simple hand axe that, although not unknown in the Indian trade, appears often in colonial sites.

The consistent feature of this type is the eye, or hole for the handle, is rectangular or oval rather than round. The shape of the head may be traditional with a straight top and the lower edge curving down or a rectangular shape, often called a rifleman's axe. This type became standard issue in the American army in the nineteenth century. (Hanson 1981:22. Kuck 1977:86).

An interesting example, which appears to exhibit both characteristics, was found at the Ackia battleground near Tupelo, Mississippi. This 1736 battle was between French forces and the Cherokee. The axe is identified as a French type (Russell 1967:269-270).

1710-1730

1720-1758

HALBERD

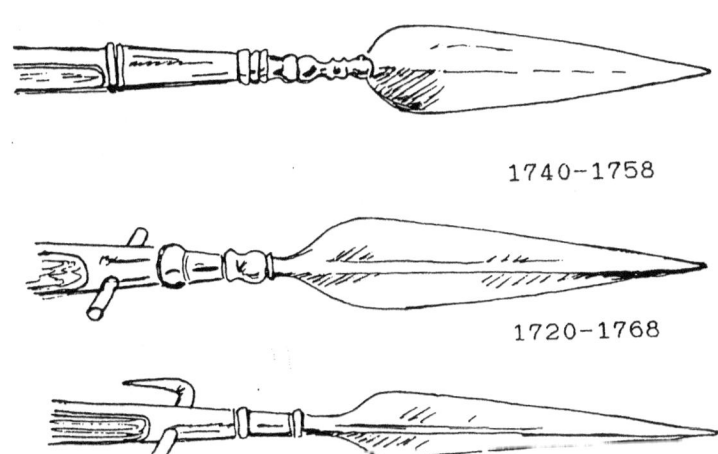

1740-1758

1720-1768

1720-1758

SPONTOON

Halberd

The halberd was the pole arm carried by a sergeant, although it may have also been used by guards (Proulx 1971:14). It was a symbol of his rank and, as it was approximately seven feet in length, extended above the level of the muskets, allowing the sergeant to be located during battle. Toward the end of the final French and Indian War (1758) sergeants of the French army were carrying muskets rather than halberds (Funcken 1977:66). Marine sergeants with North American frontier service may well have replaced their halberds long before this.

French halberds were distinct from the "axe" variety carried in the English and German armies. They had a dagger-shaped blade. At the base of the blade there was a stylized sunburst. The head taken as a whole resembles a fleur-de-lis. The pole was fitted into a socket (Neumann 1973:208).

Spontoon

The spontoon was the pole arm that identified its carrier as an officer. The French spontoon was simpler in design than the halberd. They generally had a leaf-shaped blade and a crossbar. Period regulations called for a total length of eighty-seven to ninety-six inches (Neumann 1973:220).

By the close of the final French and Indian war the use of the spontoon officially ended. An ordinance dated October 31, 1758, ordered army officers to carry fusils. This followed a report written April 7, of that year that stated, "There is not a single spontoon remaining in the entire infantry" (Kennett 1967:117). If the army in Europe was abandoning this arm it is certain that marine officers, mostly Canadians, would have discarded this arm.

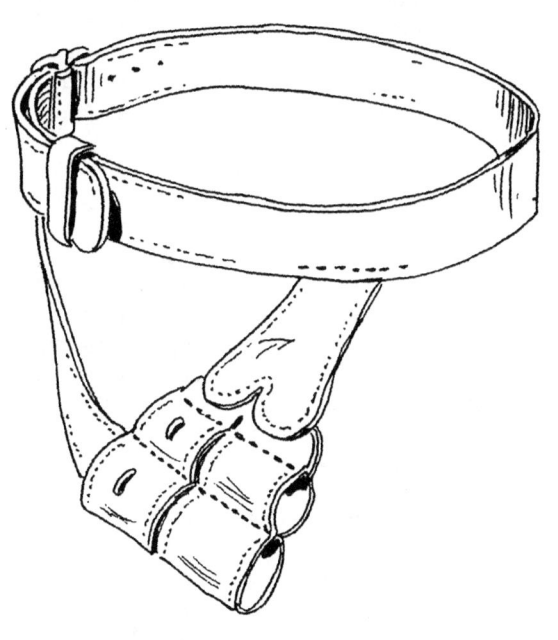

BELT with FROG

OTHER EQUIPMENT

Le Ceinturon (Belt)

Belts were of cowskin and had a brass buckle. A line of stitching followed the top and bottom edges. A frog was attached to the left side for the bayonet and sword (the sword was probably replaced with a tomahawk on campaign). The belt was worn over the vest (Petard 1976:26).

Le Haversac (Haversack/Knapsack)

Louisbourg records show knapsacks were issued to the troops beginning in 1747 (Proulx 1971:14). The need for this item in garrison is limited and this date suggests the issue may well be related to the conflict with Britain and an anticipated call for campaign travel. It is likely that a marine would have had some sort of bag as he was supposed to have extra shoes and shirts.

The issue knapsack was a large rectangular linen bag with a two-piece leather strap sewn to the sides of the bag about halfway between the bottom and open top. The strap buckled together to form a sling for carrying the bag from the right shoulder. The bag was packed, the top secured, and it was folded at the sling. The closure may have been by one of three methods. The top may have been gathered, wrapped with a cord, and tied. There may have been a drawstring as part of the top. These methods of closure had the tendency to cause the sack to take on a round shape. A third method closed the sack with buttons. This would maintain the rectangular shape. There are documentary references to a haversack being large enough for the soldier to use as a sleeping bag.

A *petit sac* was also used. It was a rectangular bag, probably leather with the fur still attached. It had a flap that folded and buttoned, or a drawstring. This was carried in the large bag and used for the soldier's

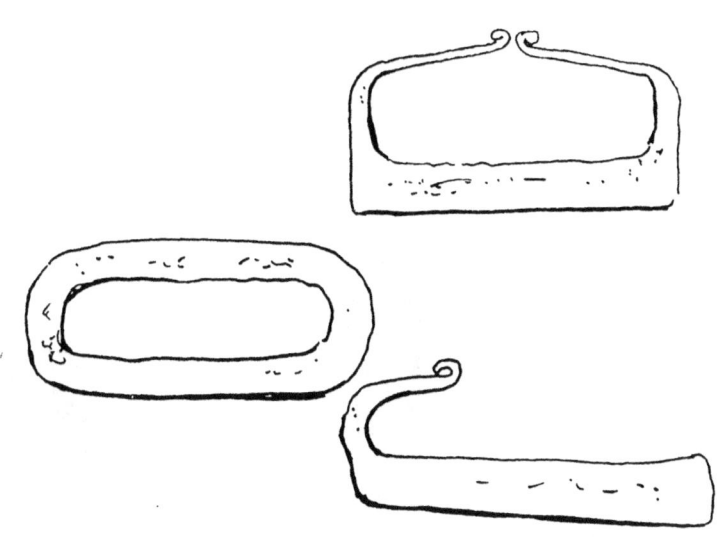

STRIKERS

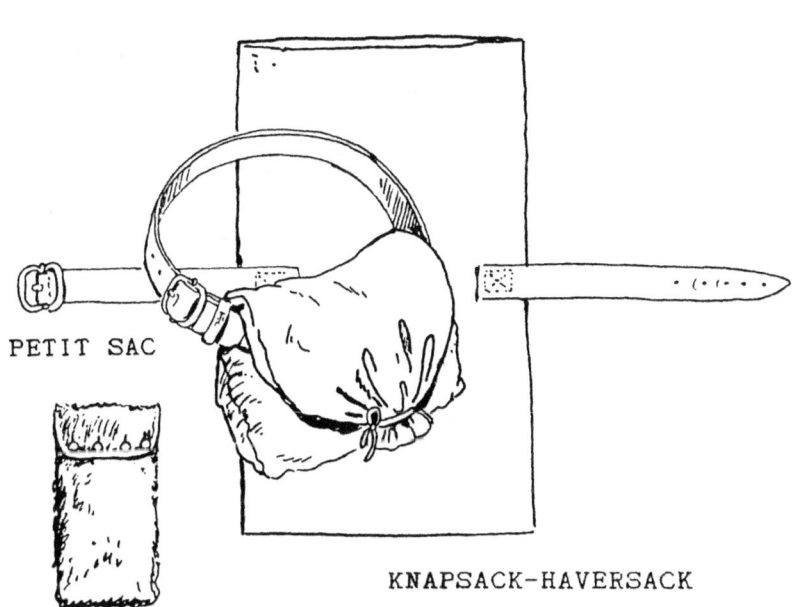

PETIT SAC

KNAPSACK-HAVERSACK

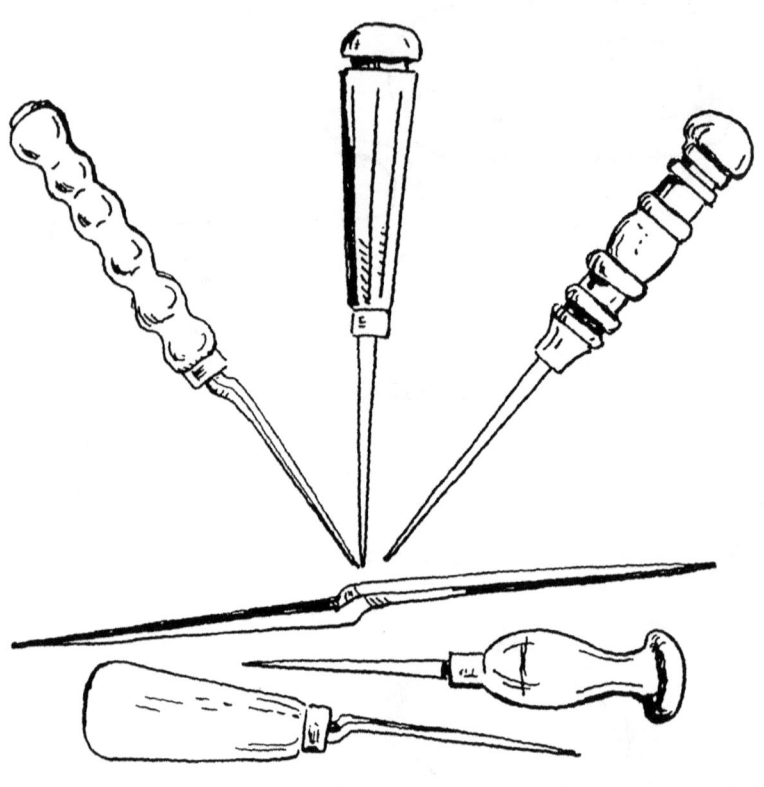

AWLS

"toilet" articles (Petard 1985:93. Anderson 1988:2).

Small Items

The toilet articles included a box wood comb, four to five inches long, sewing needles and thread, and Marseilles mottling soap. The soldier received two livres (1 livre = 1.08 pounds) of soap per year (Proulx 1971:13). He may have also packed an awl, tinderbox, and possibly a razor, although razors were company property kept by the surgeon (Bougainville 1964:87. Wright 1990:11).

The French in Canada were clean shaven (Kalm 1987:449). This was probably true of the marines, although sergeants and artillerymen may have worn mustaches (Protz and Marsala 1989:1). Six razors have been recovered at Michilimackinac. The blades form an elongated triangle tapering to the end that would attach to the case, presumably made of wood. One example, however, has a narrow steel shank (Stone 1974:139-140).

The hair style of the marine was probably the military fashion shown in period illustrations. The hair was long and gathered at the back of the neck. It was fastened at this point and the excess braided and/or wrapped (Hamilton 1967:52). Officers may have worn wigs (page 71).

Tinder boxes were metal, although wood may have been used. The box often contained a metal flint striker and flint, as well as the tinder. Based on the archaeological evidence at Michilimackinac, the strikers were either the open end or oval varieties (Stone 1974:186-188).

Awls were of two types. One was straight, tapering toward each end, the other was offset near the middle. Michilimackinac has recovered both types in the French context. The straight type was associated with the French guardhouse (Stone 1974:156-157). Also, contracts for supplies for the Louisiana colony specify straight and crooked awls (Brain 1979:297).

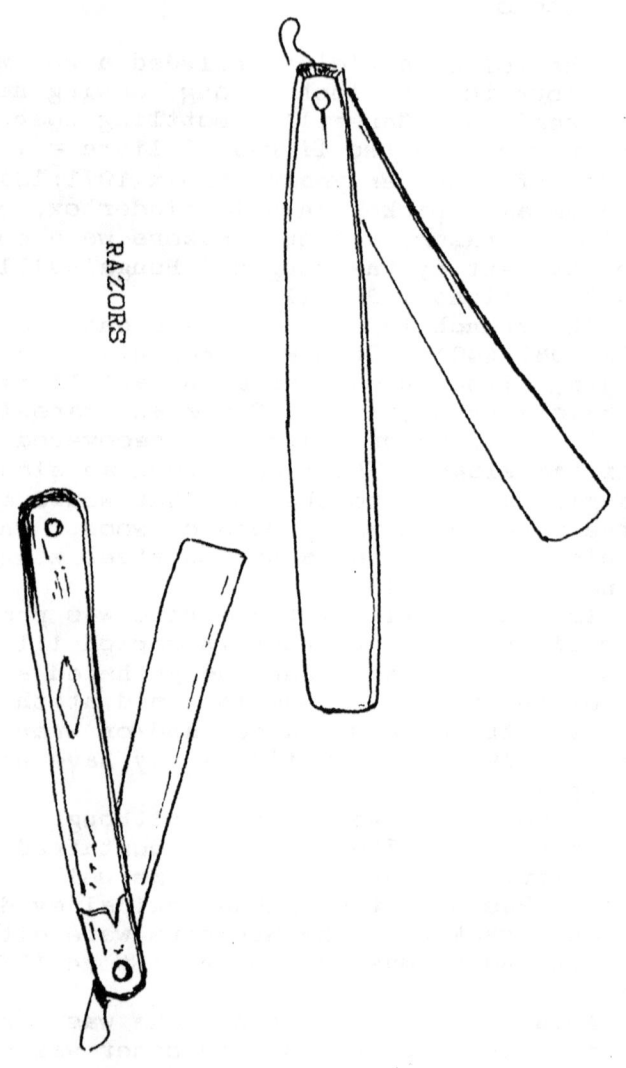

RAZORS

EYEGLASSES

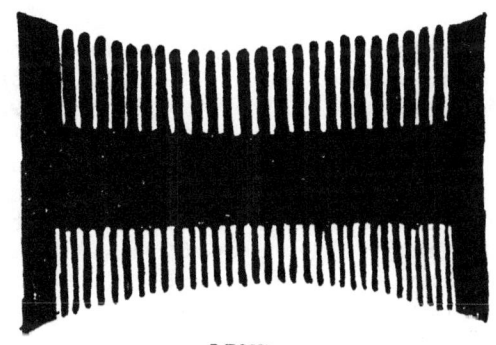

COMB

There is no evidence as to whether eyeglasses were available to marines or if they were affordable. Eyeglasses, c.1750, had oval or round lenses and the temple bars were hinged. The temple bars had loops at the end for a ribbon that held the glasses at the back of the head (Neumann and Kravic 1975:247).

Gourd (Canteen)

There is no information concerning the canteen carried by the marine. As with the knapsack, this item had little value to garrison troops. It is quite possible that, like the knapsack, canteens were not issued until the late 1740's or 1750's in anticipation of campaigning. They were issued to the regulars on a company, rather than an individual, basis. This may have been the case in the marines.

The French word for canteen is gourd and it has been suggested that this item was used. However, the French had the industry to manufacture this item from tin or wood in a style common with other military forces.

Knives

The knife was the most common tool in colonial North America. The marine carried and used a knife for a variety of reasons. As important as this tool may be, there is only one reference to it being issued. In 1757, the equipment list for the soldiers of an expedition included a butcher's knife and two siamese knives (Bougainville 1964:87). A siamese knife was a folding knife with wooden handles (Waselkov 1988).

There is ample archaeological evidence that the marine had a choice of fixed blade (case knife) or folding knives. The maker's name is stamped on the blades of many French knives (Stone 1974:262-275. Wheeler 1985:60). The numbers of archaeological specimens at Michilimackinac are the same for the two types, although the folding knife dominates the earlier, pre-1740, period (Stone 1974:273). "Each

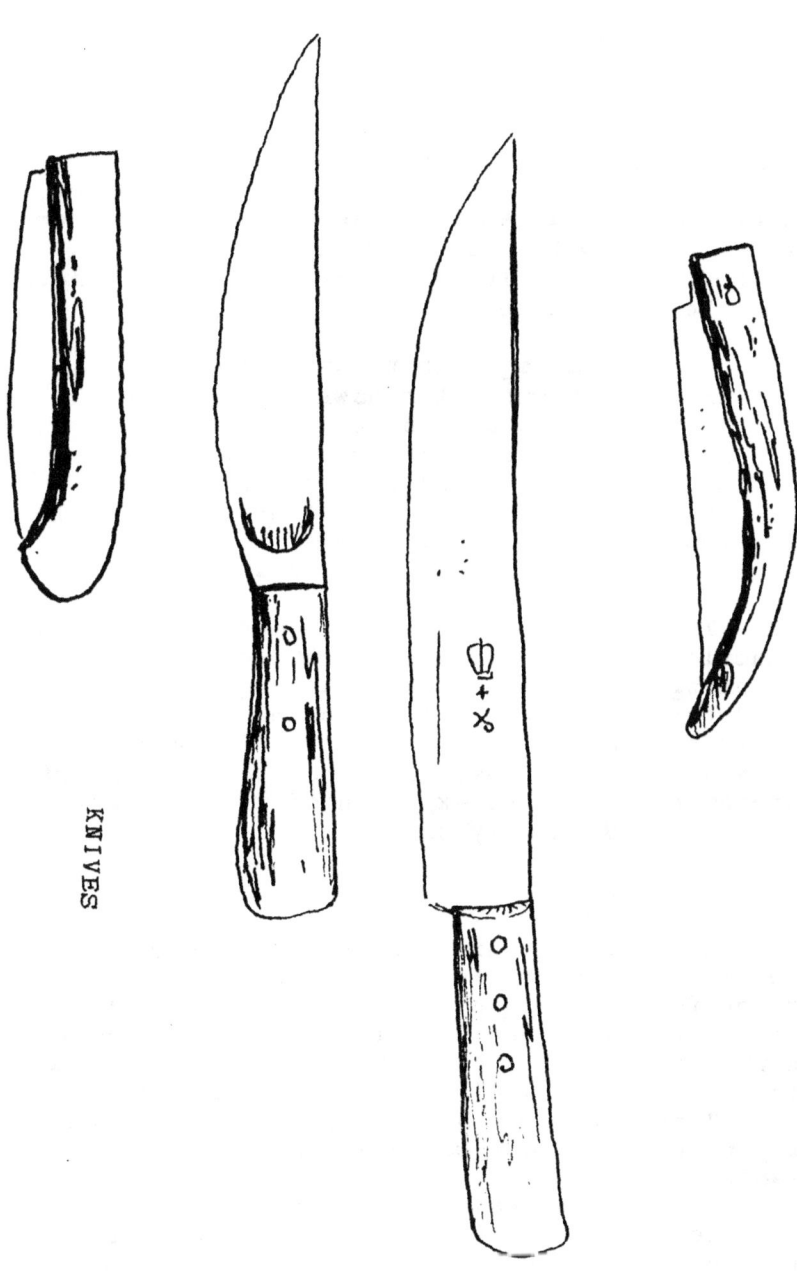

KNIVES

person here (Quebec) produces and ordinary clasped knife from his pocket, which serves him for every use; and, when they have dined or supped, they wipe and return it..." (Knox 1980:224).

The marine may have carried the folding knife; however, he also used a hunting knife. Charles Bonin makes this clear in his hand-to-hand combat with a bear (Bonin 1941:51). Although this marine had only one knife, others were better equipped.

> When savages go to war, they are armed with guns, tomahawks, and knives. They usually have three knives; one hung around the neck, one in the belt, and one fastened in the garter on the outside of the leg. Canadians arm themselves in the same way, as a precaution or safeguard (Bonin 1941:147).

The three knives may have served separate functions. They may have included a skinning/scalping knife and a large blade for hand-to-hand combat, although the tomahawk would have served this purpose. If three knives were a necessity, rather than a form of adornment, then the experienced marine might have adopted this system.

Mess Equipment

Marines at Louisbourg had one large pot for each seven or eight men. The pot had a spoon for each man attached. There were also mess tins that were used for beer. This equipment was minimal. In 1738, a request was made that a mess tin and canteen be issued for each "mess" of seven men and two water buckets and a frying pan for each barracks room (Louisbourg 1981:78).

If he used them, the marine probably obtained his own dishes and eating utensils from civilian sources. Dishes/bowls may have been tin, wood, or ceramic. Of interest are specimens at Michilimackinac of a brown and

MATERIAL CULTURE

white ceramic attributed to French manufacture and having a high frequency in the area of the guardhouse, c.1720-1750 (Stone 1974:166).

The inventory of stores at Fort de Chartres at the time it was turned over to the English (1765) includes eight plates, knives, and forks found in the guardhouse (Keefe 1992:44). If these items were used by the soldiers, it indicates a change in foodways from the earlier "common pot" of the Louisbourg example. (This change in foodways may indicate a fundamental change in lifestyle. See Deetz 1977:122-125.)

Each regular soldier was to receive, upon landing in Quebec, a knife, fork, and spoon. The company was to receive mess tins (Papiers 1754). It is possible that the marines were given a similar issue.

Blankets/Bedding

At Louisbourg the soldiers' bedding was a straw tick. Mattresses were expensive and the wet climate would cause rot. The material was sent from France and sewn by local women. White wool blankets were decorated with an embroidered or painted blue fleur-de-lis in the center (Louisbourg 1981:76, 77).

Supplies for the Louisiana colony (1733) included inexpensive "dog's hair blankets of two pieces 5 ft. 2 in. long and 4 ft. 6 in. wide with bars at both ends as per sample" (Brain 1979:297). It is not clear if these blankets were made from dog hair, which can be spun and woven, or if the term defines a quality of wool and/or workmanship. Dog's hair blankets were used by slaves in the Louisiana colony (Waselkov:1988). Wool blankets from Rouen and Bazas were also on the list for contracts (Brain 1979:298, 300). As the Ministry of the Marine provided supplies for settlers and the Indian trade, which blankets were issued to the marine soldier is unknown.

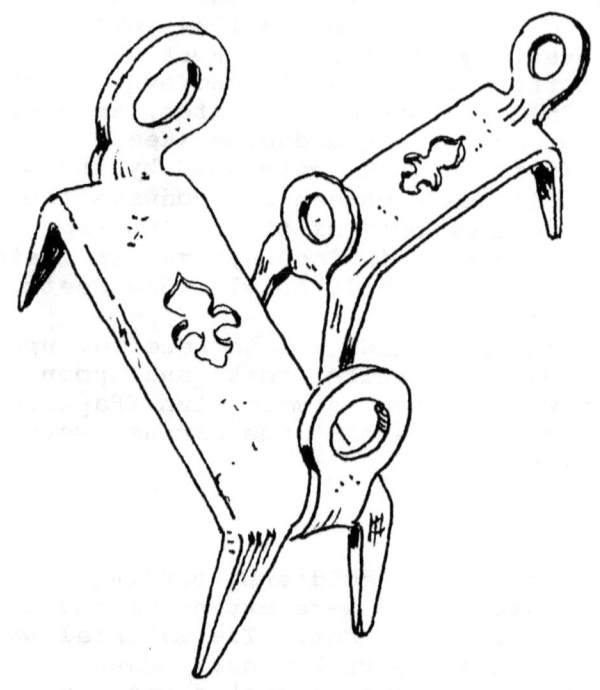

ICE CREEPERS

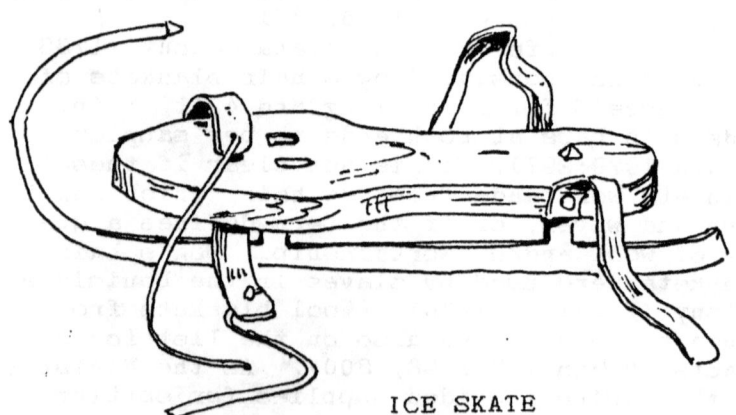

ICE SKATE

MATERIAL CULTURE

Ice Creepers/Ice Skates

Ice creepers are flat metal bars cut and bent at each end to provide two downward pointing prongs (to bite into the ice) and one flange, bent up, which was drilled or punched so a leather thong could tie the creeper to the shoe (Stone 1974:83, 86). A specimen stamped with a fleur-de-lis is in the collection of Louisbourg (Neumann and Kravic 1975:162). The English, while occupying Quebec during the winter of 1759-1760, issued creepers from captured stores (Knox 1980:231).

The use of ice skates by soldiers in North America is well documented (Bonin 1941:54. Rogers 1966:11). An iron blade was mounted to a wooden platform which was strapped to the shoe. An archaeological specimen of an ice skate blade was found at Michilimackinac (Stone 1974:83, 87). There is an artist's conception of a period skate taken from a specimen at William Henry illustrated in an article about Rogers' Rangers (Zaboly 1978:9). Another specimen is pictured in the Collector's Encyclopedia of the American Revolution (Neumann and Kravic 1975:162).

Snowshoes

A marine's snowshoes, like moccasins, could have been of Indian, French Canadian, or his own manufacture. Therefore the shape and lacing pattern may have varied. A period illustration [1722] shows a Canadian on pear-shaped snowshoes and Bonin describes snowshoes as pear-shaped (Osgood and Hurley 1975:15. Bonin 1941:41).

Traine (Sled)

There is ample evidence that the marine became well acquainted with the "traine" during the last decade of the French rule of Canada. Like snowshoes, he probably had ample experience long before that time. The 500-man expedition to establish Fort Duquesne left Montreal

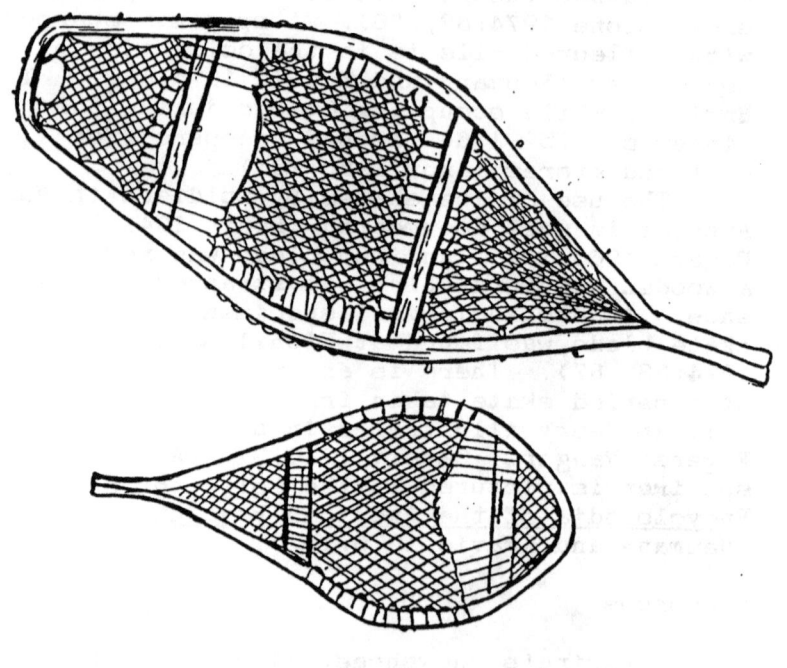

SNOWSHOES

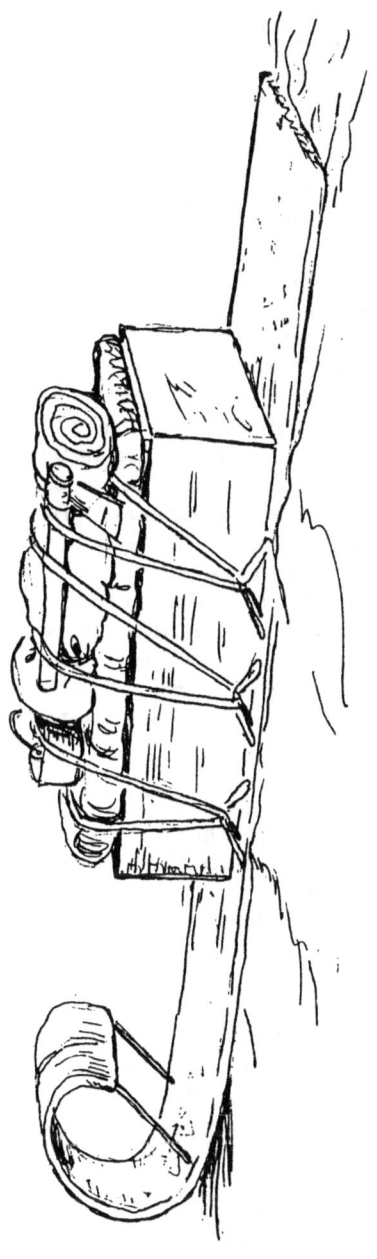

TRAINE

in January 1754, each man had a "traine" (Bonin 1941:54).
The traine was very similar to a toboggan.

> The traine is a thin plank, six to nine feet in length, and twelve to fifteen inches in width. It is bent at one end into a half circle, called a hood, to which a strap called a collar is attached - made of birch withes about eighteen feet long. The center part is about three of four inches wide and sixteen to eighteen inches long. This collar is also used to haul a load. The thick middle piece of the collar rests on the forehead, or sometimes slantingly across the chest and shoulders. The traine has, down its length and sides, sinews of animal hide into which a cord is laced to hold the goods loaded on the traine. Two or three hundred leagues can be covered in this way over snow and ice (Bonin 1941:41).

It was common for the settlers to use dogs to draw the traine. In the early years of Canada, horses were scarce and dogs were substituted and referred to as the "poor man's horse" (Kalm 1987:475-476).

Carts

The "poor man's horse" was also used to draw small carts. Larger carts used horses singly or harnessed in tandem (Kalm 1987:475, 476). Some French carts were apparently designed for human power (Diderot I 1959:plate 5).
The cart in Canada, due to the availability of waterways for shipping and the limited road network, was probably used only for short trips, transferring cargo from the harbor to the storehouse, bringing crops from the field, or conducting commerce between nearby towns. Period illustrations are of a simple two-

MATERIAL CULTURE

wheeled vehicle with solid or rail sides (Diderot I 1959:plate 5. Petersen 1968:18). The tradition is seen later in the Red River carts (Wheeler 1985:36).

Tents

There is no evidence concerning tents used by marines on a regular basis. As garrison troops they would have used barracks of some form. In *le petit guerre*, minimum equipment was the rule and tents would not have been common. Joseph Marin did use a tent on his travels, 1753 to 1754, and reported on May 10, 1754, "All these nations [Foxes, La Roche River Sakis, Sioux, and Illinois] assembled in my tent" (Bailey 1975:98). The 1754, Pean expedition to Michilimacinac did transport tents for the men. Lery's journal provides a description of the camp at Detroit.

> The officers placed their tents on the first line along the side which faced the water, and the troops and militia back of them in four lines (De Lery 1940:57).

Tents were used by the French regulars on campaign and the marines associated with the campaigns probably had access to this item. Bougainville mentions conical tents, two-by-two tents (for officers), and large duck tents for the field hospital. Winter expeditions issued a large tarpaulin to every four men (Bougainville 1964:21, 22, 61, 87). The tarpaulin may have been used as a tent or a groundcloth. Although issued to four men, guard duty may have limited actual use of the tarpaulin to two men at a time.

A period illustration of French tents shows conical, wedge, and wall varieties (Petersen 1968:10). The conical variety appear in two sizes. The smaller may be a bell of arms.

TENTS

A MARINE'S LIFE

The reason a man joined a marine company in the eighteenth century is probably the same as a person enlisting in the armed forces today. Economic need, adventure, personal patriotism, or to avoid a worse fate, such as criminal prosecution, are only a few possibilities. Service in the marines offered an advantage available in the modern armed forces: It gave a recruit hope that he would be better off when discharged than he was at the time of enlistment.

Service in the marines was different than that of the army. The army traveled on campaign, marines were garrison troops. The marines were, however, the regular army of Canada. Consequently, on occasion, they conducted expeditions for various reasons. Yet, due to their small numbers and organizational structure, they could not mount a sustained campaign against the English colonies to the south, or withstand a general Indian uprising. They had a police function in respect to the fur trade, but more important, they were a symbol of the French presence.

Enlistment in the marines was usually for life; this was preferred by the crown. However, shorter contracts were offered. This is not to suggest that the soldier expected to die in the ranks; there was retirement and a reward for service.

> The soldiers who are sent hither from France commonly serve till they are forty or fifty years old, after which they are honorably discharged and allowed to settle upon and cultivate a piece of ground. But if they have agreed on their arrival to serve no longer than a certain number of years, they are dismissed at the expiration of their term. Those who are born here commonly agree to serve the crown during six, eight, or ten

years, after which they are (honorably) discharged and settle down as farmers in the country. The King presents each discharged soldier with a piece of land, being commonly 40 arpents long and but three broad, if the soil be of equal goodness throughout; but they get somewhat more, if it be poorer. As soon as the soldier settles to cultivate such a piece of land, he is first assisted by the King, who supplies him, his wife and children with provisions during the first three or four years. The King likewise gives him a cow and the most necessary instruments for agriculture. Some soldiers are sent to assist him in building a house, for which the King pays them. These are of great help to a poor man who begins to keep house, and it seems that in a country where the troops are so highly distinguished by royal favor, the King cannot be at a loss for soldiers. For the better cultivation and population of Canada, a plan was proposed some years ago for sending three hundred men over from France every year, by which means the old soldiers might always be retired, marry and settle in the country. The land which was allotted to the soldiers about this place, was very good, consisting throughout of a deep mould, mixed with clay (Kalm 1987:382-383).

The policy of settling soldiers in the colony was begun with the Carignan Saliere Regiment in the seventeenth century. This was a great opportunity for the common soldier. It offered a better life than what he could expect if he returned to France. The crown also benefited by keeping experienced soldiers in the colony, in essence a "ready reserve".

The marine recruit was usually between twenty and thirty years old (Petard 1976:21). Therefore, to obtain his farm, he faced a mini-

A MARINE'S LIFE

mum of two decades of service. The reward justified the commitment. For many it was a second chance at life.

As was the custom in French military service, the new soldier received a *nom de guerre*, his soldier name (this name follows the word *dit* in period documents). His true identity was not officially discarded but to his comrades he became Softy, Orange, Pearl, Mug, Ready to Drink, or Happy (Petard 1976:21). The name may have been only a part of the rites of passage into his new life. Probably, his reputation would be built on his action from that point.

When the new marine boarded a transport for Canada he faced a three-month voyage to Quebec. The trip would have been interesting, if not frightening, for a young man who had never traveled beyond the small village near the farm where he was born and raised.

At Quebec he would receive a dunking in the river if he did not pay for his release (Kalm 1987:426). He would then be introduced to a foreign country and people.

> Unlike the peasant in France who spent his life sweating, scrimping, cheating, and saving to put aside enough money to buy a small piece of land or to purchase exemption from manorial obligation, and who had to keep his little hoard well hidden, wearing rags, living in a hovel, giving every appearance of near starvation to prevent the tax collectors from seizing his savings, the Canadian could spend what he had earned without a care. He could buy land for his sons so as to have them near him and spare them the necessity of clearing virgin forest on a new seigneury, or he could spend his earnings on consumer goods and entertainment. Whereas the economics of the situation would tend to make the French peasants mean and grasping, the Canadian could afford to be openhanded,

and with little care for the morrow
(Eccles 1974:95).

Perhaps the young recruit was sent further west. He watched the farms along the banks of the Saint Lawrence become less frequent as a Canadian described this place where he was to serve, Michilimackinac. Past Montreal all habitations disappeared. Day upon day of travel on the Ottawa, Mattawa, and French rivers. His world was now endless forests, portages, and weather that was getting colder by the day. Then this strange bark craft entered a lake, larger than any he had seen before, where the canoemen constantly watched the weather. Finally, he arrived at a wooden fort placed so deep in the wilderness that desertion was out of the question. Add to this the native people who were, in appearance and custom, frightening and unlike any people he had ever known.

The customary welcome of the firing of muskets and shouts of *Vive le Roi* would not have eased his anxiety (Kalm 1987:580). This strange environment probably bonded him to his fellow soldiers. It seems reasonable that he made friends with the area settlers. Many of these settlers may have gone native, including adopting native-style clothing and the custom of tattooing various parts of their bodies (Kalm 1987:577). "One would not pass for a man among the Indians of the Far West if he had not had himself tattooed" (Bougainville 1968:288). Through these friendships he may have been introduced to individual Indians and gradually become more at ease with this post and duty.

A marine had time to make these adjustments. Unlike most European soldiers, he was not subjected to endless campaigns in summer and drilling in winter cantonments. Guard duty was the main activity and he could hire a substitute (Louisbourg 1981:75). Although it varied according to local situations, a marine in many instances had more time off duty than on, and he was free to engage in trading, farming,

carpentry, hunting, or other activities that would provide him with enjoyment or profit.
The ability to make adjustments to the wilderness environment seems clear.

> Fort Michilimackinac is situated at the foot of Lake Huron. This lake is said to be three hundred and fifty leagues in circumference, and triangular in form. The fort is surrounded by a stockade, mounted with six cannon, and had thirty men in garrison who are changed every three years, if they wish. Their only remuneration is powder and lead bullets. This is enough, because they cultivate maize or Indian corn, and go hunting and fishing, thus supplying their needs. Anyone who is content there, and asks not to be transferred from this post, is permitted to remain. I saw two men there who had stayed on, one for twenty years, and another, a Parisian, for thirty years. The latter was sixty years old. The soldiers in this garrison usually trade with neighboring savages. It is known that some, when transferred from this post, have collected and taken with them, two, three, or four bundles of pelts, which they have obtained by their trade with the savages. These they sell for as much as ninety francs a pack - more or less, according to the number of furs. This will procure additional comforts for them in the place they are garrisoning (Bonin 1941:37-38).

Trading and hunting were common elsewhere. When accused of desertion, soldiers from Fort Sandoske claimed they were only out turkey hunting, the equipment for which included a sizable amount of trade goods (Wright 1990:11). At Fort Toulouse, in the Louisiana colony, trading was important to survival. Governor Vaudreuil wrote in 1745 that "...we send nothing but flour for the subsistence of the garrison and which most frequently is in the situation of lacking it so that the garrison must necessarily trade in order to get a living..." (in Waselkov 1988). These examples, and the Michilimackinac description, suggest that trading was a regular activity of the marine at the frontier posts.

Food

The marine's diet in Canada depended on the place he was stationed. At Louisbourg in 1718, the soldier received a livre and a half of bread, four onces of pork (or half a livre of beef), and four onces of vegetables per day. He also got a quarter livre of butter and five livres of molasses each month. The meat, vegetables, butter, and molasses were issued every fifteen days; the bread was issued every four days (Louisbourg 1981:76, 77).

Soldiers received ammunition for hunting and, as posts were in the vicinity of water, they fished. Louisbourg marines hunted moose, caribou, bear, seal, passenger pigeon, duck, partridge, and rabbit. The area also provided a variety of berries (Louisbourg 1981:77, 78).

The frontier posts were provided with an adequate supply of meat from the game of the surrounding area. The archaeology at Michilimackinac presents faunal evidence that suggests 60% of the meat consumed at the fort was wild game (Petersen 1968:25). The appearance of any domesticated animals is only evident after the rebuilding of the fort in the 1730's (Scott 1985:205). The soldier's garden, produce from farmers, and wild foods such as rice, gathered by the soldier or local Indians, provided a good diet for this period of history. At Niagara, the soldiers collected ducks, apparently killed in accidents involving the falls (Kalm 1987:702).

Similarly, the marine garrisoning the more settled areas seems to have fared well.

A MARINE'S LIFE

> The soldiery enjoy such advantages here [Quebec] as they are allowed in any part of the world. Those who form the garrison of this place had a very plentiful allowance from their government. They get every day a pound and a half of wheat bread, which is almost more than they can eat. They likewise get plenty of peas, bacon, and salt or dried meat. Sometimes they kill oxen and other cattle, the flesh of which is distributed among the soldiers. All the officers kept cows, at the expense of the king, and the milk they gave was more than sufficient to supply them. The soldiers had each a small garden outside the fort, which they were allowed to attend and to plant in it whatever they liked. Some of them had built summerhouses in them and planted all kinds of vegetables. The governor told me that it was a general custom to allow the soldiers a small plot of ground for kitchen gardens, as such of the French forts hereabouts as were not situated near great towns, from whence they could be supplied. In time of peace the soldiers have very little guard duty when at the fort; and as the lake close by was full of fish, and the woods abounded with birds and animals, those amongst them who chose to be diligent could live extremely well and like a lord in regard to food (Kalm 1987:381).

Although it seems that food was usually abundant and available to all, there were hard times. Food problems appeared in the 1750's and had a profound effect on the defense of Canada. The problems involved crop failures, farmers being called to military duty, transportation being commandeered by the military, and the difficulty of the government to adjust to other aspects of wartime conditions.

From all our posts great complaints
of the bad quality of the food
(Bougainville 1968:6).

On the eleventh of this month
[October, 1756] the Marquis de Montcalm
received an order from the Marquis de
Vaudreuil, dated the third, to change
the field ration in this garrison [St.
Frederic] immediately. This decrease
was because of the lack of provisions
in the storehouses, this year's poor
harvest, the feeble resources of the
colony, and the uncertainty of help
from France (Bougainville 1968:63).

There were attempts to adapt to the shortages. Oats and peas were mixed with the flour to make bread. When the adaptation included issuing horse meat a line was drawn. The women of Montreal threw the horse meat at the feet of the Governor. The next day the marines followed their example when it was apparent that the Governor's threat of imprisoning and hanging the women would not be carried out (Bougainville 1968:70, 71-72, 195. Douville and Casanova 1968:96).

The posts in the far west fared better. In 1757, Detroit expected to be able to send flour, maize, and salt pork to Fort Duquesne (Bougainville 1968:90). The posts in Illinois said they could help.

There is word from the Illinois
country that they can supply Fort
Duquesne with two thousand
hundredweight of flour and five hundred quarters of salt pork, considered
to be sufficient provisions for five
hundred men for six months, including
extra employees and the visits of
Indians (Bougainville 1968:105).

Charles Bonin, a member of the Fort Duquesne garrison, recorded that in July 1758, ten tons of supplies arrived from the Louisiana colony. It included two tons of tobacco. This abundance did not necessarily mean that the men would be supplied. The tobacco belonged to the guide of the supply boats and was for private sale. In an earlier incident, the distribution of supplies was very particular. During the building of the fort at Presque Isle the men lived on a diet of salt meat, sea biscuits, and water. The officers, however, had bread, fresh game, wine, and brandy. Bonin, as commissary clerk, was able to "appropriate" from the officers' supplies for some of the sick. His success indicates there was enough on hand to cover what he was stealing (Bonin 1941:32, 101).

The marine in Canada shared food shortages with the civilian population. Evidence would suggest that periods of shortages were infrequent. There was a famine in 1737 that forced the population to eat "the buds of trees, potatoes and other foods never intended to be used as food for human beings" (Douville and Casanova 1968:55). Problems in the 1750's were magnified by the war and, perhaps, because the quantity of documentary evidence is greater. Shortages of food were certainly not unique to eighteenth-century Canada. By the standards of this time period a marine in Canada ate well.

Health

The diet of the marine in Canada may well have been the best of any soldier in the world. This contributed to the good health he enjoyed. The Canadian diet was, in comparison to that of the French peasant, greater in vitamin and protein content (Eccles 1974:95-96). The voyage to Canada was more of a risk to his health than the period after. Except in time of war, the hospital in Quebec only saw soldiers from the arriving replacements (Kalm 1987:446). The recruit in France knew that if he had a choice between Canada and Louisiana, Canada would prove healthier (Bonin 1941:1). Corporal Jean Casse dit St. Aubin came to Detroit in 1707. He died there in 1759, at the age of 100

(Thwaites 1959:306 note). Canada seems to have been the healthiest place on earth.

The French who are born in France are said to enjoy better health in Canada than in their native country, and to attain to a greater age than the French born in Canada. I was likewise assured that the European Frenchmen can do more work, and perform more journeys in winter, without prejudice to their health than those born in this country. The intermittent fever which attacks the Europeans on their arrival in Pennsylvania, and which as it were, hardens them to the climate, is not known here, and the people are as well after their arrival as before. The English have frequently observed that those who are born in America of European parents can hardly ever bear sea voyages or move to different parts of America with as healthy results as those born in Europe. The French born in Canada have the same constitutions, and when any of them go to West India Islands, such as Martinique, Domingo, etc., and make a long stay there, they commonly fall sick and die soon after: those who fall ill seldom recover, unless they are brought back to Canada. On the contrary, those who go from France directly to those islands can more easily bear the climate, and attain a great age there; this I heard confirmed in many parts of Canada (Kalm 1987:376-377).

It is questionable if Kalm's observations would hold up to quantitative analysis. The ability of a European to do more work than a Canadian may be more a result of motivation than "constitution". Likewise, anyone traveling into a tropical climate would be subject to more problems, including insect borne diseases, a situation that even a modern traveler experiences.

Canada, by comparison to other places in the eighteenth-century world, may well have been a healthy place to live. Still, the marine was subject to the same sicknesses as the general population. Pleurisy was common, as was venereal disease and tapeworm (Kalm 1987:389-391). Certain areas saw malaria and tuberculosis. In 1749, the twenty-two man garrison of Fort des Miamis was ill with fever (Eccles 1974:159). Dietary deficiencies in winter may have caused a weakening to the resistance to disease. At Fort Presque Isle in 1753, 200 men were sick with scurvy (Bonin 1941:32). Records of Detroit show dysentery, typhus, smallpox, and typhoid fever. A lack of knowledge concerning personal sanitation may have spread the sickness once it was established (Anderson 1951:4).

The Ministry of the Marine did make an effort to meet the medical needs of the colony and the troops. A school of naval hygiene was established at Rochefort in 1722. Similar schools were started at Toulon in 1725 and Brest in 1734. A student was trained as a physician, surgeon, apothecary, and dentist. Twenty-eight graduates were sent to Canada in one year, 1740. In 1757, Bougainville reported that the King maintained a physician and ten surgeons at Quebec, one physician at Montreal, one at Three Rivers, and surgeons at some frontier posts including Detroit. There were two hospitals at Quebec and Montreal, and one at Three Rivers. The hospitals were administered by nuns (Anderson 1951:8).

The service provided at a hospital at Quebec is described by Kalm.

> The King has erected a hospital for sick soldiers here. The sick person is there provided with everything he wants, and the king pays twelve sols every day for his keep, attendants, etc. The surgeons are paid by the king. When an officer is brought to

this hospital, who has fallen sick in the service of the crown, he receives victals and attendance gratis; but if he has gotten a sickness in the execution of private concerns, and comes to be cured here, he must pay it out of his own purse. When there is room enough in the hospital, they likewise take in some of the sick inhabitants of the town and country. They have the medicines and the attendance of the surgeon gratis, but must pay twelve sols per day for meat, etc (Kalm 1987:413).

Medical treatment in eighteenth-century Canada was based on the same superstitions and primitive practices that were prevalent in Europe. Herbal remedies used in Europe, such as garlic to prevent cholera, were brought to the New World. Some experimentation was done with the herbal remedies of the Native Americans. The clear golden pitch of the fir balsam was a remedy for frostbite and sores (Anderson 1951:14). Thuya (white cedar) was used to ease rheumatic pains and to cure cough (Kalm 1987:469).

Medical treatment for the sick was probably similar to that found in France. Yet, from a preventative standpoint, a marine was quite possibly better off in Canada. He ate better than he would have in France. Germ-laden pollution was less in Canada. Also, the smaller concentrations of people in Canada enhanced his chances of not acquiring a communicable disease.

Relaxation

> ...and the soldiers are always there drinking, playing cards and smoking (quoted in Louisbourg 1981:68).

As discussed above, marines had an ample amount of free time to spend hunting, fishing, trading, and working in their gardens. It

A MARINE'S LIFE

seems probable not all soldiers were this industrious and the long, harsh Canadian winter would curtail the activities of those who were. What activity filled the winter months?

Not unlike other eighteenth-century soldiers, or soldiers of any time, marines drank and sought female companionship. The writings of the Jesuits make this abundantly clear. Wine and brandy was imported and there was some domestic production. In terms of companionship, it would be rare to find a village or town, if located near a military installation, that did not have a few women who entertained soldiers for a fee.

In one account three soldiers fortified with wine, had a Sunday rendezvous with a woman in a field behind the barachois; in this particular incident a fight resulted between these men and two sailors who came along (Louisbourg 1981:75).

Drinking among the civilian population was moderate. Breakfast for a Canadian was bread dipped in brandy or eaten with brandy on the side. Dinner, the noon meal, and supper included wine and spruce beer. Water was said to be the most common drink (Kalm 1987:473-475). Coffee was imported and tea rarely used.

Although Kalm suggests moderate drinking, he dined with upper-class people. The soldier probably had the diet of the surrounding population; however, temperance was not part of the formula: "...the soldiers, for their part, often preferred to spend their money on drinking, rather than paying for their uniforms" (Proulx 1971:2).

> Of the 16 livres this soldier earned, 6 were spent on drink with two companions, 2 on tobacco, then several quarts of liquor were purchased and shared with some soldiers, and 15 sols spent on transportation. At the end of the day only 2 livres remained (Louisbourg 1981:74).

PIPES

The frontier posts, like Michilimackinac, saw activity, aside from trading, that included drinking, gambling, and lechery (Eccles 1974:90). Louisbourg, and probably other posts, had canteens which sold wine, spirits, and tobacco. These establishments were operated by officers and in 1739 each company had its own canteen (Louisbourg 1981:80).

Smoking was a pastime in Canada in which the marine probably regularly indulged. The kaolin clay pipe was the usual smoking device (page 148). Archaeological evidence shows that clay pipes were imported, but there was also a Canadian clay pipe industry. There are a large variety of designs in evidence at Louisbourg and Michilimackinac including pipes of Dutch manufacture (Walker 1971:64. Stone 1974:150).

Although clay pipes were the most frequent, micmac and other styles were used (Stone 1974:151). Kalm describes a soft gray stone which was carved into pipe heads and blackened. He gives the French name as "Pierre a Calumet". The popular use of the term, calumet, usually applies to a pipe of red pipestone. Kalm's description, however, suggests these pipes were of the micmac type (Kalm 1987:498). The stems for the pipes were made from the *bois de calumet*, shoots of dogwood (Kalm 1987:588. See Hanson 1981:34).

A sealskin (Kalm may mean otter) pouch was used by many Canadians to carry their tobacco (page 150). The hair was left on the skin (Kalm 1987:395). Pouches were also made of otter, martin, or other small mammals. The Canadians apparently copied the Indian style.

> The native's way of protecting and carrying their tobacco with them was to cut it up and place it in the skin of an otter, a marten, or some other small animal. The feet, where they join the body, had been sewed up and an opening left under the chin. In other respects the skin was complete, as it had been taken from the animal, with head legs, and feet. The hairy

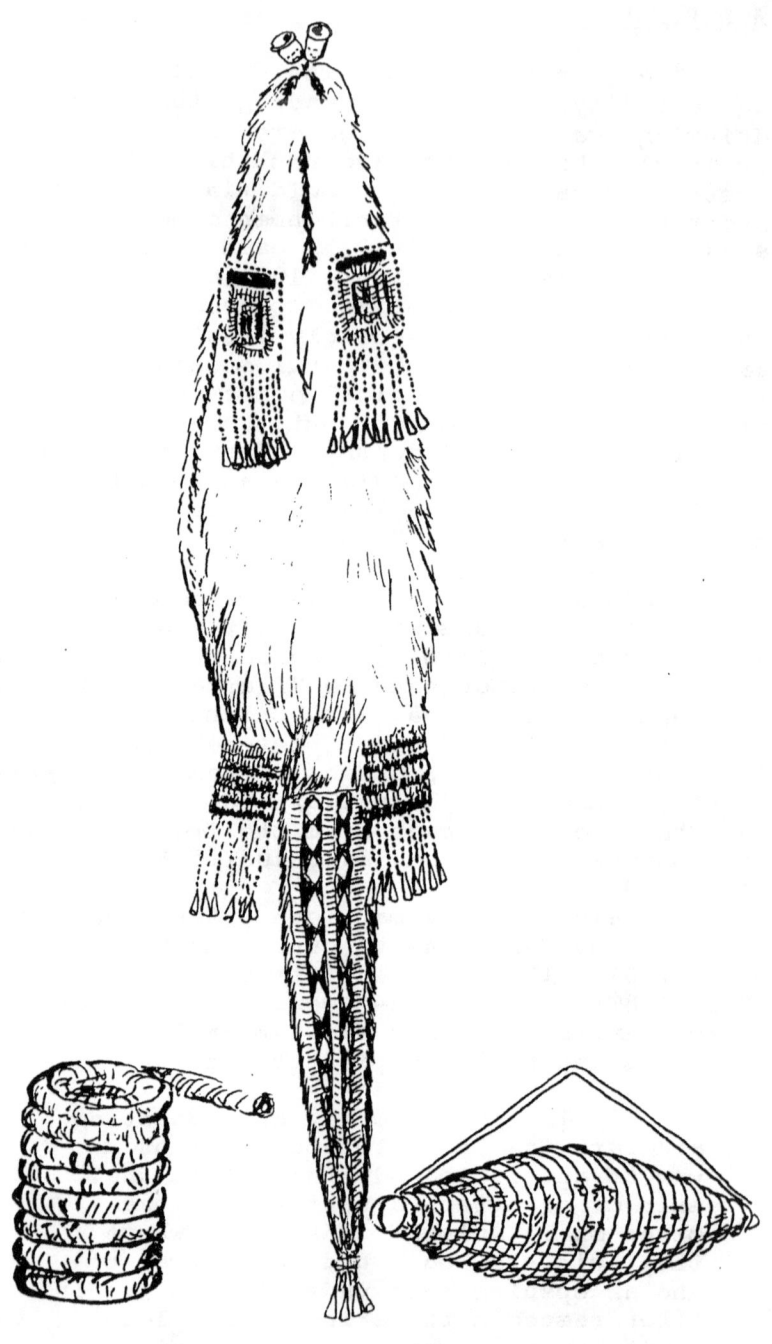

TOBACCO BAG and TOBACCO

side was on the outside. These skin
pouches were adorned on the outside
with red tassels, tin and brass
trimmings. The Indian carried this
tobacco pouch upon his arm, along with
his tinder box and pipe, wherever he
went. As a rule the ordinary Frenchman
made use of this same custom and the
pouch of otter skin was most commonly
used. A skin prepared thus cost thirty
sous (Kalm 1987:573. See Hanson
1981:33)

Tobacco was a domestic product, sometimes blended with natural additives.

Every farmer plants a quantity
of tobacco near his house, in proportion to the size of his family. It is
necessary that one should plant
tobacco, because it is so universally
smoked by the common people. Boys of
ten or twelve years of age, as well as
old people, run about with a pipe in
their mouth. Persons of the better
class do not refuse either to smoke a
pipe now and then. In the northern
parts of Canada they generally smoke
pure tobacco; but further north and
around Montreal, they take the inner
bark of the red Cornelian cherry
(Cornus sanguinea L.) crush it, and mix
it with the tobacco, to make it weaker
(Kalm 1987:510).

The bear berries (Arbutus uva
ursi L.) grow in great abundance here.
The Indians, French, English and Dutch,
in those parts of North America which I
have seen, call them Sagackhomi, and
mix the leaves with the tobacco for
their own use (Kalm 1987:488-489).

Gambling is not unknown to soldiers of any time or place. Soldiers are known to be inventive as to ways and reasons to wager. Marines may have bet on shooting matches, although ammunition may have been at a premium on the frontier. Almost surely cards and dice figured in this activity.

Dice appear in the archaeological finds at Michilimackinac as do circular discs interpreted as gaming pieces. These items, and the dice, are made of bone or ivory (Stone 1974:152-154). The discs might have been used as checkers, a game popular in eighteen-century Canada (Segin 1968:xvi). The Canadian checker board was twelve squares by twelve squares (Hanson 1981:47). Also, hollow, cone-shaped objects, of bone were found and interpreted to be cups for the "cup and pin" game (Stone 1974:152-154).

Playing cards were available. France had a thriving card manufacturing industry. Each region had a particular design (Mann 1966:59).

> Some statistics on cardmaking in France seem quite overwhelming: in 1754, in one province alone, over 200,000 packs were made; the number of master cardmakers alone runs into the thousands (Mann 1966:57).

The cards were made of heavy paper stiffened with paste and laminated. The basic design was printed in black ink. Other colors were applied by hand using a stencil. One variety had suits of clubs, coins, swords, and cups (Diderot II, 1959:plates 463, 464).

The marine probably visited the neighboring villages and took part in family and community activities. Although it was condemned by the Church, the French Canadian liked to dance. There were festivals concerning the harvest and religious holidays (Segin 1968:xvi-xvii).

Money

Marine pay (see Appendix II) was five sols per day or thirty sols if he was working on fortifications or other projects for the King

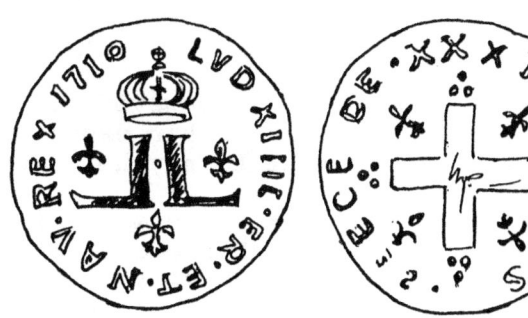

COINS

(Kalm 1987:382). His pay was, however, subject to stoppages for uniforms and other expenses. If he was at a frontier post he may not have seen currency.

Gambling or other debts incurred by a marine may have been paid with items other than hard cash. This would be especially true on the frontier. Coins, French and foreign, although not unknown in New France, were scarce. Much of the business was accomplished with paper currency hand-written on cards (page 155).

> Paper money was first introduced into Canada in 1670, to the amount of only one hundred thousand francs. In 1706, this issue of paper was increased to six hundred fifty thousand francs, and a few years later withdrawn. In 1726, it was reissued in a different form - that is on playing cards with values of ninety six francs, forty eight francs, twenty four francs, twelve francs, six francs, three livres, thirty sous, fifteen sous, and seven sous six deniers. Each card had the arms of France stamped upon it, and was personally signed by the governor, intendant, and treasurer (Bonin 1941:126).

Card money made its appearance in the seventeenth century and was withdrawn in 1719. However, in 1729, the government was again forced to use cards. In one shipment to Canada the cards, blank on each side, were damaged in transit. This required the substitution of playing cards (Hargrave 1966:314).

It was not practical to send coins or cards to frontier posts to pay the soldiers or for other debts. Consequently, payment was made with supplies and military stores (Heldman 1979:83-84). This would explain why the long-serving marines at Michilimackinac, mentioned elsewhere, took payment in ammunition.

PLAYING CARDS
CARD MONEY

Religion

The Roman Catholic Church came to New France with the earliest settlements and was a powerful force in the colony. Although the clergy was continuously critical of the lifestyle of the colonists, it seems the individual, including the soldier, had not left his faith in France.

The French, in their colonies, spend much more time in prayer and external worship than do the English and Dutch settlers in the British colonies. The latter have neither morning nor evening prayer in their ships and boats, and no difference is made between Sundays and other days. They never, or very seldom, say grace at dinner. On the contrary, the French have prayers every morning and night aboard their ships, and on Sunday they pray more than commonly. They regularly say grace both before and after their meals and cross themselves. The captain kneels in prayer at his bed in the morning, and everyone says prayers in private as soon as he gets up. At Fort St. Frederic all the soldiers assemble together for morning and evening prayers. The only fault is that most of the prayers are read in Latin, which a great part of the people do not understand (Kalm 1987:396).

Every morning as we start to row one of the soldiers read the litany to the Virgin Mary which is found in the "Livre de Vie" for Saturday, if I remember correctly. This was never overlooked. It was always read in Latin and the other soldiers always answer either with "misere nobis" or the "ora pro nobis" according to whether the prayer was directed to one of the saints or the Virgin Mary. It

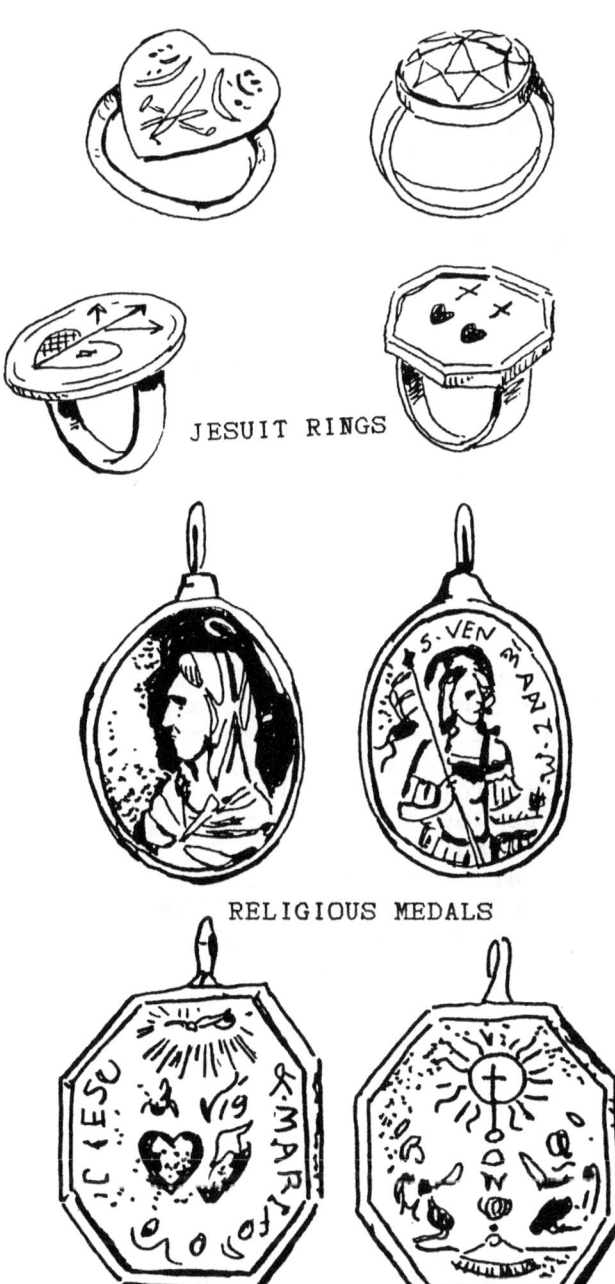

was amusing to hear them read Latin so
zealously in spite of the fact that
they did not understand the language.
I also noticed that each and all my
companions hardly failed to kneel in
prayer on arising and again at night on
retiring (Kalm 1987:578).

In each fort, which contains forty
men, the king keeps one of these monks
[Recollets] who officiates there
instead of a priest. The King gives
him lodging, provisions, servants, and
all he wants; besides two hundred
livres a year (Kalm 1987:454).

Summary

The life of a marine included a freedom
that he would not have had in France or in any
other military organization. He had an opportunity to leave the service with more material
wealth than he had upon entering. He was under
a system of discipline that was perhaps no
harsher than he would have found in France or
even as a Canadian "habitant". The danger from
sickness or that connected with his trade would
not be much greater than that of the civilian
colonist. By eighteenth-century standards, the
marine in Canada had a good life.

DISCHARGE PAPER

TAMBOUR ET FIFRE

Marine Music and Musicians

European military organization in the eighteenth century included drummers and fifers at the company level. The organization of a marine company included a fifer and one drummer for every fifty men. This ratio varied slightly during the first half of the eighteenth century (Appendix I). As with almost every other aspect of supply in North America, marine companies were often lacking musicians. It was 1741, before a fifer was part of the garrison of Louisbourg, and he was to serve the eight marine companies. In that year, there were twenty one drummers in the garrison, sixteen belonging to the marines. The marine company at that time had seventy men. (Fortier 1977:47, 48).

Drummers spent more time on duty than did the fusilier. He took his turn with the guard, which at Louisbourg was every third day. Evening retreats and changing of the guard, daily activities, required the attendance of all drummers (Fortier 1977:47).

Drummers would, of course, march with their company on campaign. The Canadian style of warfare that the marines adopted was the quick raid by a small party. A drummer would be unnecessary, or even a hindrance, to this activity. Larger expeditions, however, would require the command communication provided by the drummer. The marines who helped defeat Braddock were awakened on the battlefield by drums. "When dawn appeared, they beat the long roll of drums, and the whole force was soon up and about" (Bonin 1941:84).

The special skills of musicians set them apart from other soldiers. They received higher pay than fusiliers and had a distinctive uniform. In large garrisons, the musicians were quartered together, and supervised by a drum major, a rank equivalent to the company sergeant in the infantry (Fortier 1977:44, 47).

DRUMMER and LACE

Joe Lee
92

The drummers and fifers wore the same uniform. The justaucorps was of blue cloth lined with red serge. Pink cloth was used for ornamentation with wide braid in the King's livery. Buttons were probably brass (copper appears in translations but this may be an error). The waistcoat and breeches were red wool serge, except from 1728 to 1730 when it may have been blue. The breeches were lined with gray linen. Stockings were red. Other clothing items were the common issue (Proulx 1971:15-16).

The musician carried a sword. An example of what is thought to be a musician's sword has the hand guard removed. It is speculated that this was done to protect the drum. The musician's belt was covered with the King's livery as was the drum strap that was also lined with leather. The drum was wooden, painted blue, and decorated with yellow fleur-de-lis. Leather drum cases were used and these were painted blue (Proulx 1971:16-17).

The drum major's uniform was similar to the musician's but of finer quality. The justaucorps had velvet cuffs and the braid was the King's grand livery. The waistcoat was scarlet as were his stockings and probably his breeches. Other uniform items were those issued to other sergeants (Proulx 1971:17).

The drum major would have had many years of service. He was required to instruct the drummers in the drum calls of the service (see Appendix IX), as well as, their other duties. In addition, he had to be familiar with the calls used by foreign military establishments. As drummers were used to parley with opposing forces, it was desired that they speak other languages (Fortier 1977:44,45). Although it might be assumed that not all drummers had skill as translators, a man reaching the rank of drum major probably had ability in this area. It is not known what languages Pierre Boziac, drum major at Louisbourg, may have known, but he was literate and skilled in the social graces. He was a dancing instructor (Fortier 1977:51).

The artillery companies also had drummers. Their uniforms differed slightly from their counterparts in the infantry. The justaucorps was blue wool, with red cuffs, and red lining. Buttons were of German metal. It was decorated with braid and edging of the royal livery. The waistcoat was red wool with a wool serge lining. The buttons were the same as those on the coat, each using three dozen. The breeches were of the same material as the waistcoat and lined with linen (Proulx 1971:34).

The artillery drummers were issued a surtout. It was of blue bouracan and had eighteen buttons like those on the justaucorps. The sleeves were edged in silk with the royal livery. The drummer's hat was laced with false silver. Drummers wore red stockings and a white lace cravat.

The drummer was issued the sword worn by the canonnier. It had a German blade with a gilded brass guard and double branch hilt. This was decorated with a red, white, and blue wool sword knot with large tassels. The drummer's waistbelt and drum strap were trimmed with silk braid in the royal livery (Proulx 1971:34).

CANONNIERS-BOMBARDIERS

Eighteenth-century fortifications and artillery are inseparable. Consequently, marines, serving as garrison troops in a colony that was always short of soldiers, had to provide the personnel to man the guns. Artillery service was considered an elite position as it required greater skill than that of a fusilier. The army had a separate artillery arm. The marines in Canada had this as a separate service only during the final years of their service in the colony.

There was an artillery school in Quebec as early as 1697; however, the first artillery company raised in North America was at Louisbourg (Isle Royale) in 1743 (Devine 1990:44). This thirty-man company replaced the practice of training two soldiers from each infantry company as artillerymen (Proulx 1971:30). The first company in Canada was authorized in 1750 and a second in 1757 (Charles Bonin, who has been quoted many times in this study, states that he was a member of the second artillery company stationed in Quebec in 1751. This conflicts with the fact that the second company was not raised until 1757). These companies, like marine infantry, were part of the Ministry of Marine and not connected to the regular military establishment (Chartrand 1984;27).

It seems the artillery company had no trouble finding quality recruits. The educated and, apparently, intelligent Bonin had to use "connections" to be accepted into the company, as he was initially rejected for being too short. It is also interesting to note that at his mustering ceremony the infantry companies were also accepting new recruits (Bonin 1941:15-16). This indicates a close organizational relationship between the infantry and artillery and that both "arms" were recruiting rank and file in Canada.

Bonin spent a good deal of his time as a clerk, during which he accumulated a good deal of personal profit. He also served with a musket as he claims to have been at the defeat of Washington at Great Meadows and at Braddock's defeat the next year. This was not out of the ordinary as the artillerymen were "... elite soldiers, they served as grenadiers when not on artillery duty" (Chartrand 1984:27. Bonin 1941:15).

Unfortunately, Bonin did not talk about commonplace items of material culture. It can be assumed he wore the artillery uniform.

All companies of Canonniers - bombardiers were issued a common uniform. This consisted of a blue coat with red cuffs and lining, red vest, breeches and stockings, white metal buttons and hat lace. Each gunner was armed with a musket, a bayonet, and a brass hilted double branched sabre and equipped with a gilberne (Chartrand 1984:27).

The artilleryman's uniform included a surtout which is a plain coat with tails. It was made of blue bouracan and had eighteen buttons, the same type as found on the justaucorps (Proulx 1971:33). Bouracan (barracan) is a thick, coarse, corded wool/silk cloth which may contain angora goat's hair or other animal hair. This "undress" coat, which was not part of the infantryman's kit, would support the idea that the status of the artilleryman was higher than that of the infantryman.

Unlike the infantry companies who received the full dress uniform every other year, the artillerymen were supplied with this uniform every third year (Proulx 1971:30). Perhaps this was a perception on the part of the authorities that the duty of these men was of a less demanding nature, in terms of clothing needs, than that of the infantry. Also it is possible that this followed the custom of the regular army artillery as practiced in France.

The artillerymen left Louisbourg after the fortress surrendered in King George's War.

ARTILLERYMAN

They returned after the war when the fortress was given back to France as part of the peace settlement. During their stay in France they acquired another uniform item.

When the company returned to Rochefort after the events of 1745 at Isle Royale, a new element was added to their uniform from 1746 onwards. This was a pair of duck gaiters trimmed with ten to twelve buttons and buttonholes with two duck bows "under the buttons and buttonholes (Proulx 1971:34).

The artillerymen served a variety of guns from swivels to the heavy pieces used for fortification defense. Cannon sizes included 4, 6, 8, 12, 18, 24, and 36 pounders. Mortars were 7, 8, 9, and 12 inch. As these guns were produced for the Ministry of the Marine they were almost always made of iron, painted black. The wooden garrison carriages were painted red (Chartrand 1984:28). The fortress at Quebec had 120 iron guns of various sizes (Bonin 1942:10). The cannons used in Canada were probably manufactured in France; however, the sole Canadian ironworks near Trois Rivieres also cast cannon and mortars in addition to kettles, stoves, cannon balls, mortar bombs, and anvils. Cannon cast at the ironworks and sent to France were judged to be poor (Kalm 1987:420. Douville and Casanova 1968:172). It seems that if the ironworks was involved in casting cannon, a difficult process, there may have been a need in the colony.

The artillery at eastern Canadian forts in 1742:

Quebec

7 iron 24 pounders with 8 marine carriages.
20 iron 18 pounders with 22 carriages.
18 iron 12 pounders with 20 carriages.
26 iron 8 pounders with 28 carriages.
35 iron 6 pounders with 34 carriages.
3 iron 3 pounders with 9 field carriages.

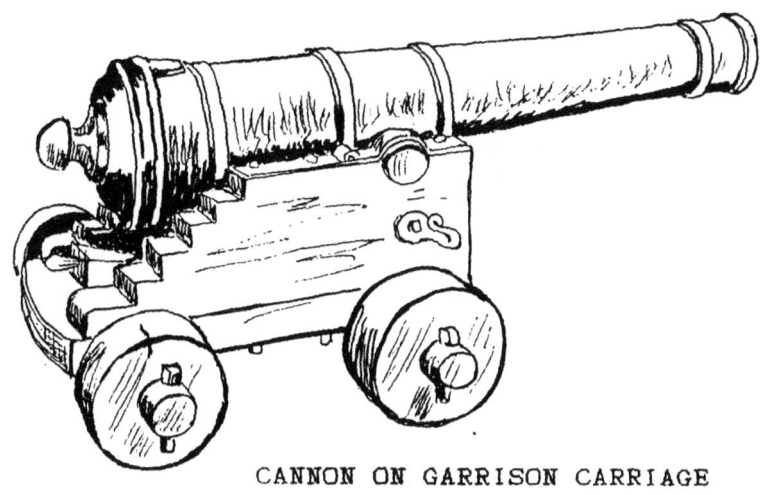

CANNON ON GARRISON CARRIAGE

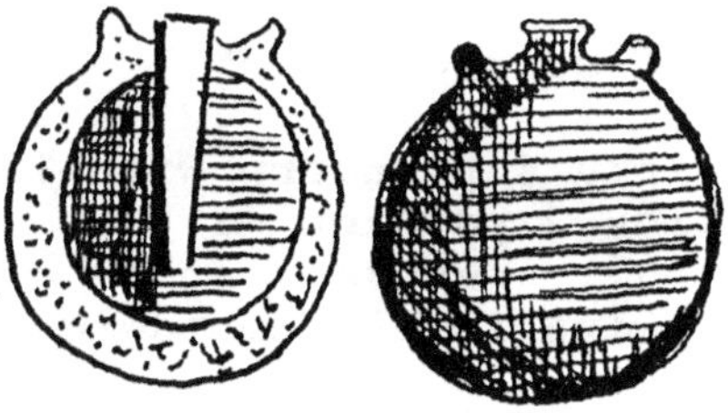

MORTAR BOMB

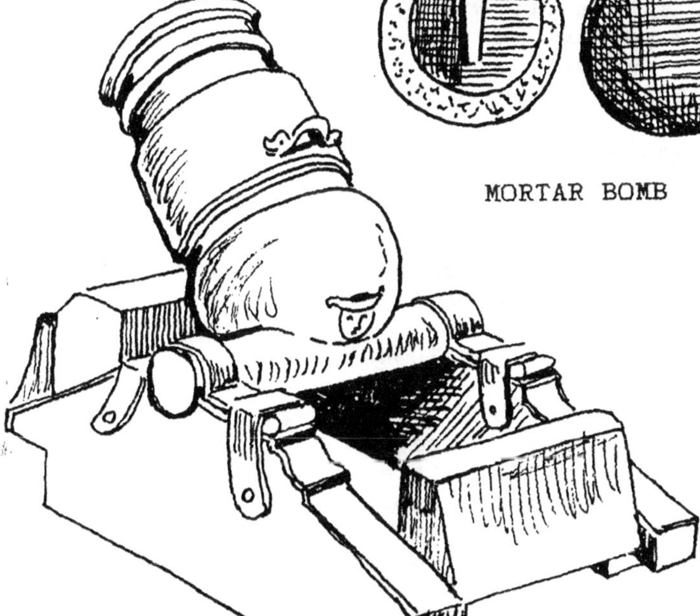

MORTAR

2 brass 4 pounders (included with this entry
and the one below, 4 field carriages and 12
limbers)
1 brass 4 pounder culverine.
1 brass 12 1/2 inch mortar with 1 carriage.
1 brass 9 1/3 inch mortar with 1 carriage.

Montreal

2 iron 4 pounders with 2 marine carriages.
2 iron 12 pounders with 2 carriages.
6 iron 8 pounders with 7 carriages.
7 iron 6 pounders with 8 carriages.

Three Rivers

1 iron 4 pounder.
8 iron 6 pounders.

St. Frederic

12 iron 4 pounders with 15 marine carriages.
1 iron 2 pounder with 1 carriage.
2 small grenade mortars with 2 carriages.
13 swivels (1/2 pounders).

Fort Chambly

2 brass 2 pounders culverines with 2 field carriages.
1 iron 1 pounder culverine with 1 carriage.
3 iron 1 pounders with 1 carriage.
12 swivels.
(O'Callaghan 1969, IX:1094-1095).

Due to need, heavy guns were limited to
the eastern posts. A report from the late
1740's or early 1750's states most of the
western posts had no guns. Detroit had "only a
few chambers" (Pargellis 1969:30-31). Chambers
were breech loading cannon, usually swivel
guns. It consisted of a barrel and a separate
breech section, the chamber, which was loaded
and inserted into the barrel. A wedge was used
to hold the chamber in place. It is very
interesting that these were found to be in use

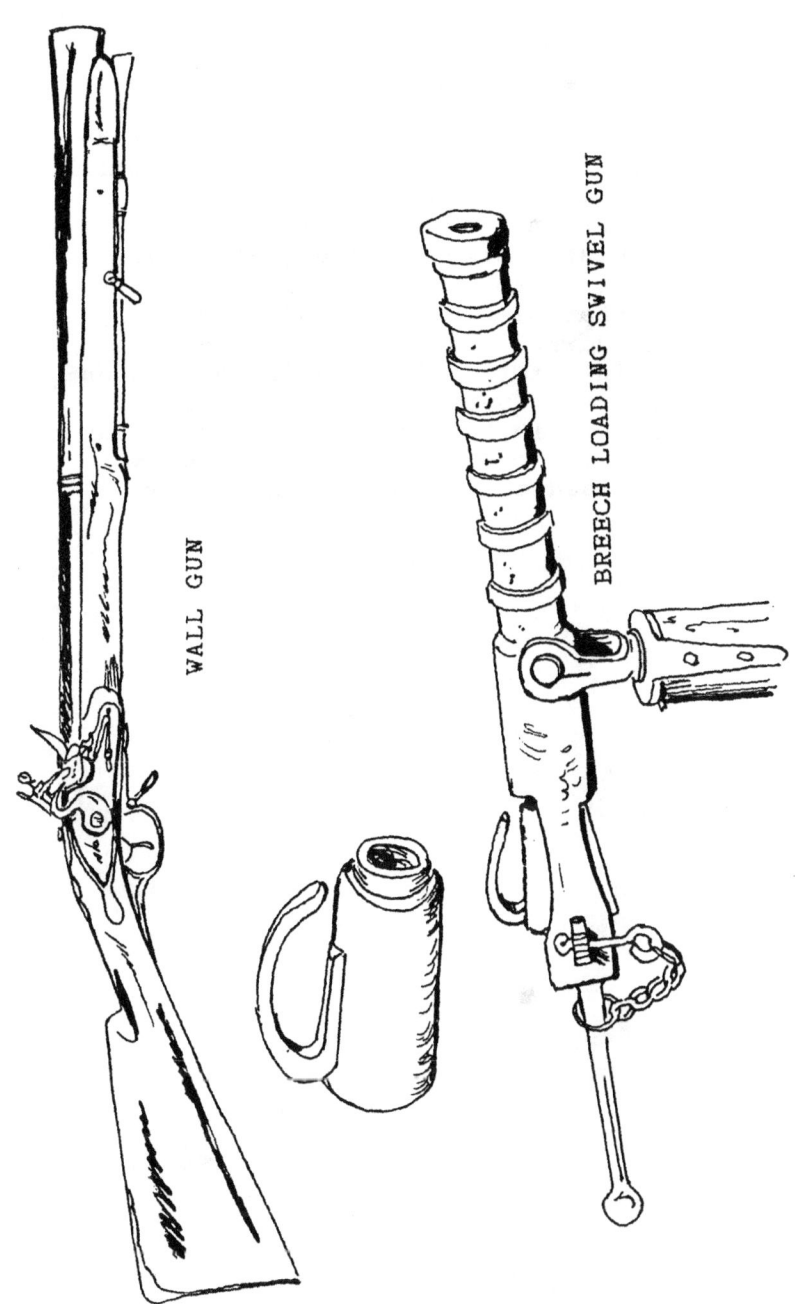

at Detroit as they were considered obsolete by this time (Gooding 1965:2).

This may be another case of inferior military equipment, in this case old stores, being disposed of in the colonies. A lack of standards allowed cannon design to be at the whim of the individual manufacturer or artillery official (Peterson 1969:48). There were attempts to standardize artillery in 1703, 1721, and 1733. The 1721 reforms produced a heavier gun that was done away with in 1733, being replaced with the lighter 1703 design. It would be interesting to know if the cannon of Louisbourg and Quebec were the result of changing designs in France. Perhaps the foundry at Trois Rivieres was producing cannon because of a need to replace "hand-me-downs" from France.

WATERCRAFT

The movement of people and goods, in quantity and with speed, in eighteenth-century North America was on the water. Roads, primitive at best, were found only near the larger settlements. The business, economic and military, of North America moved via the lakes and rivers.

The watercraft used by the marines were the canoe, pirogue, and bateau (Bonin 1941:23). These were relatively simple boats, their design based on the task to be performed and the environment in which they worked. The quality of these boats is demonstrated by their continued use, with only minor changes, into this century.

Canoe

There were two major types of canoes used in colonial Canada, the bark canoe and the dugout which the French called the pirogue. The bark canoe was widely used on the Great Lakes, the St. Lawrence River, and the tributaries of these waters. The pirogue was used in waters that were shallow or otherwise inaccessible to the canoe.

The seventeenth-century French explorers in Canada were well acquainted with the bark canoe. A description of the craft appeared at the time the first marines were about to arrive in Canada.

> ...Baron de LaHontan, gave the first reasonably complete account that has been found of the size and character of a birch-bark canoe. ... the bark canoes ranged in length from 10 to 28 pieds and were capable of carrying from 2 to 14 persons. The largest, when carrying cargo, might be handled by three men and could carry 2,000 pounds of freight (20 quintals). These large canoes were safe and never upset.

They were built of bark pealed in the winter; hot water was thrown on the bark to make it pliable, so that it could be rolled up after it was removed from the tree. The canoes were built of more than one piece of bark as a rule.

The large canoes, he reports, were 28 pieds long, 4 1/2 pieds wide and 20 pouces deep, top of the gunwale to top of frames on bottom. The last indicates "inside" measurements; in this the length over the gunwales, not overall, and the beam inside the gunwales, not extreme. He also says the canoes had a lining or sheathing of cedar "splints" or plank and, inside this, cedar ribs or frames. The bark was the thickness of an ecu (this coin, a crown, was a little less than 1/8 inch thick), the sheathing the thickness of 2 ecus, and the ribs of three. The ends of the ribs were pointed and these were seated in holes in the underside of the gunwales. There were 8 crosspieces (thwarts) between the gunwales (note: such a canoe would commonly have 9 thwarts; LaHontan may have erred here).

In translating LaHontan's measurements a pied is taken as 12.79 inches, a pounce as about 1 1/8 inches. The French fathom, or brasse, as used on colonial Canada, was the length from finger-tip to finger-tip of the arms outstretched and so varied, but may be roughly estimated as about 64 inches; this is the fathom used later in classing fur-trade canoes for length. In English measurements his large canoe would have been about 30 feet long over the gunwales and, perhaps, almost 33 feet overall, 57 1/2 inches beam inside the gunwales, or about 60 inches extreme beam. The depth inside would be 21 or 21 3/4 inches bottom to top of

WATERCRAFT

gunwale amidships. LaHontan also
described the elm-bark canoe of the
Iroquois as being large and wide enough
to carry 30 paddlers, 15 on a side,
sitting or standing. Here again a
canoe of about 40 feet is indicated.
He said that these elm-bark canoes were
crude, heavy, and slow, with low sides,
so that once he and his men reached an
open lake, he no longer feared pursuit
by the Iroquois in these slow craft
(Adney and Chapelle 1964:8).

LaHontan's description is valid for canoes
in general. There were, of course, variations
in size, construction techniques, and details,
such as the shape and height of the ends.
Bonin describes a canoe with a beam that is
exceptionally wide.

Canoes are the most frequently used
water transport in upper Canada,
because they are light enough to make
the necessary portages around the frequent rapids. They are made of small
wooden strips as thick as strong lath,
bent half double, then curved in a half
circle. They are placed four or five
inches apart, with the ends attached to
a slender pole bound with wooden straps
like barrel hoops. Five cross bars are
placed along the inside of the canoe,
which is twelve to twenty feet in
length, or more. These crossbars hold
the canoe open. It is seven to eight
feet across in the widest part, and
narrow toward both ends. The framework
is covered on the outside with birch
bark, or wild cherry bark, sewed
together with wooden withes. The seams
are then covered with gum or resin to
keep them watertight. These boats are
very light. Loaded, they are easily
managed by two men, one at each end.
More men can be put in if they are
seated. If they are large, four men

can carry the empty canoes; if small, two men are enough (Bonin 1941:23).

In 1754, Lery reports that the canoes transporting supplies on Lake Erie carry as many as fifty five packages and eight to ten men (De Lery 1940:12, 48). The traditional package weighed about ninety pounds (Nute 1955:38). The canoes also could use sails, in one instance a sail and foresail (De Lery 1940:3). Paddles used in Canada were made of maple or ash. (Kalm 1981:568, 696).

Canoes built by the Indians were distinctive to the tribal group and reflected the water conditions where they were used. Consequently, a marine at Quebec would have seen a different craft than a soldier at Ouiatenon, if it was built by Indians. However, both may have been transported by or have seen supplies moved in a French-Canadian manufactured canoe.

The expanding fur trade near the end of the seventeenth century seems to have demanded a supply of canoes that could not be met by Native American builders. The French began to build their own.

The canoe factory was located at Trois Rivieres, just below Montreal, on the St. Lawrence. A standard large canoe was built, and at the rate of 20 a year. Franquent [Military Engineer-in-Chief for New France] gives as the dimensions of the canoes the following (converted to English measurement): length 36 feet, beam about 5 1/2 feet, and depth about 33 inches. Much of this description is not clear, but it seems evident that the canoe described was very much like the grand canot, or large canoe, of the fur trade. The date at which this factory was established is unknown; it may have existed as early as 1700, as might have been required by the rapid expansion of the fur trade and other activities of the last half of the previous century. It is apparent from early comments that the French found the Indian canoe-builders unreliable, not to say most uncertain, as a source of supply. The need for large canoes for military and trade operations had forced the establishment of such a factory as soon as the Europeans could learn how to build canoes. This would, in fact, have been the only possible solution (Adney and Chapelle 1964:13).

The bark canoe was developed long before the Indians had contact with the Europeans. That the French, with their Old World technology, adopted this watercraft to their own needs highlights the canoe as a fine example of the relationship of material culture to the environment. This tool, which today is used in its traditional form, may represent the most visible contribution of a stone age culture.

Pirogue

The pirogue was the main vehicle for transporting supplies from Fort Presque Isle to Fort Duquesne. Lery also mentions this craft in use at Detroit (De Lery 1940: 95). Like other watercraft, the pirogue was found in different sizes, although the design was similar.

Pirogues are made of trunks of birch or whitewood trees from which the bark is stripped. They are hollowed like a trough, cut square at the stern with a sharp point at the bow. They are rather flattened in the bottom and underneath, but very liable to tip when a foot is put on the side (Bonin 1941:55, note 2).

Lery uses the term, middle-sized pirogue, which suggests there were differences (De Lery 1940:18). There was, however, an attempt to standardize them, at least those used to carry supplies from Lake Erie to Fort Duquesne.

M. Portneuf arrived at the camp. He had brought with him from the little lake the total amount of pirogues made, which was 79, each able to carry 30 to 35 packages (De Lery 1940:31).

Bateau

The eighteenth-century bateau in North America was a flat bottomed, double ended, cargo craft. It was built in various sizes depending on the cargo and the waterways on which it operated. In comparison to the canoe it was slower and much heavier. It also had a disadvantage in that the rower faced backward instead of forward as did a paddler.

The bateau's advantages were its initial stability (due to its flat bottom it was difficult to tip over). This helped when it was poled in shallow water or sailed on lakes and rivers. Due to the heavier materials used for construction, it was resistant to damage and it could be made larger than a canoe. The construction of the bateau demanded less skill. Also, canoe materials became scarce in the settled areas of Canada, while a bateau was made of wood that was plentiful.

> They [bateau] are always made very large here, and used for large cargoes. They are flat bottomed, and the bottom is made of red, but more commonly white oak which shows better resistance when it runs against a stone than the other wood. The sides are made of white fir, because oak would make the bateau too heavy (Kalm 1987:381).

The bateau was a common watercraft in English North America. There is no reason to believe it was different than its French-Canadian counterpart.

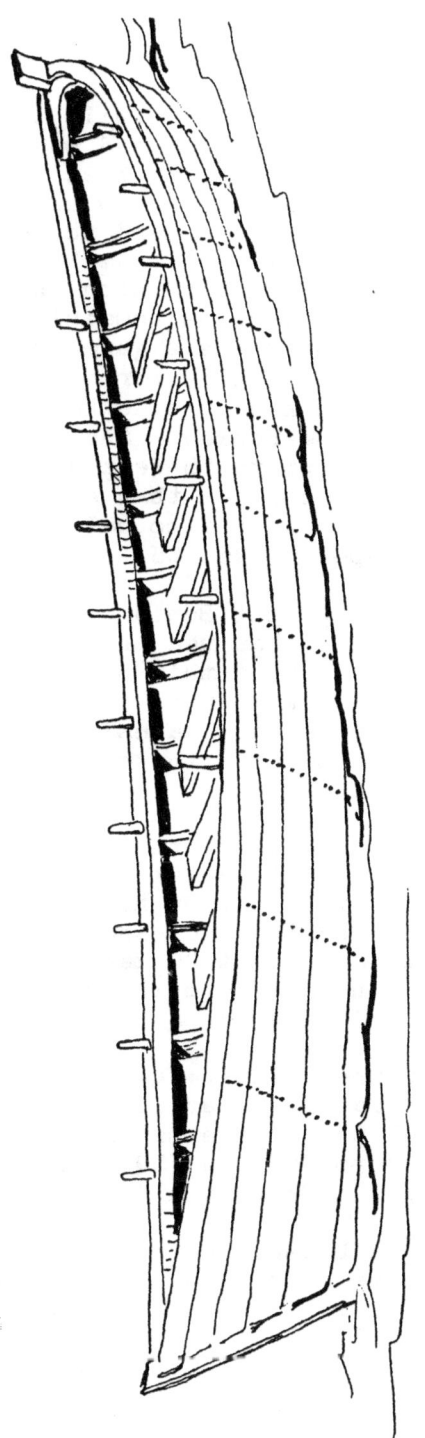

BATEAU

The colonial bateau was built in lengths up to 40 or 45 feet and was primarily a rowing or poling boat for use on rivers and lakes. A few craft of the frontier class are said to be as long as 84 feet and as short as 18 feet in the nineteenth century, which indicates the range of lengths possible in such a type. Some of the eighteenth century bateaux apparently were also fitted to sail and had outside keels to allow sailing close hauled. Such hulls, in lengths up to 75 feet and with more beam proportion than employed in frontier boats, were also called "gondolos" (Chapelle 1951:35).

It is interesting that Bonin describes the canoe but does no more than use the word bateau. This suggests that this boat was not unique. He probably saw it used in France as well as Canada. His neglect makes it necessary to turn to other sources for the military application of the craft.

In the regulations of this day, it is said that each batteau will carry twelve barrels of flour, or nine of pork, when ordered to load; and it is supposed will have about 20 men, a few more or less, in each, etc (Knox 1980:165).

The 7th [June, 1756]. At 10 o'c. there arrived [at Fort Carillon] two boats in which there were seven thousand pounds of powder and 4500 balls of all calibres,... (De Lery n.d.:38).

A draught of a bateau, dated 1776, suggest the English may have attempted to standardize the military craft with a length of about thirty feet (Chapelle 1951:34-35). There is no information to suggest that any bateau used in Canada were produced only for military purposes. It is most likely that the marines used

what was available. A source refers to bateau
having a crew of four, six, and ten men
(Bougainville 1964:10, 14, 104). Lery, posted
on Lake Erie in 1754, suggests that a boat
(bateau) carried twenty five men or 100 packages (De Lery 1940:24, 35). As stated earlier,
the Canadian bateau was designed to meet the
cargo capacity needed and the conditions found
on the local waterways.

FRENCH FORTIFICATIONS IN CANADA

The primary duty of the marine companies in Canada was to garrison forts established to protect the colony and its economic purpose. These forts were located throughout the colony from Quebec to northwestern Manitoba, although not all posts had marine troops. The life of a marine might be better understood with an understanding of what these forts were like.

There were many varieties of structures that were called forts. They ranged in size and complexity from single wooden houses to large, complex, stone fortresses. Between these extremes were forts that were geometrically "regular" and those that were an irregular shape due to the terrain. Some were meant to be permanent, some temporary.

Fortifications were expensive and therefore the form and the material used for construction was dictated by the purpose of the structure, the local environment, and the force an enemy could bring against it. French fortifications in Canada were constructed of wood, stone, and/or earth. The use of these materials was determined by availability and, most importantly, if it was believed they would have to resist enemy artillery.

By the late seventeenth century French military engineering was considered the state of the art. The development of artillery had stimulated a change in fortification techniques in Europe from the strong walls of the castle to a geometric pattern of related defensive components, organized to support each other and provide defense in depth. The master of this system was Sebastien le Prestre de Vauban, Marshal of France. The English had also adopted the Vauban methods and they were available through the writings of Coehorn and Muller.

The students of Vauban carried this fortification system to North America. The application in the New World left much to be desired. Montcalm, critical of everything in Canada, was definite in his opinion of the quality of Canadian fortification, at least one of the builders, and the cost. He states that the forts were worthless and,

> ... de Lery, senior [father of Joseph Gaspard de Lery who Montcalm thought good], a great ignoramous in his profession (it needs only a look at his works), who robbed the King like the rest (O'Callaghan 1969, X:963).

Perhaps the most important aspect of the system was its adaptability. There were differences between the battlefields of Europe and the wilderness of Canada. Foremost among these was the availability of wood. European fortifications made extensive use of stone. Although stone was available in North America and used at Quebec and Louisbourg, stone construction required skilled workmen and was time consuming. Fortifications in North America were often needed quickly, as in the case of Fort Duquense, and skilled stone masons were a premium. The builders used what was at hand, trees.

The time-consuming nature of stone construction also translated into expense. The permanence and strength of stone was not necessary on the distant frontier. The potential enemy for these posts, the Indians, did not possess artillery. Those forts that might be subjected to a formal, artillery-dominated siege had the climate as an ally. Even with heavy artillery, it took time to batter down walls. In the temperate climate of Europe, sieges continued for years. The Canadian winter did not allow continuous operations. The 1759 siege of Quebec was in large part decided by the date when the St. Lawrence river would freeze.

The use of wood in a French fort would take two basic forms. The simplest form, which dominated the western posts, was upright pickets, logs set next to one another in a trench.

FORTIFICATIONS

This method was adequate against an enemy without artillery.

If an opposing force could bring artillery to the siege, the logs were squared and laid upon one another horizontally. Two parallel walls were raised forming a "crib", which was filled with earth. The width of the crib would depend on the height of the wall. The excavation that provided the "fill" created a trench in front of the wall, the beginning of defense in depth.

The design of the fort would be based on terrain and need. In theory, the design provided the defending troops the opportunity to shoot at the enemy from protection. Each part of the structure supported another and the enemy, even if close to the wall, was not to be given a place to hide.

Forts, unless inhibited by terrain features, took a standard geometric shape such as a square, rectangle, pentagon, or triangle. These shapes were found in the stockade and the crib type. If left in this form, an enemy who reached the wall would be safe unless a defender leaned out to fire, thus exposing himself to return fire. To compensate, bastions were placed in the corners, or angles, of the fort. (Note: There is an overabundance of terminology related to military engineering. These terms are not used elsewhere in human communication and if they were used here would require a substantial glossary. As this section is not intended to cover fortifications in depth, the discussion will remain as non-technical as possible. When terms, such as bastion, are used they will be defined and illustrated, see page 186.)

The bastion was formed by extending a short section of wall at a sharp angle from the main wall. This gave the defender a clear view along one face of the fort. The bastion was completed by connecting these sections with two more sections that met at a point in line with the corner of the fort's walls. A platform might be constructed within the bastion to accommodate men and cannon.

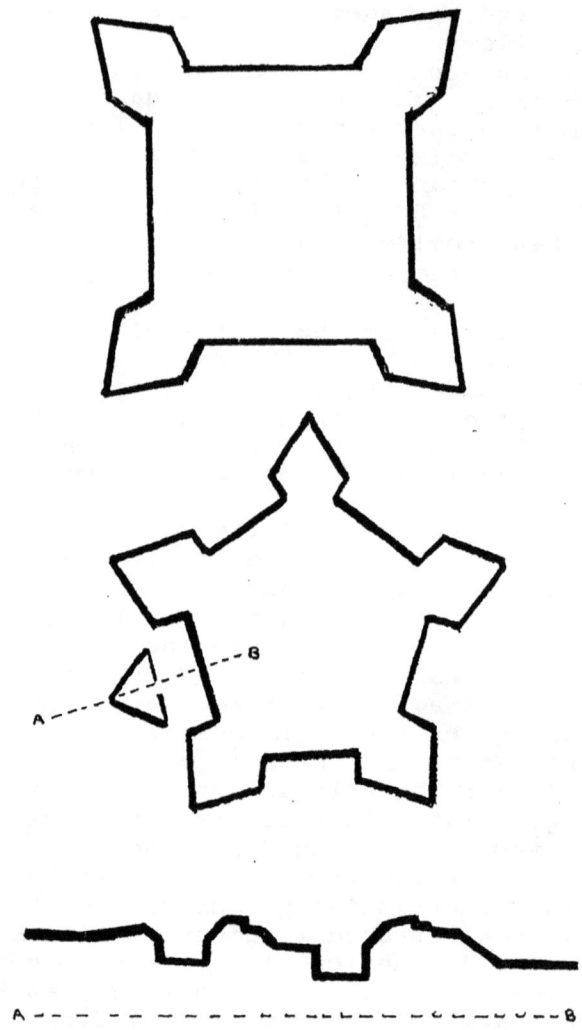

Outline of a square and a pentagon fort showing bastions. A ravilin is shown outside the gate of the pentagon fort. This outerwork protected the gate, a weak point, and could be supported from the fort's bastions. This is only one example of many kinds of outerworks which would be combined to defend the fort. A profile of the fort and the ravilin show from left to right, the glacis, ditch, ravilin, ditch, and bastion; defense in depth.

FORTIFICATIONS

The number of bastions were dependent on the number of angles in the design of the fort and the length of the wall between the angles. Depending on "the authority" the effective range of a musket was sixty to one hundred yards. Cannon had greater range. Consequently, when planning bastions the engineer had to consider the firepower he had available.

The function of a bastion may have been met by the use of a blockhouse. These covered structures would not only provide protection to the outside of the wall, but would give defenders protection if the enemy got within the walls of the fort. Blockhouses were constructed log upon log laid horizontally. They could not withstand artillery fire.

The brief description above covers the basics of North American forts. Additional features might include fortified buildings within the walls, and outerworks (fortifications, manned or unmanned, located beyond the wall and ditch, designed to keep the enemy from getting close to the main walls. This added to the defense in depth).

There were, of course, variations in the design of fortifications. Some forts with terrain advantages, such as a substantial body of water, might require fortifications only on the landward side. The opposite might be true if the threat was naval. In some cases the terrain dictated an irregular shape.

French forts usually had a dual purpose as a stronghold and a trading post. Some, like Michilimackinac, enclosed the residences of settlers. Others, Detroit, Louisbourg, and Quebec for example, had civilian structures within and outside the walls. Frontier posts that were leased to their commandants were required to maintain a priest, surgeon, and blacksmith (Eccles 1974:146). Structures were provided for the activity of these men, as well as barracks, a guardhouse, storehouses, and a dwelling for the post commander.

The structures, like the fort, were probably constructed and furnished according to their function. The marine housed in barracks had the bare necessities.

Furnishings for soldier's rooms were subject to few regulations. The Code des Armees Navales had nothing to say on the matter, and the Code Militaire, quoting an ordinance of 1716, specified only that the rooms contain as many beds as possible with a table, two benches and a fireplace. There are no plans showing room furnishings for the barracks, but there are some for other buildings in Ile Royale, a small barracks for the outpost of Port Toulouse showed five soldiers' beds lining two walls of the room with a fireplace in the third wall and a door in the fourth. The centre of the rooms was left bare, presumably for a table and benches. Such furnishings are described in an account of the barracks of the Island Battery at Louisbourg; three tables were 6 pieds long and 2 pieds wide, and six benches were 6 pieds long. There was also a folding table 4 pieds long and 2-1/2 pieds wide. In a corner of the two rooms in Port Toulouse there were small cubicles or cabinets, presumably for sergeants. A proposed new barracks for Louisbourg, drawn up in 1739, included a small sergeant's room with two beds, while the large rooms had seven beds lining two of the walls. A plan of the royal battery barracks shows bunk-beds, the only plan to do so. Finally, a plan of a redoubt in 1752 shows a room for sergeants separate from that of the soldiers (Louisbourg 1981:69-70).

French frontier architecture often lacked the solid foundation used today. The first buildings were usually constructed from posts set upright in a trench (*poteaux en terre*). Large gaps between the logs were filled with stones or pieces of wood. The wall was sealed with a clay and straw mortar (*bouzillage*). The roof was bark, wood, or, in the southern part of New France, thatch.

A second type of construction used vertical timbers set on horizontal timber sills (*poteaux sur sole*). This method would have given the wall better resistance to the environment. In some instances both methods could be found in the same building (Walthall and Benchley 1987:27).

The commanding officer's house at Michilimackinac used the *poteaux sur sole* method with refinements. The sills rested on a loose fieldstone foundation rather than in a trench. The interior walls were plastered on pine lathes. Archaeological specimens of the plaster show it to be of good quality, finished smooth, and whitewashed (Stone 1974:314).

French architecture included the use of horizontally-laid timbers. Stone construction was used at Quebec and Louisbourg for buildings as well as fortress walls. There is evidence of bricks at Michilimackinac; however, the sample is not sufficient to believe they were a factor in construction (Stone 1974:208-209).

As is common with any building, deterioration was constant. The problems would depend on the environment and the activity at a site. In Illinois, a priest constructed porches on the long sides of his house to protect the sills (Walthall and Benchley 1987:27). Michilimackinac saw new stockade walls constructed in 1735 and 1751 (dates are approximate). The first walls were built in 1715 (Stone 1974:313, 317, 319). The new walls expanded the area of the fort. The expansion is probably due to increased economic and military activity at this post. The catalyst of the new construction may have been the deterioration of the posts in the ground. The fifteen to twenty year intervals between construction may represent the life expectancy of the walls. This is speculative, however, this interval extended would predict a problem in the 1770's, which was the case (Havighurst 1966:92).

Deterioration probably resulted in plenty of work for the marine. This labor meant extra money when he worked for the government or a civilian. His own safety and comfort were other motivations for making repairs.

Comfort during the harsh Canadian winter depended upon heating the building in which the marine lived. The French used fireplaces within the building and set in an end wall. The interior type, the most efficient, seemed to dominate in Canada. The French also used iron stoves.

> In every room is either a chimney or a stove or both. The stoves have the form of an oblong square; some are entirely of iron, about two feet and a half long, one foot and a half or two feet high, and near a foot and a half broad. these iron stoves are all cast at the ironworks at Trois Rivieres. Some are made of bricks or stones, not much larger than the iron stove, but covered at the top with an iron plate. The smoke from the stoves is conveyed up the chimney by an iron pipe in which there are no dampers, so a good deal of the heat is lost. In summer the stoves are removed (Kalm 1987:460).

Canadian stoves impressed an English officer.

> The stoves that are used in this country are incomparably well adapted to the climate, and contribute, in great measure, to soften the rigour of that long-frozen season; these, with all other utensils and materials of cast-iron, are made at a foundry contiguous to the Trois Rivieres. I think these inventions would be exceedingly useful if fixed up in the halls of the old mansion-seats of the nobility and gentry of Great Britain, as the heat

may be conveyed by pipes to the most
remote apartments, which would not only
preserve these buildings, with their
furniture, from decay, but prevent
those fatal accidents that frequently
happen by fires, in the absence of the
family, by the carelessness of servants. They stand upon a square frame
of the same metal, about six or eight
inches from the ground; and, if the it
is a boarded floor, the place where it
is to be fixed should be first covered
with leaves of sheet iron; as should
likewise the edges of the holes in
wooden partitions where the pipes are
conveyed from one room to another;
which renders every thing perfectly
safe (Knox 1980:307).

It is difficult to determine how many
marines had access to stoves. Perhaps those
men stationed in major garrisons, Quebec,
Montreal, Trois Rivieres, or billeted with a
well-to-do civilian family enjoyed this comfort. The weight would have prohibited shipping this item to the frontier posts except
those on major waterways. Men at isolated
locations probably relied on warm clothes, good
blankets and a spot near the fire.
 The living quarters for a marine depended
on many variables. Although the barracks was
the norm by the mid-eighteenth century, wartime
need would overload the quartering capacity of
a fort. The extra men might use other buildings or, in good weather, use tents. In some
instances soldiers would be billeted with
civilians, a common practice of European
armies. The marine did not experience living
conditions that were any worse than would be
expected by an eighteenth-century soldier. In
many instances, he lived much better.

FINAL THOUGHTS

Those who interpret history face many problems, one of which is viewpoint. If a wide view is used, individuals and groups are often stereotyped. If the purpose of a study is to cover four centuries of history, it is impossible to focus on the activity of one percent of the population in a fifty-year period. It is likewise difficult to understand a nation's history if the narrow view is used. The activities of a few thousand selected individuals could well be misleading if projected as representative of a nation's social and cultural past. This study falls into the narrow view category. It focuses on Les Compagnie Franches de la Marine in Canada. These men are part of the history of Canada and North America, but how they fit into centuries of North American history is beyond this work.

One author of this study approached this project with the belief, found in general histories, that the marines were poor quality soldiers, as the following excerpt indicates.

> The training of the soldiers of La Marine was better than that of the militia, but the poor quality of the men, their lack of battalion organization and the small experience of many of their officers made it impossible for them to be really effective troops. They were really more policemen or gendarmes than combat soldiers (Hamilton 1962:132).

This opportunity to focus on the marines strongly suggests that Hamilton's view is not accurate. (In fairness to Edward P. Hamilton, and others, the narrow view is not a luxury available to those charged with producing general histories.) The brief history of the marines which begins this study highlights numerous examples of the combat proficiency of these men. In important engagements, British regulars and high quality provincial irregulars (Rogers' Rangers) were defeated by French forces which included marines, and were often led by marine officers. The high quality of the officer corps is not only proven in the success of the marines but also in the effectiveness of the Canadian militia and Native American allies, who were led by marine officers. The admission that the marines were better than the militia is significant. The Canadian militia was a highly effective fighting force.

> ...God knows we do not wish to disparage the value of the Canadians.... In the woods, behind trees, no troops are comparable to the natives of this country (Bougainville 1964:333).

The term "militia" creates a negative view which is very misleading in this case. As marines retired in Canada, the militia gained many experienced marines in its ranks. A study of the Canadian militia would reveal that to be compared to these citizen soldiers would be a compliment.

The view of the marine as a good soldier is reinforced by the material culture which is the main component of this study. The sources support two major related points. The marines faced a lack of support from the mother country and, despite the lack of support, they successfully adapted to the Canadian environment. Although the evidence is inconclusive as to specifics of what materiel was issued to whom, and when, the documentation produces a picture of lack of supplies and poor quality of that which was received from France. This questions the contention that the marines were irresponsible and would spend their money on drink rather than on uniforms. The drink may have kept him warmer.

Their use of the material culture found in Canada, as French supply was inadequate, was inevitable. The list of equipment provided to winter expeditions (see Bougainville 1964:87)

FINAL THOUGHTS 195

supports this idea. It is important that the marines with long Canadian service are not confused with marine companies and individual replacements arriving in Canada during the final phases of the Anglo-French conflict. The equipment and the combat record of the two groups are very different. Unfortunately, the documentation often makes it difficult to distinguish between the two.

The environmental differences between France and Canada and the isolation of the colony quickly established a Canadian identity. Bougainville found Canada a separate nation (Jenkins 1966:81). Other French officers found the same nationalism: "... the confident talk of Canadians, who believe themselves, in all respects, the first nation of the world" (O'Callaghan 1969, X:463). The conflict of French and Canadian identities may have been greater than that experienced by the British and Americans. It may have greatly contributed to the loss of the colony.

How did the marines deal with this conflict? They were born in France but expected to settle in Canada. They served under Canadian-born officers, fought beside Canadian militia, and lived in a culture that was Canadian. It is quite probable that their dress, daily activities, every aspect of their lives was Canadian. They became Canadians.

> ... the soldiers and officers often spoke together as comrades, without any ceremonies, and with a very becoming freedom (Kalm 1987:382).

> At the first movement the surprised Indians fell back to the other side of the river, but the soldiers of La Marine and the Canadians quickly fell from all directions upon the enemy... (Bougainville 1964:295).

The marines fought with the Canadians and were treated as equals. At the end, the surrender of Canada brought them together. Article XXXIX of the Capitulation stated:

> None of the Canadians, Acadians or French, who are now in Canada, and on the frontiers of the colony, on the side of Acadia, Detroit, Michillimacquinac, and other places and posts of the countries above, the married and unmarried soldiers, remaining in Canada, shall be carried or transported into the British colonies, or to Great Britain, and they shall not be troubled for having carried arms - "Granted, except with regard to the Acadians."...(Zoltvany 1969:187).

Colonial history would suggest that the combination of marines and militia in individual combat units (which was the rule rather than the exception) would be the result of manpower shortages or lack of confidence in the militia. The Canadian situation was perhaps different and unique. The combination of marines and militia in Canada was a result of their being interchangeable. The relationship of the marines and the militia was stated by Levis when he pointed out that the marines and militia camped together (Nicolai 1989:65). It is estimated that 38% of each battalion of Levis' forces in 1760 was made up Canadian militia (Nicolai 1989:72-73). The major difference between the marines and the militia was not their ability as warriors but that the militia had a responsibility at home, although this was not exclusive to the militia. Most of the marine officers were Canadian and some marines had families in Canada.

As was suggested at the end of the history section, the rearguard action by the marines and militia on the Plains of Abraham may have been fought by men with different uniforms (or perhaps no uniforms) but common purpose, the defense of their home. The marine who was established in Canada was not a French soldier.

He was, to use a designation which once seemed incorrect, the Canadian regular.

APPENDIX I

ORGANIZATION OF A MARINE COMPANY IN CANADA

Infantry

Capitaine (captain)
Lieutenant
Enseigne en pied (senior ensign)
Enseigne en deux (second ensign, added c.1730)
Cadet a' l'Aiguillete (senior cadet. The cadet system began in the 1730's. They were sons of Canadian nobility.)
Cadet (0-2 per company)
Sergent (Sergeant, 2 per company)
Caporal (Corporal, 2 per company)
Anspessade (lance corporal, 2 per company)
Fusilier (private, varied in number, 100 maximum)
Tambour (drummer, 1-2 per company)*
Fifre (fifer, 1 per company)*
Canonniers (There were two men in each company trained to serve as artillerymen after 1737)

*Ordinances called for two drummers and one fifer per company (seldom achieved). The list below illustrates the ideal.

YEAR	FUSILIERS	DRUMMERS	FIFERS
1690	100	2	1
1697	50	1	1
1702	90	2	1
1713	50	1	0
1715	35	1	1
1719	45	1	0
1725	30	1	0
1727	50	(varied from 30-60. If 60 there was to be a fifer and drummer)	
1733	80	2	1
1736	60	1	1
1739	80	2	1
1748	50	—	—
1755	100	2	1
1759	50	1	1

(Fortier 1977:48).

Artillery

Capitaine
Lieutenant
1st sergent
2nd sergent
Caporal
Canonnier (2 grades)
Tambour

There are references to other ranks found in a garrison involving more than one independent company, a garrison commander and staff was necessary to coordinate activities.

Major
Sergent Major
Barrack Sergent
Tambour Major (Sergeant of Drummers)
Chirurgien (Surgeon)

APPENDIX II

MARINE PAY

(Per year in livres, sols, denier. Brackets indicate amount left after deductions for rations and uniform. Louisbourg, 1744)

Capitaine	1080	
Lieutenant	720	
Enseigne en pied	480	
Enseigne en deux	360	
Cadet	153	[90]
Sergent	270	[156]
Caporal	162	[72]
Fusilier	108	[18]
Artillery		
1st sergent	426	[372]
2nd sergent	319	[297]
Caporal	213	[192]
Canonnier (2 grades)	191.14	[167.8]
	159.15	[139.4.6]

APPENDIX III

PRICES AND VALUES

The old regime monetary system was based on the livre tournois. There were 12 sols in the livre, 20 deniers in the sols. The sterling exchange rate varied from one shilling to one and sixpence per livre. To find the value of the livre in today's currency is extremely difficult; too many factors have altered in conflicting ways. the closest approximation that I could make is that the livre had the buying power of roughly two 1968 Canadian dollars. This estimate, despite strange anomalies, is based on prices of essential goods and services, wages and salaries, and the assumption that money has depreciated since the late seventeenth century to one-fifth of its former value (Eccles 1974:xii).

The livre and franc were the same. Three livres equaled an ecu or crown (Kalm 1987:411 note).

A pistole equalled ten francs (Bougainville 1968:197 note).

1 livre equalled 1 shilling sterling in the early 1700's. By the 1750's it had declined to 10 pence (Eccles 1987:204).

Soldiers received extra pay for additional services. They worked on fortifications or similar projects. For a fireworks display in Quebec (1752) each man received twenty-four francs (Bonin 1942:18). A marine could work for farmers or tradesmen when off duty. As was stated in this study, if stationed at a frontier post he might engage in the fur trade. Some left a post with as many as four bundles of furs which were worth ninety francs per bundle. Charles Bonin was unusually successful for a common soldier. He left Fort Duquesne with 32,400 francs worth of credit and 10,000 francs of paper money (Bonin 1941:37-38, 104).

Wages. On the farms the wages for servants and day laborers was ordinarily a little less than in the cities. They commonly give one hundred and fifty livres a year to a faithful and dilligent man servant, and to a maid servant of the same character one hundred livres. A journeyman to an artist gets three or four livres a day, and a common laboring man thirty or forty sols a day (Kalm 1987: 411).

The cost of some commodities in Canada, 1749 (Kalm 1987: 536).

horse (average quality)	40 francs
horse (good quality)	100 francs
cow	50 francs
sheep	5 livres
hog (200 pounds)	15 francs
chicken	10 sols
turkey	20 sols
wheat (minot)	40 sols
Peas (minot)	40 sols
butter (pound)	10 sols
eggs (dozen)	3 sols
watermelon	5 sols

At Detroit, c.1750, a tuque sold for 3 livres, a powder horn brought the same price (Thwaites 1959:27, 57).

CROSS OF SAINT LOUIS

APPENDIX IV

LIST OF MARINE OFFICERS

This list is unrefined. Individuals are listed by the name that appears in primary and secondary sources and may appear under more than one name due to creative spelling, inaccurate transcriptions, and/or the use of selected parts of a family name or title. An asterisk indicates that the officer may have held a marine commission but it is not clearly stated in the source.

Aubry, Charles Philippe, Sieur de (Captain, LA.). Fought British advance (Grant) near Fort Duquesne 1758. Wounded and captured at La Belle Famille 1759. Died in shipwreck 1770.

Bayeul or Bailleul (Ensign). Great Meadows 1754. Wounded at Braddock's defeat 1755. A Camet Bayeul was ensign commandant at Ouiatenon c.1757.

Bayeul (Lieutenant, Il). At Fort Necessity 1754.

Beaubassin*. May have been commandant and/or leaseholder at Point de Chagoamigon c.1757.

Beaucour (Captain). Captured on the Plains of Abraham 1759.

Beaudicourt, Drouet de. Commandant La Presentation c. 1751. (Same as Beaucour?)

Beauharnois, Charles, Marquis de. 1670-1749. Ensign 1692, Lieutenant 1696, Captain 1699, Captain de Vaisseau 1708, Chevalier de St. Louis 1727. Governor General New France, recalled 1746. Lieutenant General of Naval Forces 1747.

Beaujeu, Daniel Hyacinthe Lienard de (Captain). 1711-1755. Born in Montreal. Commandant Niagara c.1749. Killed commanding the attack on Braddock.

Beaujeu, Louis Lienard de. (See Villemonde)

Beaulac, Hertel, sieur de (Reformed [disabled] Lieutenant). At Chambly 1746.

Beaulac (Cadet). Braddock's defeat 1755.

Becancourt (Lieutenant). Commanded Canadians in Chambly/St. Jean area 1757. Built fort in the same area 1758.

Becancour, Hertel de (Lieutenant). (same as above?).

Bellestre (Bellaitre), Francois Marie Picote, sieur de (Lieutenant). 1719-1795. Born in Montreal. Served in Acadia 1745. Commandant Fort St. Joseph 1747. Raided near Albany 1757. Commandant of Detroit 1758-1760. A Bellestre was commandant at Fort Miamis 1754 and c.1757.

Bellestre, Picote de (Ensign). Killed near Fort Duquesne.

Beranger, Jean Baptiste Henry (Lieutenant). Second to Muy at Detroit and commanded temporarily after his death.

Blanville (Cadet) Braddock's defeat 1755.

Blois (Barroiz?) (Cadet).

Bleury (see Sabrevois)

Boishebert, Charles des Champs de (Captain, most junior in the colony). 1727-1797. Born in Quebec. Entered marine service 1742. Served in Acadia 1746-1747, 1757. Plains of Abraham 1759. St. Foy 1760. Went to France.

Bonne, de (Captain). Killed at Seige of Quebec 1760.

Boulascry, Chevalier de Garner de (Ensign). Niagara 1746.

Boucher de Niverville (de Montizambert or Montisambert), Joseph Claude de (Lieutenant). 1715-1804. Ensign 1742. Led attack on Fort Number Four 1747. Celoron expedition 1749. St. Pierre expedition to upper Saskatchawan 1750. Lieutenant 1756. Attacked Fort Shirley and Bigham's Fort 1756. Commanded Abenakis at William Henry 1757. Quebec 1759.

Boucherville, Herbin de (Lieutenant). Niagara 1746.

Boucherville (Junior Ensign). With Jumonville, captured 1754. Carillon 1756. Mortally wounded at St. Foy 1760.

Buisson, du (Lieutenant). Ohio 1754.

Cabanac, St. George de (Captain). Commandant Ft. Frontenac 1754. Died 1754.

Cabanac (Cadet). Braddock's defeat 1755.

Cabanas, de (Lieutenant). Ft. Frontenac 1746. (Perhaps St. George de Cabanac?)

Calaron (Celoron?) (Cadet). Braddock's defeat 1755.

Carqueville (Lieutenant). Pean expedition 1754. In Montreal winter 1754-1755. Killed at Braddock's defeat.

Celoron de Blainville, Pierre Joseph. 1693-1759. Born in Montreal. Chevalier de St. Louis 1741. Commander at Detroit (twice), Michilimackinac, and Niagara. Commanded 1749 expedition through the Ohio country. Commandant La Presentation 1751. With Dieskau 1755.

Celoron de Blainville, Jean Baptiste.
Braddock's defeat 1755. Killed near Fort
Cumberland. Pierre had a brother and son (b.
1729) with this name. An Ensign Celoron was in
the Ohio country in 1754.

Chation, de (Captain). Commandant at St. Joseph
1756.

Chevigny, sieur de (Cadet). Raided in
Pennsylvania. Killed by Cherokees 1757.

Combre, Charles Porcherson, Sieur de.
Commandant La Baye 1750.

Combre (Senior Ensign). Carillon 1756.

Courtemanche, Contemanche (Lieutenant). With
Celoron 1749. Detroit 1752, commanded company
of Sieur de Croisille. Commandant Presque Isle
1754. Braddock's defeat 1755. Commanded militia
brigade, William Henry. Quebec 1759.

Courtmanch (Cadet). Braddock's defeat 1755.

Contrecoeur, Claude Pierre Pecaudy, Sieur de
(Captain). 1706-1776. Born in New France.
Lieutenant at Niagara 1746. With Celoron 1749.
Commandant at Ft. Duquesne 1754. Chevalier de
St. Louis 1756.

Corbiere (Ensign). Ohio 1754. Braddock's defeat
1755. Raided from Ft. Duquesne 1756. Ordered to
join Langlade at Carillon 1757. Lieutenant,
mortally wounded St. Foy 1760.

Cournoyer (Lieutenant). Pean expedition 1754.
Niagara 1759.

Coutrol or Couterot, Hubert (Lieutenant).
Commandant La Baye 1756-1760. Nephew of Gov.
Vaudreuil.

Croisille, Croisil, Sieur de (Captain). Died c.
1751. Company was part of the Detroit garrison.

Cugnet*. Leased posts at Point de Chagoamigon and Kamanistigoya. Died before 1757.

D'aillebout (Sub(?) Lieutenant). A cadet Daillebout was at Braddock's defeat 1755. Genadiers, Wounded St. Foy 1760.

Dansville (first Ensign). Artillery officer.

Denys la Ronde (Lieutenant). At Carillon 1756, 1758. Captain of Grenadiers St. Foy 1760, Mortally wounded.

Darpontine (Captain). Commandant Ft. Presque Isle 1754 (This individual appears in only one source).

Debonne*. Had concession (with Repentigny) at Sault Ste. Marie c.1757.

Depeux, Second ensign Ft. Frontenac 1746.

Desillerts (Cadet, IL).

Devins (Lieutenant, IL).

Douville, Alexandre Dagneau (Lieutenant). Commandant of Presque Isle 1754. Killed in Pennsylvania soon after Braddock's defeat.

Drouillin (Ensign). With Jumonville, captured 1754.

Dubuisson, Jacques Charles Renaud (Captain). Wounded St. Foy 1760.

Dumas, Jean Daniel (Captain). Born in Agenais, France c.1712. Captain in the Agenais Regt. Came to Canada 1750 as marine captain. Braddock's defeat 1755. Winter expedition to William Henry 1757. William Henry 1757. Plains of Abraham 1759. Wounded at St. Foy 1760. Inspector General of Marine Troops in Canada 1759 (with equivalent rank of colonel). Returned to France 1760. Brigadier General 1768. Field Marshall 1780.

Du Mont (Lieutenant). Niagara 1746.

Duplessis-Faber, Francois Lefebre, Sieur. Commandant La Baye 1726. Commandant Niagara 1746. Major at Montreal. Leads force to relieve Frontinac 1758 (80 years old).

Duplessis (Junior). Second ensign Niagara 1746. An officer with a similar name was killed at Fort Necessity. Possibly the oldest son of Capt. Duplessis.

Du Sable (Cadet). With Jumonville, captured 1754.

Duverger (see St. Blain).

Falaise (Lieutenant). (May refer to Gannes). At Carillon 1756.

Ferrant (Lieutenant, IL). With Langlade 1757.

Fleurimont (Senior Ensign). Carillon 1756.

Fortenay (Cadet). Carillon 1756.

Fremont. Marine Artillery Officer

Frontenelle (Cadet). Captured on Lake George 1756.

Gannes, Michel de, sieur de Falaise. 1702 (May 2)-1752 (Oct. 23). Born at Port Royal (Annapolis Royal, N.S.). Ensign 1719, Lieutenant 1725, Captain 1730. Isle Royal 1722. Port Toulose 1726. Attack on Port Royale 1744. Captured at Louisbourg 1745. Town Major at Louisbourg 1749.

Gannes, Charles Thomas de. 1714-1765. Brother of Michel. Commandant Fort St. Jean c.1749? William Henry 1757. Carillon 1758.

Gaspe (Lieutenant). Ohio 1754. Commanded Carillon winter 1756-1757. William Henry 1757. Carillon 1758.

Godefroy (Captain). Winter expedition William Henry 1757. To Detroit and back east 1758.

Godefroy (Ensign). Ohio 1754.

Grosbois or **Groisbois** (Cadet). Carillon 1756. Mortally wounded 1757.
(Lery refers to both Grosbois suggesting 2 related Cadets.)

Hartell (Cadet). Wounded at Braddock's defeat 1755.

Herbin (Lieutenant). Commandant St. Frederic c.1749. Commandant Michilimackinac 1754.

Herbin, Louis (Cadet). With Langlade 1757. Ensign, wounded at St. Foy 1760. Wounded in Siege of Quebec 1760.

Hiche (Cadet). Carillon 1756. Ensign at St. Foy. Wounded 1760.

Hugues, de (Captain). (May be Pean) Wounded St. Foy 1760.

Jacquot (Artillery officer). With Vergor at Beausejour. Leads Montcalm's boats toward William Henry 1757.

Joncaire, or Joncaire de Chabert, Daniel (Lieutenant). Born 1714 at Repentigny (d.1771). At Niagara c.1749. Served at Detroit as an Officer and Interpreter. Built Little Fort Niagara 1751.

Joncaire, Louis Thomas de. Seignior of Chabert. 1670-1739. Born St. Remi, Provence, France. Established and Commander at Niagara 1720-1730. Prisoner of Senecas.

Joncaire, Philippe de. Commander at Machault/Venango 1753. Representative to Cayugas and Senecas.

Jumonville, Joseph Coulon de Villiers, Sieur de (Ensign). 1718-1754. Born Vercheres, New France. 1739 expedition against Louisiana Indians. Served in Acadia. Killed 1754.

Labarre (Cadet, IL).

L'Arminac, Le Chevalier de (Lieutenant). Niagara 1759.

Labourque (Cadet). Braddock's defeat 1755. A lieutenant of the same name(La Bourque?) was also present (see Le Borque).

Labrevois (Lieutenant) Wounded at St. Foy 1760.

La Chapelle, Passerat de, (Captain). Entered army c. 1752. Lieutenant, Royal Artillery 1754. Arrived in Canada 1756. Oswego 1756. Lake Champlain 1757. Duquesne and battle against Grant 1758. Quebec 1759. Second in command at Detroit 1759-1760. Retreated to Louisiana. (Apparently, sometime during his Canadian service he was transfered to the marines.)

La Chauvignerie, Michel Maray de (Lieutenant). Ohio 1754. Commandant Logstown. Commandant Fort Machault 1757.

La Chauvignerie, Michel* Son of above. Captured 1757.

La Chevrotiere, Sieur de (Second Ensign).

La Colombiere (Captain). Scouted near Ft. Edward 1756.

La Colonnerie (Cadet). Carillon 1756.

La Corne, Louis Francois. 1703-1761. Born in Montreal. 1744 Captain. 1746 Acadia. 1753 Commander post of the west. Commanded militia brigade Willam Henry 1757. St. Foy, wounded 1760. Lost at sea 1761.

La Corne, St. Luc de, or **La Corne de St. Luc.**
1712-1784. Raid on Saratoga 1747. Served in
Seven Years War. Brother of Louis Francois.
Served as Indian agent. Wounded St. Foy 1760.

La Durantay (Ensign).

Lafontaine (Cadet). Carillon 1756.

La Framboise (Cadet). Braddock's defeat 1755.

La Mouelle (Lieutenant).

La Naudiere.* Carillon 1757.

Langis (probably Langy Montegron).

Langlade, Charles Michel de. Born at
Michilimackinac. Braddock's defeat 1755(?).
Raided near Fort Edward 1757. Plains of
Abraham.

Langy Montegron (Ensign). Winter expedition
1757. Raided near Fort Edward 1757. Fought
Rogers 1758. Wounded at Carillon 1758.

Lanoix (Senior Ensign). Carillon 1756.

La Noue (La Noye) (Lieutenant IL).

La Periere (Captain). Raided near William
Henry, fall 1756. Killed on the Plains of
Abraham 1759. A Lieutenant Boucher de la
Periere was commandant of La Presentation 1752.

La Perriere, La Perrie (Lieutenant) (May be La
Periere, above). Commandant Niagara 1754-1755.

Laperiere, Chevalier de (Ensign). Wounded at
St. Foy 1760.

La Peyrade (Ensign). Killed at Braddock's
defeat 1755.

La Plante. With Indians 1757.

La Saussaie or Saussaye. (Ensign). Ohio 1754. Killed near Fort Duquesne.

La Verandry, Louis Joseph de. 1717-1761. Son-in-law of Mezieres.

La Verendrye, Pierre Gaultier de Varenne, Sieur de (Captain). 1685-1749.

La Verendrye, Jean Baptiste. 1713-1736. Killed by western Indians.

La Verendrye, Pierre. 1714-1755. Cadet a'aiguillette, 1750.

La Verendrye, Francois. 1715-1794.

Le Verrier, Louis. Commandant Fort St. Joseph c.1757.

Le Borques (Lieutenant.) Second ensign Ft. Frontenac 1746. A man with this name and his two sons were with Celoron 1749. An ensign Le Borgne is in the Ohio country 1754. A Lt. La Bourque was wounded at Braddock's defeat 1755. A lieutenant (captain?) of this name was wounded at St. Foy 1760.

LeGardeur de St. Pierre, Jacques. (Captain). 1701-1755. Born near Montreal. Commanded expedition to the west 1750. Commander Fort Le Boeuf 1753. Killed in command of Indians for Dieskau 1755.

Lery, Joseph Gaspard Chaussegros de (Captain, artillery and engineer). 1721-1797. Born in Quebec, June 21. Second Ensign 1742, Ensign 1748, Lieutenant 1751, Captain and Cross of St. Louis 1757. Built Fort Beausejour and Gaspereau (Acadia). Served at Detroit 1749, and as second in command 1754. Ft. Duquesne 1755. Carillon 1756. Led expedition to attack Fort Bull 1756. Went to France and later returned to Canada.

Ligneris (Lignery?), Francois Marchand, Sieur de (Captain, 1751). 1704-1760. Commandant at Ouiatanon 1752. Braddock's defeat 1755. At Oswego 1756. Succeeds Dumas as commander of the Ohio, 1756. Mortally wounded at La Belle Famille 1759.

Ligneris (Captain) Captured on the Plains of Abraham 1759.

Lignery, Constant Le Marchand de (same as below?).

Lignery, Le Marchand de (Cadet).

Linctot (the elder) (Cadet). Braddock's defeat 1755.

Linctot (the younger) (Cadet). Braddock's defeat 1755.

Longueuil, Joseph Dominique Emmanel de (Senior Ensign). 1738-1807. Born Soulanges, Canada. Ohio 1754. A Lieutenant (Sieur de) Longueuil was at Detroit 1752.

Longueuil, Paul Joseph le Moyne (Lemoine), Chevalier de (Captain). 1701-1778. Born near Montreal. Commander at Detroit 1743-1749. Chevalier de St. Louis 1744. Commanded Iroqouis with Villier's party 1754. Governor Three Rivers 1757-1760. Went to France.

Longueville (Longueuil?) (Ensign). Commanded Hurons of Lorette with Villier's party 1754. Braddock's defeat 1755.

Lorimer, Sieur de (Junior). Raided near Ft. Herkimer 1758. A Captain of this name wounded at St. Foy 1760.

Loumier (Captain). With Indians 1757. Wounded 1760 Ste. Foy/Quebec.

Louvigny.

St. Luc de Mezieres, Charles Francis, Chevalier de Lepervanche (Captain). A Mezieres, de (Captain) was posted at Onyatanous (?). Lery states a Lieutenant of Louisbourg troops, M. de Meziere, arrived at Detroit in 1754, on his way to replace M. des Ligneris at Oyatannons (Ouiatenon). Wounded St. Foy 1760

Lusignan, Paul Louis (Captain, 1744). 1691-? Ensign 1722. Obtains seigniory in Missiskuoy Bay 1733. Commandant Ft. St. Joseph 1735. Back to Canada 1739. Commandant La Baye 1743. Lived with the "wild rice Indians" 1745. Commandant of St. Frederic, 1749. Commandant Carillon 1756. Commandant Isle aux Noix 1759. Commandant St John 1760.

Lusignan (Lieutenant). Artillery officer at Carillon 1756.

Macarty-Mactique, Barthelemy (Captain Louisiana/Illinois). Commandant Fort de Chartres c. 1750's.

Marin, Joseph (la Malgue). Born Montreal 1719. Son of Pierre Paul. Commandant at La Baye c.1753-1754. Oswego 1756. Raided near Fort Edward 1757. Fights Rogers 1758. Captured at La Belle Famille 1759. Goes to France after the war.

Marin, Pierre Paul, Sieur de (de la Malgue). Commandant La Baye 1739. Builder and commandant Fort Presque Isle. Died 1753

Meloise (Meloneze?), des (Senior Ensign). Pean expedition 1754. Carillon 1756. A Lieutenant (Chevalier de) of the Genadiers was killed at the Seige of Quebec 1760. An adjutant of the same name was wounded.

Mercier, (Captain, Canadian Artillery Commander). Part of Bigot group. Pean expedition 1754. Great Meadows 1754. Braddock's defeat 1755. Oswego 1756. Winter expedition to William Henry 1757. Carillon 1758. Quebec 1759.

Meziere, de (see St. Luc de Meziere).

Millon, Pierre Mathurin Sieur de (Ensign). Niagara 1746. Commandant La Baye 1749-1750, drowned in Fox River.

Mommidy (Lieutenant). Braddock's defeat 1755.

Moncours, Pierre Hertel de (Cadet).

Montarville (Cadet). Carillon 1756.

Montcourt (Possibly same as Moncour). Fought in Ohio country.

Montesson (Lieutenant). Commanded Abenakis with Villiers party 1754.

Montigny, Jacques Testard de (Captain). Second ensign at Niagara 1746. Ohio 1754. Second to Lery at Fort Bull. Commander of voyaguers at Oswego 1756. Ordered to Niagara 1758. Captured at La Belle Famille 1759. (In one entry Lery uses the name M. de Montigny Cournoyer. See Cournoyer.)

Montimidy (Cadet). Sick at Niagara 1754. Fought in Ohio country.

Morandiere (Cadet). Braddock's defeat 1755.

Morambert (Lieutenant).

Muy, Jacques Pierre Daneau, sieur de. 1695-1758. Commandant Fort St. Joseph. Order of St. Louis 1754. Commandant Detroit c. 1748-1758.

Muy (Cadet). Braddock's defeat 1755.

Neuvillette. Pean expedition 1754.

Nigon (Lieutenant). From France. Wounded at Carillon 1758.

Normanville (Cadet). With the Miamis 1754. Wounded at Braddock's defeat 1755.

Noyan, Pierre Jacques Payan de, Sieur de Charvis (Captain). Born c.1698. Commandant Detroit 1739, Frontenac 1758.

Noyas, de (Captain). May be Noyan. Commandant St. Frederic 1746.

Noyelle, Charles Joseph de. A lieutenant Desnoyelles (La Noix de Noyelle) was wounded at St. Foy 1760.

Noyelles, Nicolas Joseph Fleurmont de. 1695-1761. Born in Brittany, France. Came to Canada 1710. Commander at Detroit 1720, 1728, 1738-1741 (Note Noyan above). Commandant Ft. Miami and Fox campaign, 1730. Expedition to the west 1743. Town major at Three Rivers 1751. Returned to France.

Otlas or Otelas (Cadet). Served near Carillon 1758.

Pean, Michel Jean Hugues (Captain). Born St. Ours, New France. Marine ensign 1738. Captain 1750. Ohio and expedition to Michilimackinac 1754. Major Quebec 1756. Went to France and was put in Bastille due to investigation of Bigot group. Nephew of Contrecoeur.

Pecudy (Cadet). Braddock's defeat 1755.

Portneuf, Pierre Robineau, Chevalier de. 1708-1761. Born in Quebec. Ensign of marines 1750. Established fort at Toronto. Pean expedition 1754. Oswego 1756. Commandant at Presque Isle 1756-1759. Lost at sea while returning to France 1761.

Raymond, Charles, Chevalier de (Captain). Born in Perigord, c.1706. Came to Canada as ensign 1722. Commandant of Niagara twice and Fort Miamis. With Dieskau 1755. Winter expedition William Henry 1757. Carillon 1758. Returned to France in 1760.

Repentigny, Jean Baptiste Rene Legardeur de (Captain). Commandant at Sault St. Marie 1754. Ohio 1754, identified as a Captain of the Louisbourg Company (Lery). With Dieskau 1755. Commanded militia brigade 1757. May have been commandant and/or leaseholder at Kamanistigoya c. 1757. Quebec 1759. Commanded Montreal Battalion at St. Foy 1760.

Rigauville, Sieur de. Third in command at Detroit 1754-1755.

Rimbeault (Ensign). Ohio 1754.

Rocheblave, Philippe de (Cadet) Braddock's defeat 1755. Captured a small fort beyond Fort Cumberland 1756. Scout near Loyal Hannon (PA) 1758. Raid on Fort Pitt with Marin 1759. With French force at La Belle Famille 1759, was part of guard on canoes.

Rockloyade (Lieutenant). A cadet Roctorade was at Braddock's defeat 1755.

Rouilly, de. Carillon 1757. Officer commanding party attacked by Rogers, Jan. 1757, that led to first battle on snowshoes.

Sable, du (Ensign). Ohio 1754.

Sabrevois, Bleury (Ensign). Ohio 1754. Braddock's defeat 1755. Scouted south of Carillon 1758. A lieutenant of this name was wounded 1760 Ste. Foy/Quebec.

Sabrevois. Commandant Fort St. Frederic 1747.

Sacepecs (Cadet). A cadet named Saqueped was at Braddock's defeat 1755. Carillon 1756 (De Lery refers to <u>both</u> Sacepecs suggesting 2 related Cadets.)

Saceppe (Cadet a l'aiguillette). Detroit 1752. (May be the same as Sacepecs, above)

St. Blain (St. Blin), Du Verger de (Lieutenant). Raided near Ft. Cumberland 1757. A St. Blein was Commandant of Le Boeuf 1754-1755, 1757.

St. Cherre (Cadet). Braddock's defeat 1755.

St. Leu. Commanded Indians 1760.

St. Martin, Jean Jacques, Sieur de (Lieutenant). Pean expedition 1754. Raiding near Ft. William Henry 1756. Winter expedition William Henry 1757. Quebec 1759. Captain of Grenadiers St. Foy 1760, mortally wounded.

St. Ours, Francois Xavier de (Lieutenant). 1717-1759. Born in Canada. Commandant Sandoski 1752. Pean expedition 1754. A St. Ours was commandant at Ft. St. Joseph 1754. Winter expedition William Henry 1757. Commanded Canadian militia brigade at William Henry 1757. Wounded 1757. Special mention by Montcalm for service at Carillon, 1758. Killed on Plains of Abraham.

St. Ours (Ensign). (Probably the son of Francois) With Celeron 1749. Braddock's defeat 1755. Killed near Fort Duquesne.

St. Simon (Cadet). Braddock's defeat 1755.

St. Vincent (Captain). Order of St. Louis 1754.

Ste. Thereze, Hertel (Cadet).

Saumandre (Cadet).

Soanna (Cadet). Braddock's defeat 1755.

Surville, Richerville de (Lieutenant, IL(?)). Ohio 1754.

Tonty, Charles Henri Joseph de (Captain). Commandant La Baye 1738. Commandant Frontenac 1746.

Varennes (Lieutenant) Mortally wounded St. Foy 1760.

Vassan, de. (possibly Spanish) William Henry 1757. Commander at Niagara early 1758. Captured at La Belle Famille 1759. Wounded St. Foy 1760. Bastille (Bigot group).

Vaudreuil-Cavanal, Pierre de Rigaud, Marquis de. 1704-1778. Last Governor of Canada. Held commission as marine captain.

Vaudreuil, Sieur Rigaud de (Gov. of Trois Rivieres often commanded Colony troops.) 1703-1779.

Vercheres, Jean Baptiste Jarret de. Commandant La Baye 1747. Commandant at Ft. Frontenac 1752.

Vergor, Louis Du Pont de Chambon, Sieur de. c.1712-1763. Captain the the French Army. Came to Canada 1751, Captain that year. Commandant Fort Beausejour 1754. Surrendered post in 1755. Carillon 1756. Court martialed 1757, acquitted. Commanded post at Wolfe's cove the night of the English assault. Returned to France.

Vernay, Charles de la Roche (Captain). Born Tours, France, 1728. At Detroit 1755-1757.

Verney, Oliver de Roche (Captain). Senior marine at Niagara 1759.

Villaret. Court martialed with Vergor.

Villejoint (Senior Ensign). Carillon 1756.

Villemonde, Louis Lienard Sieur Beaujeu de. 1716-1802. Born in Montreal. Brother of Daniel. Lieutenant 1744, Captain 1751, Chevalier de St. Louis 1754. Carillon 1756 (?). Commandandant at Michilimackinac 1760.

Villiers, Louis Coulon de (Captain). Ensign at La Baye 1733. Commandant at Fort Miamis 1752. Brother of Jumonville. Acadia 1753-1754. Great Meadows (Fort Necessity) 1754. Oswego 1756. Led William Henry 1757. Wounded and captured at La Belle Famille 1759.

Villiers, Coulon de, Sieur. Town Major at Three Rivers died 1751.

Villiers, Francois de, Chevalier. (Lieutenant, LA) Brother of Louis and Jumonville. Captured Fort Granville (Lewiston, PA) 1756.

Villiers, Nicolas Antoine Coulan de (Captain). Commandant Fort St. Joseph 1730. Led a combined Canadian-Louisiana campaign agaist the Fox Indians in Illinois. Commandant La Baye 1731(?)-1733, killed by Indians. Father of Louis.

Villiers, Neyon de (Captain). Major, Fort de Chartres 1760.

Villiers (see Jumonville).

APPENDIX V

IMPORTED FOOD AT LOUISBOURG

From France

Almonds
Anchovies
Artichokes
Capers
Preserves (also West Indies)
Pickles
Goose legs
Spices
Kidney beans (also New England)
Figs
Cheese ("d'Hollands", "Gruyers")
Brandied fruits (also West Indies)
Tripe and pigs' ears
Seed
Oats
White herring
Olive oil
Oysters (also New England)
Ham
Vegetables (also Quebec)
Honey
Hazelnuts
Olives
Pepper
Plums ("Prunes"-although this is the French word for plum, this item may have been dried before shipment)
Raisins
Sardines
Sausages
Vinegar (also West Indies)
Grain ("farine"-meal) (also Acadia, New England, West Indies, and Quebec)
Grain ("Millet")
Cider (also New England)
Brandies (also West Indies)
Eaux sans Pareil?
Liqueurs
Liqueurs de Villes
Syrup ("Sirop de Capilaire", "Sirop d'Orgeat")

Wines (de Nantes, de Bordeaux, de Saintonge, de Frontignac, d'Espagne, d'Aubaque, de Navarre.)

From Quebec

Eels
Biscuits (also from France and New England; probably a hardtack or ships bread)
Cheese ("petit fromage")
Preserved herbs ("Herbes Sale") ("Sale" usually refers to preservation with salt. It may also have included dried foods)
Cod oil (also Acadia and New England)
Bacon or side pork, preserved ("Lard ou Lard Sale") (also Acadia, New England, and France)
Peas (also Acadia, New England, and France)
Salmon, preserved ("Saumon sale") (also Acadia)
Tobacco (also Acadia, New England, West Indies, and France)
Grain (Oats-"Avoine") (also Acadia and New England)
Syrup ("Sirop de Capelaire")
Wine (de Bordeaux)

From New England

Beets
"Biscuit au lait" (cookie?)
Fresh beef ("Boeuf frais")
Chocolate (also France and West Indies)
Cabbage
Pumpkin
Beans
Cheese ("fromage de pays"-a country cheese) (also from Quebec)
Turnip
Walnuts (also France)
Onions
Pears
Apples (also Quebec)
hog lard ("Saindoux lard")
Grain (hay-"Foin")
Grain (bran-"Son")
Beer (also France)
Lime juice and limes
Rum

From Acadia

Butter (also from New England, France, and the West Indies)
Beef, preserved ("Boeuf, vivand sale". Probably refers to salted beef for camp/military use) (also from France and New England)
Herring
Mackarel
Cod and ? ("Morue et Goberge" [a fish?]) (also New England and Quebec)
Bread (also New England and France)
Maple bread ("D'Erable en pain, en teste") (also West Indies and France)
Grain (Indian corn-"Ble d'Inde") (also New England)
Grain (Wheat-"Bled Froment")
Grain ("Jersau Pour Pigeons"- ? for pigeons)
Grain ("Ras"-Perhaps "ris" or "riz"-rice) (also Acadia, New England, West Indies, and France)

From the West Indies

Cocoa
Cheese ("Gruyers")
Molasses
Syrup
Sugar (raw, white, and common)
Coffee
Rum ("Guildive")
Liqueurs des Isle
Liqueurs de Provence
Wine (de Provence)

(no source)

Wine (de Renar, de Champagne, de Liqueur, de Cape Breton)

(Louisbourg 1981)

APPENDIX VI

FRENCH ARTILLERY CALIBER

Caliber in weight units (Livres) of solid iron shot was the system of measurement used for cannons. One Livre equals appromimatly 1.08 pounds.

Caliber	Bore dia. (inch)	Shot dia. (inch)
1	2.09	2.02
2	2.63	2.54
3	3.00	2.90
4*	3.29	3.19
6*	3.79	3.66
8*	4.17	4.03
12*	4.77	4.61
18*	5.46	5.27
24*	6.00	5.80
36*	6.89	6.64

Mortars were sized by bore diameter in linear measurement (pouce). One pouce equals 1.0658 inches.

POUCE	(INCHES)
6	6.4
7	7.5
8*	8.5
9	9.6
12*	12.8
16*	17 (Stone Throwing)

* "Standard" sizes

APPENDIX VII

FRENCH SMALL ARMS CALIBER

Caliber of small arms was measured by quantity of balls in one livre of lead.

CALIBER	BORE (inch)	BALL (inch)	NOTES
28	.577-.623	.563	Fusil de Chasse
26	.592-.637	.577	
24	.607-.651	.593	
23	.629-.673*	.599	
22	.644-.689	.615	
21	.652-.696*	.622	
20	.659-.703*	.622	Grenadier Fusil Pistolet
18	.689-.732	.652	Army musket Navy Boucanier
16	.732-.777	.681	
14	.755-.800	.711	Gros Boucanier (coupe)
12	.800-.844	.748	Gros Boucanier (entier)

*Interpolated

APPENDIX VIII

NATIVE AMERICAN ALLIES OF THE FRENCH

Officers and soldiers of the marines had a close relationship with Native Americans. Marine officers represented the colonial government in relations with the tribes. They also were assigned to lead the Indians in battle. Marine soldiers often served with the Indian warriors in raiding parties and, like the officers, dealt with them in the fur trade.

This list is gathered from various sources. No attempt has been made to refine the information and the sources, colonial Europeans, had an imperfect understanding of the relationships of native groups. European attempts to organize the native population were based on European social and cultural norms. They attempted to recognize a feudal hierarchy in terms of individuals and groups that was opposed to the total independence of families and individual among some native people. The European structure also failed to recognize the dynamic changes within populations as groups changed geographical location, realigned with other groups (Indian and European), competed for resources, and succumbed to change brought on by European material culture and religious missionaries.

Individual native groups are often identified by various names. The name may be a European name, the name the group used to refer to itself, or a corruption of the name by European writers. In the following list native groups are found under names familiar to twentieth-century readers with other names, spellings, clans, etc. following; For example, Chippewa (Anishinabe, Ojibwa, Saulters, Saulteaux, Monsoni, Ponarak). Where groups with the same name are separately identified by geographical location the reader should not assume that this indicates cultural differences between the groups. These designations often indicate that that particular group served as a "unit" during a military campaign or action.

Abenaki (Abenaquis, Amalecites, Androscoggin,
Canibas, Cowassek, Kennebec, Malecite, Micmac,
Montagnais Pennacook, Penobscot, Pequawket,
Ossippi, Sokoki, Sourikikos, Taconnet, Wewenoc)
Abenaki from Becancour
Abenaki from Missiskoui
Abenaki from Panouameski
Abenaki from St. Frances
Adai
Akamsea (Arkansas)
Algonkin (Weskarini, Algonquin, Nipissing,
Tetes de Boule)
Algonkin from Lake
Algonkin from Lac des deux Montagnes
Algonkin from Three Rivers
Assiniboine
Bayougoula (Baygoulas)
Boloxi
Cahokia (Kaoukias)
Cahokia from Mississippi River
Catawbas
Caughnewagos
Cayuga from Oswegatchie
Cherokee
Chetimacha
Chickasaw (Chicachas)
Chippewa (Anishinabe, Ojibwa, Saulters,
Saulteaux, Monsoni, Ponarak)
Chippewa from Castor
Chippewa from Chaoschimagan
Chippewa from Chequamegon
Chippewa from Detroit
Chippewa from Kakibonock'e
Chippewa from La Carpe
Chippewa from Rainy River
Chippewa from Thunder Bay
Chippewa from Vermilion River
Cree (Kiristinons)
Creeks
Dakota (Sioux, Nadowasieux, Nadoneseronons)
Dakota from Minnesota
Delaware (Lenape, Renappi, Minisink, Mumsi,
Munsee, Unami)
Delaware from Allegheny River
Fox (Mesquakie, Utugaming, Outagamis, Renard)
Fox from Mississippi

Fox from Prairie du Chien
Huron (Wyandot, Wendat, Andostes, Tionontathes)
Huron from Detroit
Huron from Lorette
Huron from Sandusky
Illinois (Liniouek, Cahokia, Chespoussa, Chinko, Coiracoentanon, Kaskaskia, Korakoenitanon, Michigamea, Moingwena, Mora, Omouahoas, Penhenguichius, Peoria, Peouarooua, Piankashaw, Pimiteoui, Roches, Tomoroa, Tapouro, Tapouara)
Illinois from Fort Chartres
Iowa of the western sea
Iroquois (Sinnekes, Agononciosi, Agniers, Cayuga, Goyongoins, Mingo, Mohawk, Oneida, Onondaga, Oneyoutes, Seneca, Tuscarora)
Iroquois from Allegheny River
Iroquois from Caughnawaga (Sault St. Louis)
Iroquois from Lac des deux Montagnes
Iroquois from La Presentation
Kadohadacho (Caddo, Cadodaquioux) from Louisiana
Kaskaskia (Kats, Caskaskia)
Kichai
Kickapoo from Fox River
Kickapoo from Mackinaw River
Kickapoo from Ouiatenon
Kickapoo from Rock River
Kickapoo from Vermilion River
Mahican (Loups, Mahuigaus)
Menominee (Folles Avoines, Malomines)
Menominee from Green Bay
Menominee from Le Chat
Menominee from L'orignal
Menominee from Menominee River
Menominee from St. Joseph River
Miami (Maumee, Twightee, Picts, Aoreyatanouns, Kilatica, Ouabona, Ouyatanons, Painkashaw, Pepikokia, Wea)
Miami from Detroit
Miami from Mississippi River
Miami from Ouiatenon
Miami from St. Joseph
Micmac (Micmaks, Canadiens, Gasesians, Sourikios)
Micmac from Acadia

Micmac from Amalecites
Mingo
Miscoutin (Mascouten)
Miscoutin from Detroit
Miscoutin from Fox River
Miscoutin from Highlands
Miscoutin from Mississippi River
Miscoutin from Ouiatenon
Miscoutin from Macinaw
Miscoutin from Rock River
Miscoutin from Vermilion River
Missisauga from Detroit
Missisauga from La Carpe
Missisauga from La Loutre
Missisauga from Toronto
Missouri
Mohawk from Akwesasne
Mohican
Moigwena
Mugulasha
Natchez
Natchitoches
Nipissing (Sorcerers)
Nipissing from Lac des deux Montagnes
Oneyoutes
Onondaga from Oswegatchie
Osage
Ottawa (Odawa, Waghanes, Cheveux Relevez)
Ottawa from Detroit
Ottawa from Kiscacous
Ottawa from La Fourche
Ottawa from L'isle au Castor
Ottawa from Magnonjan
Ottawa from Michilimackinac
Ottawa from Saginaw Bay
Ottawa from Sinago
Paducah
Pawnee
Penhenguichius
Peoria
Peouarooua
Piankashaw from Mississippi River
Piankashaw from Vincennes
Piankashaw from Highlands
Pimiteoui
Potawatomi (Pouteouatamis, Poux)

Potawatomi from Green Bay
Potawatomi from Michigan
Potawatomi from St. Joseph River
Potawatomi from Detroit
Roches
Seneca
Sauk (Sakis)
Sauk from Detroit
Sauk from Prairie du Chien
Shawnee (Shavanose, Shawanese, Kispotaka, Piqua, Chalagotghwa, Makujay, Talegwa, Kispoko, Hathawakela)
Shawnee from Allegheny river
Shawnee from Mississippi River
Taensa
Tamaroa (Tamarousa, Tamarouha)
Tamaroa from Mississippi River
Taouayas
Tawakoni
Teton
Tionontati (Nation du Petun, Tobacco)
Tunica
Wababakis (Passumaquoddy, Penobscot, Micmac, Maliseet)
Wea from Mississippi River
Wea from Ouiatenon
Wichita
Winnebago (Puans)
Winnebago from Green Bay
Winnebago from Lake Winnebago
Yscanis

APPENDIX IX

FRENCH DUTY CALLS FOR THE DRUM

L'assemblee (The Assembly)
The assembly was used to assemble the troops to receive orders.

La Generale (The General)
This called the men to take up their arms or to assemble the garrison.

La Diane, Le Revil au Bivouac (Reville)
Beaten at daybreak to wake the troops

La Charge (The Charge)
Ordered the troops to march at double time.

L'order (The Order)
Officer's call and NCO's call.

Le Drapeau (The Colors)
Used when rendering honors to the flags.

L'appel, Le Rappel (The Call)
Used to reassemble troops after action, to close ranks, and to parley with the enemy.

Aux Champs, Le Premier (To the Fields)
March beat. Marches des Mousquetaires and La Marche Francoise were also used.

La Retraite (The Retreat)
To cease combat and/or withdraw. Also used at the end of the day.

La Prier, La Messe (Call to Prayer)
Call to mass.

L'enterrement (The Burial)
For funerals. The drums were covered in black wool serge.

La Descente des Arms (Dismissal)
To dismiss troops or at the end of the day.

La Guarde (The Guard)
Used to change the guard.

La Fascine, La Breloque (The Fort)
Used to start or stop work and mess call.

La Ban (The Announcement)
Call to pay attention to orders or announcements.

APPENDIX X

A LIST OF FRENCH FORTS AND THEIR GARRISONS

This list represents posts that appear most often in the sources used for this study. There were many other posts, especially in the west, that maintained garrisons of probably less than twenty men. The size of the garrison would vary greatly depending on the season of the year and the needs of the grand campaign of any particular year.

FORT	GARRISON (YEAR)	SOURCE
QUEBEC (PQ)	2400 (c.1751)	Bonin
	12 companies (1754)	O'Callaghan
	300 (1754)	Forbes**
	(other troops in area)	
MONTREAL (PQ)	14 companies (1754)	O'Callaghan
	220* (1754)	Forbes**
	1200* (1759)	Bougainville
	(in vicinity)	
LOUISBOURG (NS)	16 companies (c.1741)	Fortier
	1017 (1758)	Knox
ST. FREDERIC (NY)	93 (1746)	O'Callaghan
	50 (1756)	Bougainville
	100* (winter 1756-57)	Bougainville
CARILLON (NY)	100* (winter 1756-57)	Bougainville
	150 (July 8, 1758)	Bougainville
	2651* (July 13, 1758)	Bougainville
CHAMBLY (PQ)	6 (1746)	O'Callaghan
ST. JEAN	14 (winter 1755-56)	Bougainville
	35 (winter 1756-57)	Bougainville
	50 (1756)	Bougainville
LA PRESENTATION	30	Roberts

FRONTENAC	35	(1746)	O'Callaghan
(ONT)	30	(1753)	Bonin
	110*	(1758)	Peckham
NIAGARA	37	(1746)	O'Callaghan
(NY)	80	(1753)	Bonin
	25	(1754)	Forbes**
	100*	(1754)	Bonin
	40 militia (1757)		Roberts
	183 (garr. 486, 1759)		Dunnigan
PRESQUE ISLE	150*	(1753)	Bonin
(Erie, PA)	30	(1754)	Forbes**
	50-60 (c.1757)		Bougainville
	200*	(1754)	Bonin
LE BOEUF	20	(1754)	Forbes**
(Waterford, PA)			
MACHAULT	200*	(1759)	O'Callaghan
(Franklin, PA)	50	(1757)	Chauvignerie
	40*		Washlaski 1984
DUQUESNE	1400*	(May 1754)	Forbes**
(Pittsburgh)	400	(October 1754)	Forbes**
	500	(1757)	Washlaski 1984
SANDOSKI	8	(c.1749)	Defievre
(near Port Clinton, OH)			
DETROIT	27	(c.1723)	Peyser
(MI)	35	(c.1749)	Defievre
MICHILIMACKINAC	27	(c.1723)	Peyser
(MI)	30	(1754)	Bonin
ST. JOSEPH	18	(c.1723)	Peyser
(Niles, MI)			

MIAMIS
(Ft. Wayne, IN)

OUIATENON
(West Lafayette, IN)

VINCENNES
(Vincennes, IN)

LA BAYE   18 (c.1723)   Peyser
(Green Bay, WI)

CHARTRES   6 companies   Bougainville
(Prairie du Rocher, IL) (These companies served
the entire Illinois region)

 * Marines and militia.
** Thomas Forbes's narrative is found in Gist.

TERMS

accouterments: Equipment directly involved in the use of the musket including a cartridge box, bayonet, and related scabbards and belts.

arpent: Ten (10) perches. 191.838 feet (English). In land measurement (square or carré), .845 acres.

artifact: A man-made item.

aune: A measurement of cloth, 47.244 English inches.

barrel band: A cylindrical metal strap that encircles the barrel and stock of a musket binding the two pieces together.

barrel channel: The groove in a gunstock in which the barrel rests.

battalion: Part of a regiment. An eighteenth-century military regiment would be composed of two or more battalions. Each battalion would be composed of eight to ten companies.

bayonet lug: A piece of metal attached to a gun barrel near the muzzle that engages a slot in the socket of the bayonet fixing it to the musket.

breechcloth: A garment made from a rectangular piece of cloth. It was worn between the legs, the ends passing over a belt in back and in front of the body.

bridle: Metal part used to strengthen a component of a gun lock.

bulb of percussion: A bulge found on a piece of flint that has been struck from a larger piece.

cadets: Men in training to be military officers. Marine cadets were young men from the Canadian nobility. Their rank was equivalent to a senior soldier.

caliber: A measure of the bore of a gun barrel equal to hundreths of an inch. Example: 50 calibre equals .50 inches (1/2 inch).

campaign: The activities of an army, in a specific geographical area, over a period of time. This can apply to the entire army such as the British Campaign of 1759 in North America. This would include separate campaigns such as Amherst's Lake Champlain campaign and Wolfe's campaign against Quebec.

cantonment: A place where an army camps for a long period of time. In the eighteenth century, armies seldom, if ever, campaigned in the winter. They would usually establish a winter cantonment.

carré: (see arpent)

Caudebec style hats: Caudebecs were fine Normandy hats. Marine hats defined as being of this style suggests that they followed the appearance of the Normandy hat but may well have been of lesser quality.

cock spring: The main, internal spring in a gun lock. It powers the cock (the part that holds the flint) forward allowing the flint to strike the frizzen causing sparks.

cockade: A decorative feature of a military hat made from ribbon. It usually took the form of a bow or a rosette.

condemned: a term used to signify that certain supplies were unfit for use and should be disposed.

TERMS

coureur de bois: Canadians who made a living in the Indian trade outside the "official" system (an outlaw). They spent most, if not all, of their lives on the frontier. Their lifestyle made them adept in guerilla warfare.

culverin: A type of cannon with above average range and accuracy.

denier: A division of the French monetary system equal to 1/12th of a sol.

duffle: A thick, coarse woolen cloth.

ecu: A silver coin (French) equal to 3 livres. Also known as a "crown".

fathom (or brasse): A division of marine measurement equal to 6 feet.

fatigue duty: Military work other than combat, guard, or drill. This would include: gathering wood, repairing fortifications, and moving supplies.

"fixed ammunition": Gunpowder and musket ball combined in a rolled paper cartridge.

flats: Sides of a gun barrel.

fowling pieces: Smoothbore firearms designed for hunting waterfowl and small game.

francs: A division of the French monetary system that replaced livres.

frizzen: The part of the gun lock that produced sparks when struck with the flint. This term is post-eighteenth century. Eighteenth-century terms for this part are hammer, and battery.

frizzen spring: An external spring which holds the frizzen in place until it is struck by the flint.

frog: The leather pieces that are attached to the waistbelt or shoulder sling to hold the bayonet and sword scabbards.

furniture: Metal parts of a firearm other than the lock, barrel, trigger, and ramrod. Includes the buttplate, sideplate, triggerguard, and ramrod pipes.

fusil a'domino: "A soldier's musket with the barrel attached to the stock by bands which superseded the older method of "pinning" in the early 1740's" (Ravenshear 1986:44) The term a'domino may indicate that the barrel and other metal parts of the musket were blued or browned.

fusil de chasse: A lightweight hunting gun.

fusilier: A soldier (private).

fuzee: A fusil, musket.

garrison: A military site, usually fortified. The group of men stationed at the site.

garter: A strap to hold up stockings or a strap worn over leggings below the knee. Military garters were leather with a buckle.

gauge: A method of describing the size of the bore of a gun barrel. The gauge is a number of balls in a pound. Example: A twenty gauge barrel would use balls of a size that twenty would weigh one pound.

gilberne: French term for a shoulder-slung cartridge box.

gorget: A crescent-shaped piece of metal worn at the throat as identification of an officer.

grenadiers: The elite soldiers of an eighteenth-century army.

gun worm: A device resembling a cork screw. It was used to remove a charge from a gun barrel.

habitants: The common people of French Canada.

hammer stall: A piece of leather that fit over the frizzen of a gun lock. It prevented accidental discharges.

hammer: The frizzen (18th century).

Huguenot: French Protestant.

inch (French): (see point)

intermittent fever: Undetermined common ailment in French Canada.

Iroquois Confederacy: Alliance of six Native American tribes living in New York. The confederacy included the Cayuga, Mohawk, Onandaga, Onieda, Tuscarora and Seneca.

kaolin: A white clay used for smoker's pipes.

King's livery: A particular design used on decorative lace for military musician's uniforms.

lace: A ribbon used to decorate military uniforms. The location and color of the lace would indicate the battalion and rank of the wearer.

lead or leather cap: A piece of material wrapped around a gunflint which helped hold the flint in the gunlock.

league: French measurement of distance. In the eighteenth century the marine league was equal to 1/20 of a degree of latitude (95 arpents, 3.45 English miles). The common league was 76 arpents or 2.76 English miles.

lignes: A division of French linear measurement equal to 1/12 of a French inch.

living history: a method of history interpretation involving interpreters using reproductions of historic material culture and depicting the lifeways of people during a particular historic period.

livres (currency): The standard French monetary unit in the eighteenth century.

livres (weight): A common French unit of weight in the eighteenth century equal to 1.08 English pounds.

lock plate: The part of a gun lock upon which the other components are attached.

Lodeve cloth: French cloth is identified by its place of manufacture.

Louisiana: The southern part of New France. It extended from the Gulf of Mexico to the southern end of Lake Michigan and included the southern part of present day Indiana.

lugs: Piece of metal attached to the bottom of a gun barrel which received the pins that held the barrel to the stock.

material culture: The man-made items (artifacts) of a particular group of people found in a particular time period. Example: Eighteenth-century French material culture.

mazamet: Twilled woolen serge with a nap on one side.

neck: The section of a bayonet which connects (and offsets) the blade from the socket.

nodule: The large irregular round flint from which other pieces are struck.

octagon-to-round: A gun barrel with eight sides extending a short distance from the breech then becoming round to the muzzle.

TERMS

pan: The part of the gun lock that holds the priming powder.

pan brush: A small brush used to clean the pan of a flintlock.

pan cover: Part of the frizzen, located at the base, that is perpendicular to the frizzen face. When in the firing position the cover closes the pan protecting the powder. When the frizzen is struck the cover is lifted to expose the powder to the spark.

parade: The formation of troops for inspection or review.

patched ball: A piece of cloth wrapped around the ball creates a seal with the interior of the barrel. This would provide superior performance. This is in contrast to using a military paper cartridge which would speed the loading process but would allow much of the propellant gases to escape around the projectile.

perche: Three (3) toise, 19.184 feet.

pied: A division of French linear measurement equal to 12.79 English inches.

pins: Pieces of wire that held the barrel to the stock of a firearm.

point: .0074 inches (English).

poll axe: A hatchet that had a head for driving nails as well as a cutting blade.

portage: The process of carrying a watercraft and cargo on land to avoid a dangerous rapids or to get from a lake or river to another where there is no connecting waterway.

pounce: A division of French linear measurement equal to 1/12th of a pied.

pounder: The system of classifying cannon by the weight of the cannon ball. Example: A 12-pounder used a 12-pound ball.

powder measure: A device to insure a consistent amount of gunpowder is used in loading a firearm.

powder quality: The power produced by a given amount of eighteenth-century gunpowder would vary from lot to lot. Consequently, a soldier receiving cartridges produced from two lots of powder might find them containing very different amounts of powder.

primary sources: Historical documents or illustrations including, journals, diaries, military record books, personal letters, paintings, sketches etc., prepared by participants in specific events or their contemporaries.

proofmark: A symbol stamped, or otherwise applied, on an item to signify it has been inspected and meets contractual specifications.

quintals: 100 French pounds, equal to approximately 108 English pounds.

ramrod: Rod of wood or metal used to push a ball or other projectile down the gun barrel.

ramrod pipes: Metal tubes attached to the bottom of a gun stock providing a place to carry the ramrod.

Rangers: Term used for scouts who moved (ranged) ahead of an army to guard against attack and collect intelligence. Rangers were skilled at irregular warfare.

reenactors: Participants in living history programs.

regiments: The primary military unit in the eighteenth century. It was made up of two or more battalions. Individual battalions often served separately.

regular: A trained soldier of a national army. He served on a permanent basis for a fixed number of years. This is in contrast to the militiaman who was a civilian obligated to serve in time of need in the area in which he lived.

rites of passage: Ceremonies or tasks performed by an individual allowing him/her to be part of a group.

Saint Etienne: A French military manufacturing armory.

sea service/shipboard marines: In addition to troops for colony service the Ministry of the Marine provided men for French ships who provided ship security and would fight in naval actions.

side plate: A metal plate inletted in the stock of a weapon opposite the lock. It protects the stock from the heads of the lock screws.

sling swivels: Metal rings attached to the musket stock on which the gun sling was mounted.

socket: Part of the bayonet that fit over the muzzle of the musket.

sol (sous): Unit of French currency equal to 1/20th of a livre.

spalls: Pieces of flint struck from a nodule that would be worked into an individual gunflint. Contrasts with the technique of striking off a long blade that would be broken into individual gunflints.

surgeon: A medical person with less training than a physician.

swivels: Small cannon mounted on a wall of a fortification by means of a yoke and pin.

tang: The end of a firearm's butt plate, triggerguard, or breechplug.
tenon: (same as lug).

thimbles: (same as ramrod pipe)

trade cloth: Cloth used in the Indian trade including wool, linen, and cotton.

trigger guard: The metal piece that bows over and protects a weapons trigger.

Tulle: French arms manufactory that supplied most of the arms purchased by the Ministry of Marine.

turn backs: Eighteenth-century military fashion of connecting the bottom corners of the side panels of uniform coats.

vent pick: Piece of wire used to clear the touchhole of a musket.

victals: Eighteenth-century term for food.

voyageurs: Canadian boatmen engaged in the fur trade.

wedding band: Grooves around a gunbarrel. Common on octagon-to-round barrels.

BIBLIOGRAPHY

REFERENCES CITED AND CONSULTED

Acker, Kim. "The French Capote". *Newsletter for Voyaguers*. Vol. 5, No. 1, 1982.

Adams, Blaine. "The Construction and Occupation of the Barracks of the King's Bastion at Louisbourg." *Contributions from the Fortress of Louisbourg*, No. 3. Parks Canada, 1978.

Adney, Edwin Tappen and Howard I. Chapelle. *The Bark Canoes and Skin Boats of North America*. Washington D.C.: Smithsonian Institution, 1964.

Alberts, Robert C. *The Most Extraodinary Adventures of Major Robert Stobo*. Boston: Houghton Mifflin Co., 1965.

Anderson, Dean L. "Variability in Trade at French Outposts During the Eighteenth Century." Paper presented at the Conference on French Colonial Archaeology. Springfield, Illinois. April 8-9, 1988.

Anderson, Fannie. *Doctors Under Three Flags*. Detroit: Wayne State University Press, 1951.

Anderson, Jay. *Time Machines, The World of Living History*. Nashville: The American Association for State and Local History, 1984.

Anderson, Stephen K. "Le Haversac." *Journal of the Forces of Montcalm and Wolfe*. Vol. 1, No. 3, 1988.

_____. "18th Century Weight and Measurement Conversions." *Journal of the Forces of Montcalm and Wolfe*. Vol. 1, No. 4, 1988.

Armour, David A. *Made in Mackinac. Crafts at Fort Michilimackinac.* Illustrated Vignettes Series, No. 8. Mackinac Island, Michigan: Mackinac Island State Park Commission, 1966.

Bailey, Kenneth P., editor. *Journal of Joseph Marin.* Published by Kenneth P. Bailey, 1975.

Barth, Claire Hoffman. "French Christmas Customs." *Newsletter of the Forces of Montcalm and Wolfe.* Vol. 2, No. 2, 1985.

Bonin, Jolicoeur Charles. *Travels in New France by J.C.B.* S.K. Stevens, Donald H. Kent, and Emma Edith Woods, Editors. Harrisburg: Pennsylvania Historical Commission, 1941.

Bouchard, Russel. *Les Fusils de Tulle en Nouvelle France 1691-1741.* Chicoutimi, Quebec: Journal des Armes enr., 1980.

Bougainville, Louis Antoine de. *Adventure in the Wilderness.* The American Journals of Louis Antonie de Bougainville 1756-1760. Edward P. Hamilton, editor and translator. Norman: University of Oklahoma Press, 1964.

_____. "French Posts in the West." *Journal of the Forces of Montcalm and Wolfe.* Vol. 3, No. 2, 1990.

Bourlamarque, Louis Antoine de. Bourlamarque Papers, Vol. 6, 2nd part (1756-60). Public Archives of Canada.

Brain, Jeffery P. *Tunica Treasure.* Cambridge: Harvard University, 1979.

Brown, Craig. *The Illustrated History of Canada.* Toronto: Lester and Orpen Dennys Ltd., 1987.

BIBLIOGRAPHY

Brown, Lloyd A. *Early Maps of the Ohio Valley, a Selection of Maps, Plans, and Views made by Indians and Colonials from 1763 to 1783.* Pittsburgh: University of Pittsburgh Press, 1959.

Brown, M.L. *Firearms in Colonial America.* Washington: Smithsonian Institution Press, 1980.

Brown, Margaret Kimball and Lawrie Cena Dean, editors. *The Village of Chartres in Colonial Illinois 1720-1763.* New Orleans: Polyanthos, Inc., 1977.

Buchmann, Randall C., editor. *The Historic Indian in Ohio.* Columbus: Ohio Historical Society, 1976.

Campau, Jean Bte as greffier (court clerk). Judicial Process at Detroit against Francois Soisron dit St-Francois, Henry d'Avoud La Fonde, Esquire acuuvais dit L'Eveille accused of the crime of desertion and rebellion. 10 Jan. 1752.

Cardin, Richard E. "Early Blacks in New France." *Journal of the Forces of Montcalm and Wolfe.* Vol. 1, No. 4, 1988.

_____. "The Mysterious French Marine." *Compagnie Franche de la Marine du Detroit Newsletter.* May 1988.

_____. "Joseph Gaspard Chaussegros de Lery." *Journal of the Forces of Montcalm and Wolfe.* Vol. 1, No. 2, 1988.

_____. "French Marine Flags in Canada." *Journal of the Forces of Montcalm and Wolfe.* Vol. 3, No. 1, 1990.

Chapelle, Howard I. *American Small Sailing Craft.* New York: W.W. Norton, 1951.

Chartrand, Rene. *The French Soldier in Colonial America*. Historical Arms Series. No. 18. Ottawa: Museum Restoration Service, 1984.

_____. *Louis XIV's Army*. Men at Arms Series. London: Osprey, 1988.

Christofferson, David J. *Batteau, Battoe, A Pictorial Collection*. Vol. I. St. Paul: Fox in a Circle Productions, 1986.

_____. *Batteau, Battoe*. Vol. II. St. Paul: Fox in a Circle Productions, 1987.

Costain, Thomas B. *The White and the Gold*. Garden City: Doubleday and Company, Inc., 1954.

Coulter, Jon. "The Tulle, Fusil de Chasse." *Muzzle Blasts*, June 1985.

Deetz, James. *In Small Things Forgotten*. Garden City: Anchor Books, 1977.

De Briquet, M. *Code Militaire, ou Compilation des Ordonnances des Rois de France, Concernans les Gens de Guerre*. Paris: Chez Durand, 1761.

De Lery, Gaspard-Joseph Chaussegros. *Journal of Chaussegros de Lery*. Harrisburg: Pennsylvania Historical Commission, 1940

_____. (De Lery diary May 8th to July 2nd, 1756) in, *The Bulletin of the Fort Ticoneroga Museum*, n.d.

Derleth, August. *Vincennes: Portal to the West*. Englewood Cliffs, NJ: Prentice-Hall, Inc., 1968.

De Ville, Winston. *French Troops in the Mississippi Valley and on the Gulf Coast: 1745*. Ville Platte, Louisiana, 1986.

BIBLIOGRAPHY

Devine, Ed. "Le Canonniers-Bombadiers, Le Compagnie Franche De La Marine Of His Most Christian Majesty King Louis XV." *Journal and Newsletter, Seven Years War Association*. Vol. 5, No. 2, 1990.

Douville, Raymond and Jacques-Donat Casanova. *Daily Life in Early Canada*. New York: Macmillan, 1968.

Diderot, Denis. *A Diderot Pictorial Encyclopedia of Trades and Industry*. Charles C. Gillespie, editor. New York: Dover, 1959.

Downes, Randolph C. *Council Fires on the Upper Ohio*. Pittsburgh: University of Pittsburgh Press, 1968.

Dunnigan, Brian Leigh. *Seige 1759. The Campaign Against Niagara*. Youngstown, N.Y.: Old Fort Niagara Assn., 1986.

_____. *Glorius Old Relic. The French Castle and Old Fort Niagara*. Youngstown, N.Y.: Old Fort Niagara Assn., 1987.

Eccles, W.J. *France in America*. Fitzhenry and Whiteside, Ltd., 1972.

_____. *The Canadian Frontier 1534-1760*. Albuquerque: University of New Mexico Press, 1974.

_____. "The Social, Economic and Political Significance of the Military Establishment in New France." *Essays on New France*. Toronto: Oxford University Press, 1987.

Egli, Bruce J. "A Shirt of Roussi Cloth." *F&I War*. Vol. 1, No. 1, 1982.

_____. "French Marine Uniforms in North America." *F&I War*. Vol. 2, No. 2, 1984.

Encyclopedia Britannica, or a Dictionary of Arts and Sciences. 3 vols. Edinburgh: A. Bell and C. Macfarquhar, 1769-1771.

Farmer, Dennis P. "The French Model 1728 Musket." *Old Fort Niagara Newsletter,* 1989.

Fortier, Margaret. *Eighteenth Century French Drumming.* Fortress of Louisbourg, 1977.

Fredrickson, N. Jaye. *The Covenant Chain. Indian Ceremonial and Trade Silver.* Ottawa: National Museums of Canada, 1980.

Fregault, Guy. *Canada: the war of conquest.* Toronto: Oxford University Press, 1969.

Funcken, Liliane and Fred Funcken. *The Lace Wars.* Part 1. Ward Lock Ltd. 1977.

Galbreath, C.B. *Expedition of Cerloron to the Ohio Country in 1749.* Columbus, Ohio: F.J. Heer Printing Co. 1921.

Gallup, Andy. "Boats Used in the Lake Champlain Campaigns of 1758 & 1759." *Journal of the Forces of Montcalm and Wolfe.* Vol. 3, No. 2, 1990.

Gist, Christopher. *Christopher Gist's Journals.* New York: Argonaut Press Ltd, 1966.

Gilman, Carolyn. *Where Two Worlds Meet, The Great Lakes Fur Trade.* St. Paul: Minnesota Historical Society, 1982.

Good, Mary Elizabeth. *Guebert Site: An 18th Century, Historic Kaskaskia Indian Village in Randolph Co. IL.* The Central States Archaeological Societies, Inc., 1972.

Gooding, S. James. *An Introduction to British Artillery in North America.* Ottawa: Museum Restoration Service, 1965.

BIBLIOGRAPHY 255

Gousse, Andre. Letter to D.F. Shaffer concerning Noiret (marine). October 23, 1991.

_____. Letter to D. Shaffer concerning musket tools and French ceramics. 1992.

Gowing, Lawrence. *Paintings in the Louvre*. New York: Stewart, Tobori, and Chang,. 1987.

Graves, Donald E. *French Military Terminology 1670-1815. A Technical Glossary*. The New Brunswick Museum, 1979.

Gringhuis, Dirk. *In Grey-White and Blue. French Troops at Fort Michilimackinac. 1715-1760*. Mackinac History Vignette Leaflet. No. 12. Mackinac Island, Michigan: Mackinac Island State Park Commission, 1969.

_____. *Indian Costume at Mackinac: Seventeenth and Eighteenth Century*. Illustrated Vignette Series Vol. II, No. 1. Mackinac Island, Michigan: Mackinac Island State Park Commission, 1972.

Hagerty, Gilbert. *Massacre at Fort Bull, the DeLery Expedition Against Onieda Carry 1756*. Providence: Mobray Co., 1971.

Hamilton, Charles. *Braddock's Defeat*. Norman: University of Oklahoma Press, 1959.

Hamilton, Edward P. *The French and Indian Wars*. Garden City: Doubleday and Company, Inc., 1962.

_____. *The French Army in America and The Musketry Drill of 1755*. Historical Arms Series. No. 7. Ottawa: Museum Restoration Service, 1967.

Hamilton, T.M. *Early Indian Trade Guns: 1625-1775*. Contributions of the Museum of the Great Plains, No. 3. Lawton, Oklahoma. 1968.

_____. *Firearms on the Frontier: Guns at Fort Michilimackinac, 1715-1781*. Reports in Mackinac History and Archaeology. No. 5. Mackinac Island State Park Commission, 1976.

_____. *Colonial Frontier Guns*. Chadron, Nebraska: The Fur Press, 1980.

_____. *Trade Guns*. Union City, Tennessee: Pioneer Press, 1982.

Hamilton, T.M. and Bruce W. Fry. "A Survey of Louisbourg Gunflints." *Canadian Historic Sites: Occasional Papers in Archaeology and History*, No. 12. Ottawa: National Historic Sites Service, 1975.

Hanson, James A. *Voyager's Sketchbook*. Chadron, Nebraska: The Fur Press, 1981.

_____. *The Long Hunter's Sketch Book*. Chadron, Nebraska: The Fur Press, 1983.

Hargrave, Catherine Perry. *A History of Playing Cards and Bibliography of Cards and Gaming*. New York: Dover, 1966.

Harrington, J. C. *New Lights on Washington's Fort Necessity*. Richmond: The Eastern National Park and Monument Association, 1957.

Hauser, Judith Ann. *Jesuit Rings from Fort Michilimackinac and Other European Contact Sites*. Mackinac Island, Michigan: Mackinac Island State Park Commission, 1982.

Havighurst, Walter. *Three Flags at the Straits*. Englewood Cliffs, N.J.: Prentice Hall, Inc., 1966.

Held, Robert. *The Age of Firearms, A Pictorial History*. Northfield, IL: The Gun Digest Co., 1970.

BIBLIOGRAPHY

Heldman, Donald P. "Coins at Michilimackinac." *Historical Archaeology.* Vol. 14, 1979.

Hicks, Major James E. *French Military Weapons 1717-1938.* N. Flayderman and Co., 1964.

Hill, R. Douglas. Letter to D. Shaffer concerning medical instruments. December 30, 1991.

_____. Letter to D. Shaffer concerning medical instruments. January 13, 1992.

Houlding, J.A. *French Arms Drill of the 18th Century.* Historical Arms Series. No. 19. Ottawa, Ontario: Museum Restoration Service, 1988.

Hughes, Quentin. *Military Architecture.* New York: St. Martin's Press, 1974.

Hupp, Nancy. "French Log Home in New France." *Newsletter of the Forces of Montcalm and Wolfe.* Vol. 1, No. 3, 1985.

Innis, Harold A. *The Fur Trade in Canada.* Toronto: University of Toronto Press, 1970.

Jacobs, Wilber R. *Wilderness Politics and Indian Gifts: The Northern Colonial Frontier, 1748-1763.* Lincoln: University of Nebraska Press, 1950.

Jenkins, Kathleen. *Montreal, Island City of the St. Lawrence.* Garden City: Doubleday and Company, Inc., 1966.

Johnson, Mary Moyars, Judy Forbes, and Kathy Delany. *Historic Colonial French Dress.* West Lafayette, IN: Ouabache Press, 1982.

Johnson, Michael G. *American Woodland Indians.* London: Osprey Publishing, Ltd., 1990.

Kalm, Peter. *Travels in North America, 1748-1751.* New York: Dover, 1987.

Kastner, George. *Manuel General de Musique Militaire, A L'usage De Armees Francaises.* (Minkoff Reprint.) 1848.

Kauffman, Henry J. *American Axes, A Survey of Their Development and Their Makers.* Battleboro, Vt.: The Stephen Greene Press, 1972.

Kavanagh, Martin. *La Verendrye, His Life and Times.* Brandon, Manitoba: M. Kavanagh, 1968.

Keefe, James F. "The Inventory of Fort Des Chartres." *Muzzleloader.* Vol. 18, No.6, 1992.

Keene, David. "Mercantilism and the Structure of Colonial Settlements in Eighteenth Century New France." Unpublished Manuscript. n.d.

Kellogg, Louise P., Editor and Translator. "La Chapelle's Remarkable Retreat Through the Mississippi Valley, 1760-61." *Mississippi Valley Historical Review.* Vol. 22, 1936.

Kent, Donald H. *The French Invasion of Western Pennsylvania 1753.* Pennsylvania Historical and Museum Commission. Harrisburg: Commonwealth of Pennsylvania, 1981.

Kent, Timothy J. Letter to D. Shaffer concerning dugout canoes. January 31, 1992.

Klinger, Robert L. *Sketchbook 76.* Arlington, Virginia: Robert L. Klinger, 1967.

Kennett, Lee. *The French Armies in the Seven Years War.* Durham, NC: Duke University Press, 1967.

BIBLIOGRAPHY

Knox, John. *The Journal of Captain John Knox.*
  Vols. 1 and 3. New York: Greenwood Press,
  1968.

_____. *The Seige of Quebec.* Mississauga,
  Ontario: Pendragon House, 1980.

Kopperman, Paul E. *Braddock at the Monongahela.*
  Pittsburgh: University of Pittsburgh
  Press, 1977.

Kraft, Herbert, editor. *The Lenape Indian, A
  Symposium.* Archaeological Research Center.
  South Orange, NJ: Seton Hall University,
  1984.

Kubiak, William J. *Great Lakes Indians, A
  Pictorial Guide.* New York: Bonanza Books,
  1970.

Kuck, Robert. *Tomahawks Illustrated.* Xenia,
  Ohio: Aldine Printing Co, 1977.

Le Verendrye. *Journals of La Verendrye.*
  New York: Greenwood Press, 1968.

LeBlond, Guillaume. *A Treatise of Artillery.*
  London: E. Cave, 1746

Leliepvre, Eugene and Rene Chartrand. "French
  Colonial Infantry and Artillery, 1740
  -1763." *Military Uniforms in America; The
  Era of the American Revolution, 1755-1795.*
  San Rafeo: Presidio Press, 1974.

Lenk, Torsten. *The Flintlock: Its Origin and
  Development.* New York: Bramhall House,
  1965.

Lewis, W.H. *The Splendid Century, Life in the
  France of Louis XIV.* New York: Morrow,
  1971.

Lloyd, Christopher. *The Capture of Quebec.* New
  York: MacMillian Co., 1959.

Louisbourg, Fortress of. "Soldier's Manual."
    Unpublished. 1981.

McLennan, J.S. *Louisbourg from its Foundation
    to its Fall.* Toronto: The Bryant Press,
    Ltd., 1983.

Macdonald, Robert R. *The Sun King Louis XIV and
    the New World.* The Louisiana Museum
    Foundation, 1984.

Manucy, Albert. *Artillery Through the Ages.*
    Washington, DC: National Park Service,
    1949.

Mann, Sylvia. *Collecting Playing Cards.* New
    York: Crown Publ., 1966.

Margerand, J. *Armement et Equipment de
    L'Infanterie Francais de XVI e au XX e
    Siecle.* Paris. n.d.

May, George S. *The Mess at Mackinac.* Mackinac
    Island, Michigan: Mackinac Island State
    Park Commission, 1964.

Mitford, Nancy. *The Sun King. Louis XIV at
    Versailles.* Crescent Books,. 1982.

Mollo, John. *Uniforms of the Seven Years War
    1756 -1763.* New York: Hippocrene Books,
    1977.

Moogk, Peter N. *Building a House in New France.*
    Toronto: McClelland and Stewart Limited,
    1977.

Moore, James T. *Indian and Jesuit a Seventeenth
    Century Encounter.* Chicago: Loyola
    University Press, 1982.

Moore, Warren. *Weapons of the American
    Revolution.* New York: Promentory Press,
    1967.

BIBLIOGRAPHY

Morse, Eric W. *Fur Trade Routes of Canada, Then and Now.* Toronto: University of Toronto Press, 1979.

Muller, John. *A Treatise Containing the Elementary Part of Fortification.* Ottawa: Museum Restoration Service, 1968.

Myers, Robert C. and Joseph L. Peyser. "Four Flags Over Fort St. Joseph." *Michigan History Magazine,* 1991.

Nemnich, Philip Andrew. *Universal European Dictionary of Merchandise.* 1799.

Neumann, George C. and Frank J. Kravic. *Collector's Encyclopedia of the American Revolution.* Harrisburg: Stackpole, 1975.

Neumann, George C. *The History of the Weapons of the American Revolution.* New York: Bonanza Books, 1967.

_____. *Swords and Blades of the American Revolution.* Harrisburg: Stackpole, 1973.

Newsletter for Voyaguers. Vol. 5, No. 1, 1982.

Nicolai, Martin L. "A Different Kind of Courage: The French Military and the Canadian Irregular Soldier during the Seven Years' War." *Canadian Historical Review.* Vol. LXX, No. 1. Toronto: University of Toronto Press, 1989.

Nixon, David D. "Powder Horn." *Newsletter for Voyageurs.* Vol. 3, No. 2, 1980.

Noble, Vergil E. "Discovering Fort Ouiatenon: Its History and Archaeology." *Tippecanoe Tales.* No. 6. Lafayette, IN: Tippecanoe County Historical Assn. n.d.

Nute, Grace Lee. *The Voyaguer.* St. Paul: Minnesota Historical Society, 1955.

O'Callaghan, E.B., editor. *Documents Relative to the Colonial History of the State of New York*. Vols. IX and X. New York: AMS Press, 1969.

O'Meara, Walter. *Guns at the Forks*. Englewood Cliffs, N.J.: Prentice-Hall Inc., 1965.

Osgood, William and Leslie Hurley. *The Snowshoe Book*. Brattleboro, Vermont: The Stephen Greene Press, 1975.

Papiers La Pause. Regulations for supplying the French regulars in Canada. 1754.

Pargellis, Stanley. *Military Affairs in North America. 1748-1765*. Archon Books, 1969.

Peck, Anne Merriman. *The Pagent of Canadian History*. David McKay Co., Inc., 1963.

Peckham, Howard H. *The Colonial Wars*. Chicago: University of Chicago Press, 1964.

Penny, David W. *Great Lakes Indian Art*. Detroit: Wayne State University Press, 1989.

Petard, Michel and Rene Chartrand. "L'Homme de 1690. L'infantrie des Colonies en Nouvelle France." *Gazette des Uniforms*. No. 28. Nov.-Dec. 1975.

Petard, Michel. "L'Homme de 1751. Les Compagnies Franches de la Marine." *Gazette des Uniforms*. No. 34. Nov.-Dec. 1976.

_____. *Equipments Militaires de 1600 a' 1750*. Tome I. 1984.

_____. *Equipments Militaires de 1600 a' 1750*. Tome II. 1985.

Petersen, Eugene T. *Clay Pipes: A Footnote to Mackinac's History.* Illustrated Vignettes Series, No. 1. Mackinac Island, Michigan: Mackinac Island State Park Commission, 1963.

_____. *Gentlemen on the Frontier, A Pictorial Record of the Culture of Michilimackinac.* Mackinac Island, Michigan: Mackinac Island State Park Commission, 1964.

_____. *France at Mackinac.* Mackinac Island, Michigan: Mackinac Island State Park Commission, 1968.

Peterson, Harold L. *Arms and Armor in Colonial America 1526-1783.* Bramwell House, 1956.

_____. *American Indian Tomahawks.* Museum of the American Indian. Heye Foundation. 1965.

_____. *Round Shot and Rammers.* Harrisburg: Stackpole Books, 1969.

Pick, Albert. *Standard Catalog of World Paper Money.* Iola, WI: Krause Publications, 1990.

Pope, Tukemas/Hank. *Shawnee Nation United Remnant Band - A Brief History of the Present Day Shawnee Tribe of Ohio.* 1989.

Porterie, M. de la. *Institutions Militarires pour la Cavalerie et les Dragons.* Paris: Chez Guillyn, 1754.

Protz, Bill and Jim Marsala. "Summary of Some Points of Interest from the Rene Chartrand Seminar. July 1, 1989." *Journal of the Forces of Montcalm and Wolfe.* Vol. 2, No. 2, 1989.

Proulx, Gilles. "Study of Military Costume at Louisburg." (Unpublished) 1971.

Ravenshear, Kit. "The Gunsmith as Detective - Tracing the Tulle Contract Marine Musket." *Man at Arms*. Vol. 1, No. 3, 1979.

_____. "The Guns of Tulle. Some Updated Information and Comment." *Muzzleloader*. March-April 1989.

Riddel, William Renwick. "A Late Official Report on the French Posts in the Northern Part of North America." *Michigan History Magazine*. Vol. XVI, No. 1. Lansing: Michigan Historical Commission, 1932.

Roberts, Robert B. *New York's Forts in the Revolution*. Cranbury, NJ: Associated University Presses, Inc., 1980.

Robinson, Percy J. *Toronto Under the French Regime*. Toronto: University of Toronto Press, 1965.

Rogers, Robert. *Journals of Major Robert Rogers*. Readex Microprint, 1966.

Roosevelt, George E. "Dos Blanc." *F&I War*. Vol. 1, No. 3, 1983.

Russell, Carl P. *Firearms, Traps, and Tools of the Mountain Men*. Albuquerque: University of New Mexico Press, 1967

_____. *Guns on the Early Frontier*. Lincoln: University of Nebraska Press, 1980.

Saint-Remy, Pierre. *Memoires d'Artillerie*. 1697.

_____. *Memoires d'Artillerie*. 1702.

Scott, Elizabeth M. *French Subsistence at Fort Michilimackinac 1715-1781. The Clergy and the Traders*. Archaeological Completion Report Series, No. 9. Mackinac Island State Park Commission, 1985.

BIBLIOGRAPHY

Seguin, Robert-Lionel. *Les Divertissements en Nouvelle France.* Bulletin No. 227. Ottawa: Musee National du Canada, 1968.

_____. *Le Costume Civil en Nouvelle France.* Bulletin No. 215. Ottawa: Musee National du Canada, 1968.

Seno, William Joseph. *Up Country, Voices from the Great Lakes.* Minoqua, WI: Heartland Press, 1989.

Shaffer, Donald F. "The French Paper Cartridge." *Journal of the Forces of Montcalm and Wolfe.* Vol. 2, No. 1, 1989.

_____. "Le Rois Orders." *Journal of the Forces of Montcalm and Wolfe.* Vol. 3, No. 3, 1990.

_____. "Caliber vs: Calibre - Artillery." *Journal of the Forces of Montcalm and Wolfe.* Vol. 4, No. 1, 1991.

Smith, James. *Scoouwa: James Smith's Indian Captivity Narrative.* Columbus: Ohio Historical Society, 1978.

Stanley, George F.G. *Canada's Soldiers, The Military History of an Unmilitary People.* Toronto: The MacMillian Company of Canada Limited, 1960.

_____. *New France, The Last Phase 1744-1760.* Toronto: McClelland and Stewart Limited, 1968.

Steele, I.K. *Guerilla and Grenadiers, The Struggle for Canada 1689-1760.* Toronto: The Ryerson Press, 1969.

Steiner, Roger J. *The New College French and English Dictionary.* New York: Amsco School Publications, 1972.

Stevens, Sylvester K. and Donald H. Kent. *Wilderness Chronicles of Northwestern Pennsylvania*. Harrisburg: Pennsylvania Historical Commission, 1941.

Stone, Lyle M. *Fort Michilimackinac 1715-1781. An Archaeological Perspective on the Revolutionary Frontier*. East Lansing: Museum, Michigan State University, 1974.

Sullivan, Catherine. *L'heritage du Machault une collection d'artefacts du XVIII e siecle*. Ministre des Approvisionnments et Services Canada, 1986

Suthren, Victor J. H. "Louisbourg Troup de la Marine: A Guide for Animation." Fortress of Louisbourg, 1973.

Swayze, Nathan L. *Engraved Powder Horns of the French and Indian War and the Revolutionary War Period*. Dallas: Taylor Publishing Co., 1978.

Tanner, Helen Hornbeck. *Atlas of Great Lake Indian History*. Norman: University of Oklahoma Press, 1987.

Thatcher, Joseph. *Cast for War: A History of Muzzle Loading Artillery*. New York State Bureau of Historic Sites, 1985.

Thibault, H. Paul. *Dictionary of Canadian Biography*. Vol. III. Toronto: University of Toronto Press, 1974.

Thomas, Jean-Louis. Letter to D.F. Shaffer concerning Noiret (marine). November 10, 1987.

_____. Letter to D.F. Shaffer concerning French musket cartridges. 1988.

Thorburn, W.A. *French Army Regiments and Uniforms*. New York: Hippocrene Books, Inc., 1976.

BIBLIOGRAPHY

Thwaites, Reuben Gold. *The Jesuit Relations and Allied Documents*. Vol. LXX. New York: Pagent Book Company, 1959.

Tocco, Tom. "French Posts in the West." *Newsletter of the Forces of Montcalm and Wolfe*. Vol. 2, No. 3, 1986.

_____. "The Result Has Not Fulfilled Our Expectation." *Journal of the Forces of Montcalm and Wolfe*. Vol. 2, No. 3, 1989.

Vadeboncoeur, Guy. "Compangnie Franche de la Marine (1683). The Arrival of the First Compagnies Franches de la Marine and Their Mission." *F&I War*. Vol. 2, No. 1, 1983.

_____. "Compangnie Franche de la Marine (1683). The Arrival of the First Compagnies Franches de la Marine and Their Mission." *F&I War*. Vol. 2, No. 3, 1984.

_____. Letter to D.F. Shaffer concerning Noiret (marine). Oct. 21, 1987.

Vidler, Virginia. *American Indian Antiques. Arts and Artifacts of the Northeast*. Cranbury, N.J.: A.S. Barnes and Co., 1976.

Walker, Iain C. "An Archaeological Study of Clay Pipes from the King's Bastion, Fortress of Louisbourg." *Canadian Historic Sites: Occasional Papers in Archaeology and History* No. 2. Ottawa: National Historic Sites Service, 1971.

Wallace, W. Stewart. *The MacMillian Dictionary of Canadian Biography*. London: MacMillian. 1963.

Walthall, John A. and Elizabeth D. Benchley. *The River L'Abbe Mission*. Studies in Illinois Archaeology. No. 2. Springfield: Illinois Historic Preservation Agency, 1987.

Waselkov, Gregory A. "French Colonial Trade in the Upper Creek Country." Paper presented at the Conference on French Colonial Archeology. Springfield, Illinois. April 9, 1988.

Washlaski, Raymond A. "French Clothing - Men's Shirt." *F&I War*. Vol. 2, No. 1, 1985.

_____. "Interrogation of Michael La Chauvignerie, Jr. A French Officer from Fort Machault." *F&I War*. Vol. 1, No. 2, 1982.

Wheeler, Robert C. *A Toast to the Fur Trade. A Pictorial Essay on Its Material Culture*. St. Paul: Wheeler Productions, 1985.

Windrow, Martin. *Montcalm's Army*. Men at Arms Series. Reading, England: Osprey, 1981.

Wood, George A. "Celoron de Blainville and French Expansion in the Ohio Valley." *Mississippi Valley Historical Review*. Cedar Rapids, Iowa: The Torch Press, 1923.

Woodward, Arthur. *Denominators of the Fur Trade*. Pasadena: Westernlore Press, 1970.

Wright, Mark. "Deserters from Fort Sandoske." *Journal of Montcalm and Wolfe*. Vol. 3, No. 3, 1990.

Wrong, George M. *The Rise and Fall of New France*. Two volumes. New York: Octagon Books, 1970.

Yeoman, R. S. *A Guide Book of United States Coins*. Kenneth Bressett, editor. Racine: Western Publishing Co., 1986.

Zaboly, Gary. "Wilderness Commados, the dress, weapons, and accoutrements of Rogers' Rangers." *Muzzle Blasts*. Vol. 39, No. 10, 1978.

Zoltvany, Yves F., editor. *The French Tradition in America*. New York: Harper and Row, Inc., 1969.

INDEX

Abenakis 27, 41
Acadia, 9
Algonkins, 27
Artillery, 165-172
Aubrey (Sieur de), Charles Philippe, 45, 47, 48
Awls, 120-121
Battle on Snowshoes, 35-36
Bayonet, 94
Beaujeu, Daniel Hyacinthe de Lienard de, 28, 29
Bedding, 127
Bellestre (Sieur de) 24
Bougainville, Louis-Antoine de, 19, 39, 42, 44, 46
Braddock, Edward, 28-31
Canada
  Government 10, 36, 40
Canteen, 124
Carignan Salieres, 10, 11
Cart, 132-133
Cartridge, 96
Cartridge box, 96, 97, 99
Celoron (de Blainville) Pierre Joseph, 24, 31
Colbert, Jean Baptiste, 10
Comb, 121
Contrecoeur (Sieur de) Claude Pierre Pecaudy, 27, 28
Cooking/eating equipment, 126-127
Delaware (tribe), 23
Dieskau (battle at Lake George), 31-34
Dumas, Jean, 29, 31, 32, 37, 39, 45, 48
Eyeglasses, 123-124
Flints, 105-108
Food, 26, 140-143
Forks of the Ohio, 25, 26
Fortifications, 183-191
Forts
  Bull, 32-33
  Beausejour, 94
  Carillon (Ticonderoga), 34, 35, 38, 39, 41-44, 45, 48
  Detroit, 13, 19, 23, 24, 28, 47
  Duquesne, 25, 26-27, 28, 32, 34, 45, 46
  Frontenac 32, 45

Le Bouef, 24, 26
Louisbourg, 11, 14, 17, 21, 24, 46, 51, 54, 161, 187, 188
Machault (Venango) 24, 26, 46
Miamis, 23
Michilimackinac, 19, 23, 24, 87, 88, 139, 187
Necessity (Great Meadows), 28
Niagara 19, 24, 26, 32, 46-48, 90
Presque Isle, 24, 26, 46, 145
Sandoske, 76, 140
William Henry, 14, 36, 38-39, 40
Fox Wars, 21
Fur trade, 9, 19, 23, 25, 32
Groghan, George, 23
Halberd, 115-116
Hammerstall, 102-104
Health/medicine, 143-146
Hurons, 27
Ice creepers, 128-129
Ice skates, 128-129
Iroquois, 9, 10, 11, 18, 23, 41, 51
Jumonville (Sieur de), 27
King George's War, 21
Knapsack, 118-119
Knives, 124-126
La Belle Famille, 47-48
La Galissoniere, Governor, 24, 25
La Marine, 11
  Adaptation to Canada, 19, 20, 139, 194-195
  Discharge, 50, 135, 196
  Off-duty activity, 20-21, 138-139, 146-152
  Officers, 13, 18, 19, 20
  Organization (company), 13-14, (battalion), 38, 39, 40, 45
  Rank and file, 15-17, 46, 135, (praised) 40, 42, 43, 44
Langlade, Charles, 24, 36, 38, 40
Langy Montegron, 43
Le petite guerre, 17, 36
Lery, Joseph Gaspard Chaussegros de, 28, 32, 33, 35, 40, 176, 177-178
Levis, 39, 43, 44, 49
Ligneris, Francois Marie le Marchand de, 45, 47, 48
Living history, 2-6
Longueil, 37

Louis XIV, 9
Louisiana, 13, 17, 27, 50, 56, 68
Marin,
   Joseph, 18-19, 20, 38, 40, 47, 48, 133
   Pierre Paul, 24
Mercier, 20, 37, 40, 42
Miami (tribe), 23
Money, 152-155
Montcalm, 14, 16, 18, 19, 32, 33, 34, 36, 37,
   38, 39, 40, 41, 43, 44, 45
Montreal 14, 20, 24, 25, 49-50, 191
Musket, 84-94, 110
Musket tools, 102, 104-105
Music, 161-164
Nepissing, 27
Ohio (region), 23-32, 45
Oswego, 32-34, 40, 47
Pennsylvania, 24, 25, 31, 32
Pickawillaney, 24
Pistol, 108-109
Portneuf, de, 54, 178
Powder flask, 99-102
Quebec, 9, 10, 14, 46, 48-49, 51, 145-146, 187,
   191
Raymond (Comte de), 23, 31, 42, 43
Razors, 121-122
Religion, 156-158
Rigaud, 37, 38, 39, 40
Rogers' Rangers (Robert Rogers), 36, 40, 41,
   92, 194
Roger's Rock (battle), 40-41
St. Etienne (arms factory), 88-89
Sandusky (area), 23
Shawnee, 23
Sled (traine), 129, 131-132
Snowshoes, 129-130
Spontoon, 115-116
Strikers, 121
Sword 110-112
Tent, 133-134
Three Rivers, 14, 168, 176, 190, 191
Tomahawk, 112-114
Tracy, Alexandre de Pouville, 10
Tulle (arms factory), 85
Uniforms, 53-84, 162-164, 166-168

Vaudreuil-Cavagnal (Marquis de) Pierre-Francois de Rigaud, 14, 16, 17-18, 32, 35, 41, 42, 43, 44, 49
Villiers
  Francois de, 28, 32
  Louis Coulon de, 27, 28, 33, 39, 40, 112
Villiers Volunteers, 39-40
Waistbelt, 117-118
Watercraft, 173-181
Washington, George, 25, 27, 28, 31, 46
Winter Equipment, 78
Wyandot, 23

ERRATA

La Marine, The French Colonial Soldier in Canada 1745-1761.

Page

vii   J.C.B. is "Jolicoeur" Charles Bonin. He appears as a *canonnier* on a 1755 list of troops going to Fort Duquesne (*The French Invasion of Western Pennsylvania.* Donald H. Kent. Harrisburg: Pennsylvania Historical Commission 1954. Page 59, note 34).

ix   Jim Marsalles should read Jim Marsala. Sincere apologies.

10   Colbert was not, of course, Governor of Canada. Sincere embarrassment.

24   The site of Fort Machault (Venango) was occupied in 1753 but the Fort was not constructed until the following year.

27   Mousseaux, the survivor of Jumonville's party, is found as Monceau in other sources.

40   Langly (in quote) should read Langy.

217   Muy was commandant at Detroit 1754-1758. He began as a temporary replacement for Celoron.

227   The ball size of the 22 caliber should read .629.

www.ingramcontent.com/pod-product-compliance
Lightning Source LLC
Chambersburg PA
CBHW070726160426
43192CB00009B/1336